New Casebooks

POETRY

WILLIAM BLAKE Edited by David Punter
CHAUCER Edited by Valerie Allen and Aries Axiotis
COLERIDGE, KEATS AND SHELLEY Edited by Peter J. Kitson
JOHN DONNE Edited by Andrew Mousley
SEAMUS HEANEY Edited by Michael Allen
PHILIP LARKIN Edited by Stephen Regan
DYLAN THOMAS Edited by John Goodby and Chris Wigginton
VICTORIAN WOMEN POETS Edited by Joseph Bristow
WORDSWORTH Edited by John Williams
PARADISE LOST Edited by William Zunder

NOVELS AND PROSE

AUSTEN: *Emma* Edited by David Monaghan
AUSTEN: *Mansfield Park* and *Persuasion* Edited by Judy Simons
AUSTEN: *Sense and Sensibility* and *Pride and Prejudice* Edited by Robert Clark
CHARLOTTE BRONTË: *Jane Eyre* Edited by Heather Glen
CHARLOTTE BRONTË: *Villette* Edited by Pauline Nestor
EMILY BRONTË: *Wuthering Heights* Edited by Patsy Stoneman
ANGELA CARTER Edited by Alison Easton
WILKIE COLLINS Edited by Lyn Pykett
JOSEPH CONRAD Edited by Elaine Jordan
DICKENS: *Bleak House* Edited by Jeremy Tambling
DICKENS: *David Copperfield* and *Hard Times* Edited by John Peck
DICKENS: *Great Expectations* Edited by Roger Sell
ELIOT: *The Mill on the Floss* and *Silas Marner* Edited by Nahem Yousaf and Andrew Maunder
ELIOT: *Middlemarch* Edited by John Peck
E.M. FORSTER Edited by Jeremy Tambling
HARDY: *Jude the Obscure* Edited by Penny Boumelha
HARDY: *The Mayor of Casterbridge* Edited by Julian Wolfreys
HARDY: *Tess of the D'Urbervilles* Edited by Peter Widdowson
JAMES: *Turn of the Screw* and *What Maisie Knew* Edited by Neil Cornwell and Maggie Malone
LAWRENCE: *Sons and Lovers* Edited by Rick Rylance
TONI MORRISON Edited by Linden Peach
GEORGE ORWELL Edited by Bryan Loughrey and Graham Holderness
SHELLEY: *Frankenstein* Edited by Fred Botting
STOKER: *Dracula* Edited by Glennis Byron
WOOLF: *Mrs Dalloway* and *To the Lighthouse* Edited by Su Reid

(continued overleaf)

DRAMA

BECKETT: *Waiting for Godot* and *Endgame* Edited by Steven Connor
APHRA BEHN Edited by Janet Todd
REVENGE TRAGEDY Edited by Stevie Simkin
SHAKESPEARE: *Antony and Cleopatra* Edited by John Drakakis
SHAKESPEARE: *Hamlet* Edited by Martin Coyle
SHAKESPEARE: *Julius Caesar* Edited by Richard Wilson
SHAKESPEARE: *King Lear* Edited by Kiernan Ryan
SHAKESPEARE: *Macbeth* Edited by Alan Sinfield
SHAKESPEARE: *The Merchant of Venice* Edited by Martin Coyle
SHAKESPEARE: *A Midsummer Night's Dream* Edited by Richard Dutton
SHAKESPEARE: *Much Ado About Nothing* and *The Taming of the Shrew*
  Edited by Marion Wynne-Davies
SHAKESPEARE: *Romeo and Juliet* Edited by R. S. White
SHAKESPEARE: *The Tempest* Edited by R. S. White
SHAKESPEARE: *Twelfth Night* Edited by R. S. White
SHAKESPEARE, FEMINISM AND GENDER: Edited by Kate Chedgzoy
SHAKESPEARE ON FILM Edited by Robert Shaughnessy
SHAKESPEARE IN PERFORMANCE Edited by Robert Shaughnessy
SHAKESPEARE'S HISTORY PLAYS Edited by Graham Holderness
SHAKESPEARE'S TRAGEDIES Edited by Susan Zimmerman
JOHN WEBSTER: *The Duchess of Malfi* Edited by Dympna Callaghan

GENERAL THEMES

FEMINIST THEATRE AND THEORY Edited by Helene Keyssar
POST-COLONIAL LITERATURES Edited by Michael Parker and Roger Starkey

---

New Casebooks Series
Series Standing Order
ISBN 0–333–71702–3 hardcover
ISBN 0–333–69345–0 paperback
(outside North America only)

You can receive future titles in this series as they are published by placing a standing order. Please contact your bookseller or, in case of difficulty, write to us at the address below with your name and address, the title of the series and the ISBN quoted above.

Customer Services Department, Macmillan Distribution Ltd
Houndmills, Basingstoke, Hampshire RG21 6XS, England

New Casebooks

SHAKESPEARE ON FILM

EDITED BY ROBERT SHAUGHNESSY

Published by
PALGRAVE
Houndmills, Basingstoke, Hampshire RG21 6XS and
175 Fifth Avenue, New York, N. Y. 10010
Companies and representatives throughout the world

PALGRAVE is the new global academic imprint of
St. Martin's Press LLC Scholarly and Reference Division and
Palgrave Publishers Ltd (formerly Macmillan Press Ltd).

Outside North America
ISBN 0–333–72016–4 hardcover
ISBN 0–333–72017–2 paperback

Inside North America
ISBN 0–312–21447–2 cloth
ISBN 0–333–21448–0 paperback

This book is printed on paper suitable for recycling and
made from fully managed and sustained forest sources.

A catalogue record for this book is available
from the British Library.

Cataloging-in-Publication data is available from the Library of Congress

Typeset by EXPO Holdings, Malaysia

Printed and bound in Great Britain by
Antony Rowe Ltd, Chippenham and Eastbourne

For Kevin, Gary and Kay Shaughnessy

Contents

Acknowledgements

The editor and publishers wish to thank the following for permission to use copyright material:

Catherine Belsey, for 'Shakespeare and Film: A Question of Perspective', *Literature/Film Quarterly*, XI (1983), by permission of Literature/Film Quarterly; Curtis Breight, for 'Branagh and the Prince, or 'a royal fellowship of death', *Critical Quarterly*, 33: 4 (1991), by permission of Manchester University Press; John Collick, for 'Symbolism in Shakespeare Film' from *Shakespeare, Cinema and Society* (1989), by permission of Manchester University Press; Anthony Davies, for 'Laurence Olivier's *Henry V*' from *Filming Shakespeare's Plays* (1988), by permission of Cambridge University Press; Peter S. Donaldson, for 'Olivier, Hamlet and Freud' from *Shakespearean Films/Shakespearean Directors* (1990), by permission of Routledge; Barbara Hodgdon, for material from 'Katherina Bound; or Play(K)ating the Strictures of Everyday Life', *PMLA*, 107 (1992), by permission of Modern Language Association of America; Graham Holderness for material from 'Radical Potentiality and Institutional Closure' in *Political Shakespeare: New Essays in Cultural Materialism*, ed. Jonathan Dollimore and Alan Sinfield (1985), by permission of Manchester University Press; Jack J. Jorgens, for 'Realizing Shakespeare on Film' from *Shakespeare on Film*, Indiana University Press (1977), by permission of the author; Douglas Lanier for 'Drowning the Book: *Prospero's Books* and the Textual Shakespeare' from *Shakespeare, Theory and Performance*, ed. James C. Bulman (1996), by permission of Routledge; Colin MacCabe, for 'A Post-National European Cinema: A Consideration of Derek Jarman's *The Tempest* and *Edward II*', from *Screening Europe: Image and Identity in Contemporary European Cinema*, ed. Duncan Petrie, British Film Institute (1992), by permission of the author.

General Editors' Preface

The purpose of this series of New Casebooks is to reveal some of the ways in which contemporary criticism has changed our understanding of commonly studied texts and writers and, indeed, of the nature of criticism itself. Central to the series is a concern with modern critical theory and its effect on current approaches to the study of literature. Each New Casebook editor has been asked to select a sequence of essays which will introduce the reader to the new critical approaches to the text or texts being discussed in the volume and also illuminate the rich interchange between critical theory and critical practice that characterises so much current writing about literature.

In this focus on modern critical thinking and practice New Casebooks aim not only to inform but also to stimulate, with volumes seeking to reflect both the controversy and the excitement of current criticism. Because much of this criticism is difficult and often employs an unfamiliar critical language, editors have been asked to give the reader as much help as they feel is appropriate, but without simplifying the essays or the issues they raise. Again, editors have been asked to supply a list of further reading which will enable readers to follow up issues raised by the essays in the volume.

The project of New Casebooks, then, is to bring together in an illuminating way those critics who best illustrate the ways in which contemporary criticism has established new methods of analysing texts and who have reinvigorated the important debate about how we 'read' literature. The hope is, of course, that New Casebooks will not only open up this debate to a wider audience, but will also encourage students to extend their own ideas, and think afresh about their responses to the texts they are studying.

John Peck and Martin Coyle
University of Wales, Cardiff

Introduction

ROBERT SHAUGHNESSY

I

The 1993 film *Last Action Hero* tells the story of Danny, a young teenager obsessed with violent action movies, and in particular with the muscle-bound, gun-toting, monosyllabic movie hero Jack Slater, played by Arnold Schwarzenegger as a self-parody of the screen role he has perfected from *The Terminator* onwards. Early in the film, having sat through an all-night screening of Jack Slater films, Danny is seen in a school English class, as the teacher struggles vainly to interest her pupils in Shakespeare's *Hamlet* by showing a clip from Laurence Olivier's film version.[1] As the class sniggers, the camera closes in on an impatient and irritated Danny, who urges Olivier's contemplative, soliloquising Prince: 'Don't talk, just do it!' In a variation upon the film-within-film conceit around which *Last Action Hero* is constructed, Danny fantasises a trailer for the kind of *Hamlet* he'd really like to see. Olivier dissolves into the armoured and heavily armed figure of Arnie himself who, lifting Claudius by the lapels and growling, 'You killed my father. *Big mistake*', proceeds to wreak his accustomed mayhem, as he launches Claudius through a stained-glass window, hurls Yorick's skull at an attacker, and stabs, slashes and shoots his way through the court. 'To be or not to be', he muses, and then, lighting a cigar butt, 'not to be', as Elsinore explodes in flames behind him.

The comic strategies of this sequence are fairly easy to identify. The substitution of Schwarzenegger for Olivier effects a faintly camp comedy of incongruity as the generic traits associated with the former are brought into juxtaposition with the cultural values associated with the latter. 'Something is rotten in the state of Denmark', intones a voice-over, 'and Hamlet is taking out the trash', and it is precisely this confrontation between classics and trash that produces the laughs. Whereas Olivier portrays the Prince as the most sensitive and articulate yet most ineffectual of Shakespeare's action heroes, Schwarzenegger displays the amoral, visceral decisiveness that the action genre demands. On the one hand is intellect, sensibility and poetry; on the other, the body and violent, gratuitous spectacle; even Shakespeare's most celebrated lines are twisted into the mordant one-liners that have become Schwarzenegger's trademark. In the context of a film which makes great play with the relations between genre, spectatorship, and the various levels of cinematic artifice (and which also traces a vaguely *Hamlet*-like exploration of heroism), this sequence is an amusing enough generic spoof; but it also sets out, in commendably succinct terms, some of the problems which have haunted the production, reception and discussion of Shakespeare on film from the outset. It is hardly stretching the point to read the violence that the Schwarzenegger fantasy *Hamlet* inflicts upon the play's traditional iconography as the dream (or nightmare) scenario of what Hollywood might do (and, some would say, has done) to Shakespeare in the interests of attracting a mass audience, as poetry, character and narrative are cut to pieces. The joke for the audience is that it knows that such an appropriation of *Hamlet*, by making the concessions to taste and to generic consistency that Danny demands, would also be an absurd travesty.

Underpinning the joke, however, is a deeper sense of a potentially irreconcilable antagonism between cinematic and Shakespearean values. For most of this century Shakespeare scholarship has, at the very least, been distinctly wary of Shakespeare on screen. Although a wide variety of cinematic versions, treatments, adaptations of, and borrowings from Shakespeare's plays have been part of the film industry's stock-in-trade from its earliest days (the first recorded instance of Shakespearean film being Beerbohm Tree's one-reel record of his celebrated stage production of *King John* in 1898), these were comprehensively ignored by academic criticism until the 1930s. The advent of sound provided a turning point, as did the critical discussion provoked by the Warner Brothers' 1935 *A Midsummer Night's Dream*. The critical response to this film, as later summarised by one commentator, indicates one of the major points of contention: 'there was a difference of opinion as to whether it was a good film. All critics agreed it was not good Shakespeare.'[2] The belief that there may be a fundamental and irreconcilable antipathy between film (good or bad) and Shakespeare has persisted; and a central element in this has been the sense that the economic priorities and standards of taste of the cinema industry as a medium of mass entertainment are necessarily at odds with the integrity of Shakespeare's art. As another, more recent, critic put it, the 'chronic problems' that have plagued Shakespeare on film are 'casting directed by box-office economics, the need to make Shakespeare popular through whatever Philistine distortion of his thought, and the timidity of producers who, while sensing that Shakespeare will sell, recoil from the notion that he might sell without gimmickry and press-agentry'.[3] There has, meanwhile, been a vigorous tradition of arguing against this view, which rather than situating Shakespeare's work outside the grubby machinations of capitalism, as the myth demands, places it heartily in the thick of it: thus in 1936 Allardyce Nicoll robustly proclaimed that 'the Elizabethan stage occupied a position by no means dissimilar to that taken in our own time by the cinema'.[4] Cognate with this is the populist argument that Shakespearean cinema is a truly global and inclusive medium for the plays, addressing the kind of mass, non-elite audience of which theatre practitioners can only dream. A further development of this position is to argue that Shakespeare's work is actually at its best in the cinema – that it is an instance of what Henri Lemaitre calls 'pre-cinema'[5] – a conviction that is at its most wistfully conjectural in the almost proverbial maxim that, if Shakespeare were alive today, he would be writing film scripts.

II

At the heart of much of the discussion has been the issue of language; that is, of the relationship between a poetic discourse which was initiated within the context of the non-illusionist, non-realist, extravagantly rhetorical early modern theatre and a predominantly realist visual medium. The notion that Shakespeare's rhetorical and figurative language, whether read or spoken, works best when left to the imagination has been a tenacious one; and for extreme bardolators, and defenders of Shakespeare's literary reputation, the very idea of filming Shakespeare is either a monstrous affront or a self-evident absurdity – hence, to a large extent, the derision and contempt which has been directed at the considerable body of Shakespearean film produced during the silent era, which ranged

from more-or-less straight filmed scenes to travesty, parody and bur-
lesque. But if these works have been easy to dismiss, other examples
of filmed Shakespeare which sunder the link between the plays'
mise-en-scène[6] and spoken English have proved more challenging to
the assumptions of the Anglocentric Shakespearean critical tradition,
in that several of the widely acknowledged masterpieces of
Shakespearean cinema – Akira Kurosawa's *Kumonosu Jo* (known in
the west as *Throne of Blood*), Grigori Kozintsev's *Korol Ler* (*King
Lear*) – utilise Shakespeare in translation. The various modes and
typologies of adaptation have also proved problematic and con-
tentious. For the bulk of existing commentary, 'Shakespeare on film'
points initially towards a predominantly realist mainstream, to what
is rapidly becoming an established canon of film versions of the
plays (which might run from Laurence Olivier's *Henry V*, *Hamlet*
and *Richard III*, through the works of Kozintsev and Kurosawa,
Zeffirelli's *The Taming of the Shrew* and *Romeo and Juliet*, Peter
Brook's *King Lear* to Kenneth Branagh's *Hamlet*). For the most
part, these are screen versions which acknowledge and defer to
(and exploit) the cultural authority and prestige of their source texts,
versions which conform broadly to Morris Beja's definition of the
'faithful' adaptation, which 'asks that the integrity of the original
work ... be preserved'.[7]

Faithfulness and integrity are notoriously slippery values, of
course, but in the case of Shakespeare it is more important than
usual to view them as primarily *ideological* rather than aesthetic or
ethical terms, whereby being 'true to Shakespeare' is as much about
endorsing the conservative values with which his work has been
traditionally associated – order, hierarchy, Christianity, nationalism, militarism, compulsory heterosexuality, and so on – as it is
about preserving the letter of the text. Against the mainstream,
however, there is a history of oppositional, critical and counter-
cultural appropriations of Shakespeare, where, more often than
not, the interrogation of conservative constructions of Shakespeare
means disputing the integrity of the text, and formal and stylistic
deviation from the norms of realism – the films of Orson Welles,
Derek Jarman, Celestino Coronado and Peter Greenaway being examples. Furthermore, developments in critical theory and practice
in recent years have interrogated the idea of the integrity and stability of the Shakespearean text, against which cinematic adaptations
may be graded, in fundamental terms. As Graham Holderness
pithily summarises:

For deconstruction, the text's ostensible coherence is there to be systematically discompounded. For Marxist and cultural-materialist criticism, the ideology of the text is there to be rubbed against the grain, demystified and exposed. For feminism the text's patriarchal inflections are there to be combated by an overtly ideological rereading. For New Historicism, the text's spurious individuality is to be challenged by its absorption into a general context of discursive practice. For psychoanalytic approaches the latent sub-text will reveal more meaning than the mechanism of repression that is its surface meaning. For postmodern readings the text is alive only in so far as it resists ideological closure and metanarrative authority, making its resources available for irresponsible play ...[8]

There remains yet a further caveat: what happens to the categories which have sustained discussion of Shakespeare on film when it is viewed on the broadest basis as a popular cultural phenomenon? Viewed from this perspective, Shakespeare's place within film culture loses its status of distinctive privilege and becomes subject to, and analysable within, the terms of popular film genres, encompassing a seemingly inexhaustible variety of instances of parody, quotation, displacement, translation and travesty – ranging from *To Be or Not to Be* and *Joe Macbeth* to *The Lion King* and *My Own Private Idaho*.

III

It is, perhaps, an indication of the medium's problematic status within the discipline as a whole that it was not until 1968 that the first full-length study of Shakespearean film appeared, in the shape of Robert Hamilton Ball's *Shakespeare on Silent Film*.[9] Ball's intriguing book, which is more a work of cinema history than criticism, unearthed a corpus of now-forgotten Shakespearean films from the silent popular cinema, which ranged from straightforward versions of famous scenes to travesties, sketches and burlesques. But even Ball was faintly apologetic about the significance of his project, describing it as 'a diversion ... a distraction from other and more customary forms of research and writing, a recreation'.[10] A few articles and anthologies followed in the early 1970s, and then in 1973 the journals *Shakespeare on Film Newsletter* and *Literature/Film Quarterly* started. In 1977, the first full-length critical study was published. In *Shakespeare on Film*, Jack Jorgens offered a series of enthusiastic readings of what was rapidly becoming the established canon of Shakespearean films, arguing that it was high time that scholars started to take the medium seriously: 'we need to re-examine the prides and prejudices which have driven critics and theorists of literature, theatre, and film to paint themselves into opposite corners of the room'.[11] Rather than seeing Shakespeare on film as an inevitably flawed or inferior adjunct to Shakespeare on the page or stage, he argues, critics should approach it in terms of the artistic possibilities of the cinema; the populist case for Shakespeare on film is supported by the aesthetic one.

In an obvious sense, the development of critical practice has been determined by the limits of the available technology. The first wave of criticism at the end of the 1960s was driven by the growing availability during the period of 16 mm prints of the major Shakespearean films; a further impetus was supplied by the rapid proliferation of cheap video technology at the end of the 1970s (the BBC/Time Life Complete Works of Shakespeare, which began at the same time, was another factor fuelling critical discussion). But these technological developments were themselves afforded particular significance by the contexts in which they operated. The increasing interest in Shakespeare on film not only coincided with but was to a certain extent driven by major transformations within the educational system during the 1960s and 1970s, whose impact was felt even within the rarefied field of Shakespeare studies. The social and economic changes which brought, in large numbers, an entirely new class of students into European and American universities, together with the political upheavals of the period of student protest, also created the conditions for the aims and methods of many scholarly disciplines (including the study of literature) to be called into question. At the end of the 1960s, Shakespeare studies was rapidly approaching a state of exhaustion; it has been characterised by Hugh Grady as 'a competent, informed body of work marked by timidity of spirit and a serene indifference to any larger social currents'. He goes on:

> Predictably, it was read by few outside of the field since its real purpose was to serve as a professional credential among a largely self-selected coterie. Given this professionalisation, there was virtually no pretence of operating within a sphere of public discourse, a sphere which in any case had been transformed in fundamental ways by the new electronic media.[12]

At a basic level, Shakespeare on film, as something to be both taught and studied, provided the kind of bridge between high and popular culture that, as well as appealing to the new and expanded student constituency, might also offer the means for the academic discipline to revitalise itself (the other route, widely touted at the time, was via theatrical performance). Similar processes have been at work during the expansionary periods of the 1980s and early 1990s, as film courses and film resources in universities have proliferated along with student numbers.

As it turned out, however, the body of criticism and commentary on Shakespeare on film which began to develop in the 1970s was to be abruptly sidelined at the turn of the decade by the emergence of a range of theorised and explicitly politicised critical practices which have radically challenged the traditional protocols of Shakespearean scholarship. As the combined and sometimes contending forces of poststructuralism, psychoanalysis, Marxism, new historicism, feminism and cultural materialism began to reshape Shakespeare studies during the 1980s, Shakespeare on screen for a time received rather less attention. Indeed, a significant proportion of the work on Shakespearean film that has appeared in the 1980s and 1990s has set itself against the prevailing critical wind, in that it has avoided the kind of theoretical interrogation which has been central to the discipline during the period. The opening sentence of Anthony Davies's 1988 book *Filming Shakespeare's Plays*, for example, emphatically sets it apart from the bulk of the critical work with which it is contemporaneous, claiming that 'the plays of Shakespeare have become undisputed literary classics'.[13] The fact that the 'classic' status of Shakespeare's plays (and, indeed, the very notion of the classic itself) had been subject to frequently acrimonious dispute for a decade appears to have passed this writer by.

Davies's statement is representative of a broadly Leavisite tradition of Shakespearean film criticism which has avoided engagement with debates that have been not only crucial to Shakespeare studies for well over a decade but, perhaps more importantly, central to film studies since the late 1960s. Davies's main theoretical framework is supplied by the work of André Bazin; Jorgens cites, in addition, John Howard Lawson, Robert Gessner and Susan Sontag: these are all figures whose work belongs to a body of criticism, rooted common-sense, humanist values, which, as Antony Easthope puts it, constitutes 'classic' film theory.[14] For Bazin, in particular, cinema ultimately seeks to replicate an order of the real which is given, natural and unproblematic: the aim of film is 'to give the spectator as perfect an illusion of reality as possible within the limits of the logical demands of cinematographic narrative and the current limits of technique'.[15] Moreover, cinema as an artform should attempt to replicate an order and harmony which exists in nature itself, and the ideal to which film should aspire 'would permit everything to be said without chopping the world up into little fragments, that would reveal the hidden meanings in people and things without disturbing the unity natural to them'.[16] As these remarks indicate, classic film theory reproduces the central assumptions of the humanist critical tradition, in that aesthetic worth is measured in terms of a work's organic form, its thematic, stylistic and structural unity, its logic and coherence. Since 1968, however, the major currents in film theory have sought to challenge the assumptions of classic film criticism at the most fundamental level; 'what was new', write Robert Lapsley and Michael Westlake, 'was the fact that theory no longer sought accommodation with the existing criticism and aesthetics, and was not presented as an improvement or refinement of current critical practice, but was avowedly bent on its overthrow.'[17] Post-1968 theory, defined by Stephen Heath as 'the encounter of Marxism and psychoanalysis on the terrain of semiotics',[18] politicised the analysis of film, examining both the economic, social and ideological determinants of form, style and genre, and the construction of the spectator within cinematic discourse. If traditional film criticism prized organic unity as a central principle, more recent criticism has found that the interest of a film text lies in its contradictions and self-divisions, in its gaps, silences and evasions. If, traditionally, a 'great' work of art was one which, characteristically bearing the *imprimatur* of individual authorial genius, transcends its own time, the 'classic' film might be expected to escape the limitations of genre and studio system alike (a view which has been elaborated as the *auteur* theory of film);[19] for materialist criticism, conversely, texts are to be seen as thoroughly embedded within their histories of production and reception.

Strictly speaking, the majority of essays gathered here are unrepresentative of the kind of work that has been dominant in the field of Shakespearean film criticism in recent years; for the most part, the field has been dominated by critical assumptions and methods of analysis which contemporary theory seeks to critique. Indeed, it may be that the appeal of the traditional mode of Shakespearean film criticism is that it appears to offer an antidote to theory, history and politics; much of what you need for close reading, after all, is a few videotapes, a pause button, keen powers of observation, and common sense. At least until recently, much of the theory-driven Shakespeare scholarship (particularly in the United States) has tended to concentrate upon locating Shakespeare's works in their originating period rather than examining their dissemination within contemporary culture. With the exception of the first two essays, which are representative of the best work that has been done within the traditional critical paradigm, the essays in this volume demonstrate how the critical and theoretical tools of cultural materialism may be brought to bear upon the medium through which Shakespeare's works have reached their largest and most diverse audiences in history.

IV

One of the important realignments brought about by the newly theorised work on Shakespeare on film has been that the question of whether or not a particular film version is or is not true (or faithful) to Shakespeare, which has been a recurrent preoccupation in critical discussion, has diminished in importance. If the perceived conflict between the values which are traditionally held to be Shakespearean and those of the cinema has been a critical issue in discussion of Shakespearean film, Jack Jorgens attempts to resolve this long-running dispute in the introductory chapter to *Shakespeare on Film* (essay 1 in this volume), by formulating a definition of the three types or modalities of adaptation: theatrical, realist and filmic. The theatrical mode attempts to preserve live performance on film (Stuart Burge's film of the John Dexter/Laurence Olivier *Othello* is an example). The realist mode emphasises settings, environment, period detail, and spectacle (examples are Zeffirelli's *The Taming of the Shrew* and *Romeo and Juliet*). Jorgens's main point is that it has been the weaknesses and inadequacies of these two approaches which have contributed to a large degree to the poor reputation of mainstream Shakespearean film. Whereas the theatrical mode is superficially cheap, the realist mode, which has been the dominant, popular form, is conspicuously expensive, and often vacuously spectacular: in the latter case, the text has been particularly dispensable. His preferred mode is the filmic, 'the mode of the film poet', where the emphasis is upon 'the *artifice* of film, on the expressive possibilities of distorting the surfaces of reality'.[20] By stressing the importance of treating Shakespearean film not only as film but as film *art*,

Jorgens hopes to free critical discussion from literary and theatrical biases which have tended to confine discussion to the issue of 'faithfulness', but also, in the manner of classic film theory, to emphasise the integrity and aesthetic worth of the medium itself. Within the filmic mode, the true artist or 'film poet' may (as in *auteur* theory) transcend the dictates of commerce to produce a work which, by being authentically cinematic, is paradoxically 'truest to the effect of Shakespeare's verse'.[21]

Anthony Davies appears to share Jorgens's sense of the Shakespearean film artist, and his discussion of Laurence Olivier's 1944 *Henry V* (essay 2) offers a close reading of one of the canonical works of the Shakespearean cinema. Davies's main preoccupation is with the cinematic manipulation of space and time: the spatial strategies of Olivier's *Henry V*, he argues, offer a sophisticated meditation upon the relations between theatre and cinema. In common with most commentators on this film, Davies highlights its self-conscious artifice and bold stylisation; he is concerned to demonstrate that the film's disparate styles, registers and genres are ultimately coherent and organically unified. The critical method and terminology are implicitly Leavisite, in that Davies's study seeks to demonstrate the 'greatness' of a few select works of the Shakespearean cinema (he also considers Olivier's other Shakespeare films, and those of Kurosawa and Brook) by means of detailed close readings which make little reference to the social, cultural or historical contexts of the films. The approach is, like that of Jorgens, largely appreciative, and deals with richness, complexity, organic unity – the 'life force' of the films and the plays from which they derive.[22]

Davies's enthusiastic and largely celebratory approach to his material contrasts sharply with that of Catherine Belsey (essay 3), who examines Shakespearean film in the light of poststructuralist theory. As the title of Belsey's essay suggests, the shift of perspective entailed in this is a radical one, in that it interrogates the very grounds upon which critical discussion of Shakespearean film had previously taken place. Belsey asks entirely different questions of her material to Jorgens, Davies and the majority of contributions to the journal *Literature/Film Quarterly*, where Belsey's essay first appeared. Whereas humanist film criticism assumes a common-sense, empiricist view of the role of the spectator, poststructuralist theory regards spectatorship as a position of intelligibility which is produced through and within cinematic discourse. Rather than debating the aesthetics of Shakespearean cinema, Belsey addresses the relations

between form, style and ideology, and argues that within the terms of
the realist cinema, Shakespearean film is predominantly reactionary.
In Belsey's account, the standard vocabulary of Hollywood realism
(she cites as examples Joseph L. Mankiewicz's 1953 *Julius Caesar* and
Peter Brook's 1970 *King Lear*) transforms Shakespeare's open, interrogative, non-illusionist texts into closed liberal humanist parables.

Graham Holderness (essay 4) extends Belsey's analysis of the politics of Shakespearean film by considering its potential for strategic
mobilisation and radical re-reading, specifically within the higher
educational context, while taking issue with her contention that
Shakespearean film (perhaps all film) is inevitably conservative.
Drawing a more detailed distinction between the illusionist and
non-illusionist cinema in terms of their relative capacities to
endorse, problematise or subvert ideology, Holderness insists upon
a more dialectical understanding of the relationship between the
spectator and the Shakespearean film text. By teasing out some of
the contradictions within Peter Hall's 1969 *A Midsummer Night's
Dream*, and examining the epic (as opposed to tragic) historical materialism of Akira Kurosawa's *Throne of Blood*, Holderness seeks
to demonstrate their radical potential, whilst also duly acknowledging the hegemonic ideological role of the cinema as a cultural apparatus. Holderness's work on Shakespearean film has been important
in this respect, in that he has consistently argued against the view
(prevalent when this essay first appeared in 1985, and still particularly dominant within new historicism) that Shakespeare is an inevitably conservative and reactionary cultural force: by examining
film at a time when most historicist scholarship concentrated upon
the plays in their early modern context, Holderness proposed a
practical means for Shakespeare to be put to progressive ends.

In his analysis of the Warner Brothers' *A Midsummer Night's
Dream* and Orson Welles's 1955 *Othello* (essay 5), John Collick
builds upon the historical materialist approach adopted by
Holderness, offering a detailed exposition of the economic and cultural determinants underpinning the style, form and genre of both
films. Arguing against the auteurist tendencies which have informed
much commentary on the Shakespeare films of Reinhardt and
Welles, Collick stresses the extent to which their works are implicated within and overdetermined by the generic restraints of the
Hollywood production system. Reinhardt's *Dream*, therefore,
can be regarded as a composite of Symbolist stagecraft, musical
fantasy, romantic comedy, animated cartoon and historical epic;

while Welles's *Othello*, conversely, adopts self-consciously *avant-garde* techniques, largely culled from the Expressionist cinema, in an absurdist allegory of the relationship between the creative artist and the state. Whereas Holderness foregrounds the progressive potential of Shakespeare on film, Collick places more emphasis upon the film industry's capacity for ideological containment.

Psychoanalysis has played an important part in the evolution of contemporary film theory, both as a means of probing the textual unconscious of cinematic works and as a means of theorising the relations between the spectator and the screen; Peter Donaldson's analysis of Olivier's 1947 *Hamlet* (essay 6) is a good example of the application of this methodology to a film which itself presents an overtly Freudian reading of the play. Donaldson's argument, which draws implicitly upon the distinction in Freudian dream theory between manifest and latent meaning, and effects a kind of analytic doubling by ascribing a further subtext to the film's subtext, is that Olivier's conscious Freudianism barely conceals the film's real textual unconscious, which is its exploration of the director's dysfunctional, unresolved relationship with his own father. This psychobiographical method, which restores a distinctly auteurist dimension to critical discourse, produces a highly nuanced discussion of the Oedipal dynamics of Olivier's film: Donaldson also provocatively (and contentiously) suggests that one of its recurrent motifs (the staircase) alludes to Olivier's own psychosexual conflicts.

The biography of the director/star is also brought into play in Curtis Breight's polemical critique of Kenneth Branagh's 1989 version of *Henry V* (essay 7). Branagh's film has elicited a great deal of commentary, much of it admiring, but has also seemed to provoke considerable irritation, with its ostensibly liberal credentials as an anti-war film being repeatedly called into dispute. For Breight, Branagh's *Henry V* is 'schizophrenic'[23] in the sense that the film uneasily combines an apparently egalitarian, pacifist stance with a deferential commitment to hierarchy and to the male bonding that militarism affords. Breight explores the background to the film in the form of Branagh's relationship with the Prince of Wales as explored in his autobiography; he then goes on to demonstrate how Branagh's sympathetic reading of Henry does considerable violence to the ironic and critical tendencies of Shakespeare's play. In addressing the ideology of Branagh's adaptation, Breight stresses the extent to which it draws upon, endorses and contributes to the reactionary genre of war films.

Breight's argument rests in part upon drawing comparisons between the historical provenance of Shakespeare's play and Branagh's manipulation and distortion of the text in the service of his own agenda; Colin MacCabe's discussion of Derek Jarman's 1980 *The Tempest* and 1991 adaptation of Christopher Marlowe's *Edward II* (essay 8) attempts a comparably synthetic analysis of both early modern and contemporary culture. The key difference, however, is that Jarman's appropriations of Shakespeare and Marlowe, which, with their drastic cutting, reshaping and rewriting of the texts, are far more adventurous than Branagh's (for some viewers, scandalously so), are identifiable as genuinely radical and subversive interventions in Shakespearean cinema. Drawing upon new historicist scholarship and postcolonial theory, MacCabe locates Shakespeare's *The Tempest* in the context of the formative myths of English and European colonial culture, and argues that Jarman's affirmative gay counter-reading of the play unsettles and subverts its sexual ideology. This argument is developed further with reference to Jarman's provocatively truncated and updated version of Marlowe's *Edward II*, where the links between repressive state power and the policing of sexuality are even more overtly addressed. As MacCabe suggests, by means of a direct comparison with Branagh's *Henry V*, part of the challenge of Jarman's *Edward II* is that, while loosely grouped within the genre of Shakespearean cinema, it is not *Shakespeare*, and as such it allows for critical distancing from, and reflection upon, the dominant ideologies of the genre.

V

If MacCabe's discussion moves us beyond Shakespeare by focusing upon one of the few films of Renaissance texts by other authors, Barbara Hodgdon's examination of a variety of screen versions of *The Taming of the Shrew* (essay 9) moves us into the broader reaches of Shakespearean adaptation within popular culture; like MacCabe, Hodgdon is concerned with sexual politics. Hodgdon considers the 1953 film of the Cole Porter musical *Kiss Me Kate* alongside the 1929 silent version and the 1966 version directed by Franco Zeffirelli, arguing that the play's largely misogynistic cinematic appeal in the twentieth century derives partly from its conform ity to a sado-masochistic regime of gendered spectatorship. By problematising the role and position of the spectator in relation to the pleasures that subsequent film renderings of this play may or may not afford, Hodgdon's essay makes use of feminist film theory – in particular of the concept of the cinematic gaze. As Laura Mulvey puts it, in what has become one of the most important and influential contributions to contemporary film theory, the dominant cinematic apparatus constructs 'woman as image, man as bearer of the look ... the determining male gaze projects its phantasy on to the female figure which is styled accordingly'.[24] The position of identification offered to the spectator is thus implicitly a masculine one. Hodgdon explores the visual pleasures of *The Taming of the Shrew* first by identifying a voyeuristic structure in Shakespeare's text, and then by examining how its filmic manifestations negotiate its problematic ideologies of gender and sexuality. Her rather bleak conclusion is that, if the play represents Katherina 'bound', the mainstream film tradition has endorsed rather than challenged its misogyny.

In an essay first published in 1937, Walter Benjamin argued that the age of mechanical reproduction had provoked a radical, potentially revolutionary, overhaul of the function and status of the work of art, in that the potential for widespread and instant reproducibility had stripped it of the 'aura' of uniqueness, originality and mystery with which it had traditionally been endowed, 'detach[ing] the reproduced object from the domain of tradition ... substitut[ing] a plurality of copies for a unique existence'.[25] For Benjamin, the cinema was the most developed technology of reproduction, having in it the capacity to dispense with 'outmoded concepts, such as creativity and genius, eternal value and mystery'.[26] If, according to the terms of Benjamin's thesis, the collision between Shakespeare and film has transformed the way in which the former has been understood, the onset of the age of digital reproduction opens up the possibility of an even more far-reaching transformation of the film medium itself, and hence, also, of Shakespearean cinema. In his account of Peter Greenaway's 1991 *Prospero's Books* (essay 10), Douglas Lanier addresses a Shakespearean adaptation by a filmmaker who has produced a body of work where the impact upon the art of film of computer and multi-media technologies has become increasingly, startlingly visible. According to Lanier, one of the key issues within Shakespearean performance criticism has been the simultaneously antagonistic and dependent relationship between the published, author-ised text and the imperfectly autonomous theatrical production; extended into the arena of Shakespeare on film, this problem translates as a visually explicit preoccupation with the burden of Shakespearean textuality (in Greenaway's case, this takes the form of the equation between the book and the human body). From this basis Lanier analyses *Prospero's Books* as a hyperabundant, self-reflexive and self-consciously intertextual exploration of the complex cinematic exchanges between text, image and performance, and argues that it stands as an example of 'postmodern bricolage'.[27]

Lanier calls *Prospero's Books* an instance of '"immanent theory", an artefact meditating on the theoretical grounds of its own existence'.[28] In the light of the arguments advanced in the majority of essays in this collection, this might well appear to be a highly desirable as well as historically appropriate way forward for the Shakespearean cinema as it moves into its second century. As Lapsley and Westlake point out, however, theory is inherent to any act of film-making or film-viewing: 'the spectator is not merely a passive receptacle imbibing its meanings',

> but is engaged in a succession of interpretations which depend on a whole set of background beliefs and without which the film would not make sense. On the basis of such beliefs – or theories, whether formalised or not – the spectator sees faces, telephones, desert landscapes rather than patches of colour; ascribes motives to characters; judges certain actions as good and others as bad; decides that this film is realistic and that one is not; distinguishes the happy from the unhappy ending; and so on ... Similarly, for the filmmaker, however self-consciously intuitive the approach, there is inevitably a comparable set of theories underlying the production of the film.[29]

The essays that follow demonstrate that all Shakespearean films are as underpinned by theory as are the competing schools of criticism which attend to them: theories such as Lapsley and Westlake describe, but also theories about Shakespeare's greatness or timelessness; about the construction and representation of subjectivity, gender and sexuality in his texts; about the politics of those texts; and about the right and wrong, or good and bad, ways of putting these on film. If for a long time critical discussion of Shakespeare in the cinema has been frustrated by the restrictions imposed by the last of these theoretical categories, the rapidly developing body of work sampled here affords the possibility of seeing his cinematic incarnation within the contexts of culture, history and politics – and also, perhaps, of contributing to the remaking of these contexts. For this, in the end, is what theory is for.

NOTES

1. The English teacher, in another neat metacinematic touch, is played by Joan Plowright, Olivier's widow.

2. Ian Johnson, 'Merely Players', in Charles W. Eckert (ed.), *Focus on Shakespearean Films* (Englewood Cliffs, NJ, 1972), p. 12.

3. Eckert, *Focus*, p. 3.

4. Allardyce Nicoll, *Film and Theatre* (London, 1936), p. 5.

5. Henri Lemaitre, 'Shakespeare, the Imaginary Cinema and the Pre-cinema', in Eckert, *Focus on Shakespearean Films*, p. 27.

6. The term refers to the non-verbal aspects of Shakespearean performance: setting, costume, props, the bodies of the actors, and so on.

7. Morris Beja, *Film and Literature: An Introduction* (New York, 1979), p. 82.

8. Graham Holderness, 'Shakespeare Rewound', *Shakespeare Survey*, 45 (1993), 66.

9. Robert Hamilton Ball, *Shakespeare on Silent Film: A Strange Eventful History* (London, 1968).

10. Ibid., p. 15.

11. Jack J. Jorgens, *Shakespeare on Film* (Bloomington, IN, 1977), p. 3.

12. Hugh Grady, *The Modernist Shakespeare: Critical Texts in a Material World* (Oxford, 1991), pp. 192–3.

13. Anthony Davies, *Filming Shakespeare's Plays: The Adaptations of Laurence Olivier, Orson Welles, Peter Brook and Akira Kurosawa* (Cambridge, 1988), p. xi.

14. Antony Easthope (ed.), *Contemporary Film Theory* (London, 1993), pp. 2–5.

15. André Bazin, *What is Cinema?* vol. 2, ed. and trans. Hugh Gray (Berkeley, CA, 1971), p. 26.

16. Bazin, *What is Cinema?* vol. 1, ed. and trans. Hugh Gray (Berkeley, CA, 1967), p. 38.

17. Robert Lapsley and Michael Westlake, *Film Theory: An Introduction* (Manchester, 1988), p. vii.

18. Stephen Heath, '*Jaws*, ideology and film theory', *Times Higher Education Supplement*, 26 March 1976; quoted in Easthope, *Contemporary Film Theory*, p. 8.

19. *Auteur* theory, which developed as a movement in French film criticism of the late 1950s, centres upon the idea that a particular work (or

body of works) could be ascribed personal 'authorship' on the part of the director. 'Great' films were thus read as expressions of individual genius and idiosyncrasy: the auterist film text was seen to be stylistically and thematically richer, more complex and more homogeneous than the routine products of the commercial cinema.

20. See p. 20 below.

21. See p. 21 below.

22. Davies, *Filming Shakespeare's Plays*, p. 4.

23. See p. 127 below.

24. Laura Mulvey, 'Visual Pleasure and Narrative Cinema', in Gerald Mast, Marshall Cohen and Leo Braudy (eds), *Film Theory and Criticism; Introductory Readings*, 4th edn (Oxford, 1992), p. 750.

25. Walter Benjamin, 'The Work of Art in the Age of Mechanical Reproduction', in Mast, Cohen and Braudy, *Film Theory and Criticism*, p. 668.

26. Ibid., p. 666.

27. See p. 185 below.

28. Ibid., p. 193.

29. Lapsley and Westlake, *Film Theory*, p. vi.

1

Realising Shakespeare on Film

JACK J. JORGENS

I

Critics often sort out Shakespeare films by measuring their relative distance from the language and conventions of the theatre.[1] The theatrical mode uses film as a transparent medium which 'can encapsulate any of the performing arts and render it in a film transcription'.[2] It has the look and feel of a performance worked out for a static theatrical space and a live audience. Lengthy takes in medium or long shot stress the durational quality of time, and, the frame acting as a kind of portable proscenium arch, meaning is generated largely through the words and gestures of the actors. Style in this mode derives primarily from the style of the performances, which are usually of a distinctly theatrical cast – more demonstrative, articulate, and continuous than actors are usually permitted in films. But it also derives from the manner of staging, varying from 'Elizabethan' in parts of Olivier's *Henry V*, to nineteenth-century proscenium in Burge and Dexter's *Othello*, to modern thrust stage in Dunlop's *Winter's Tale*, to Wirth's constructionist/modernist *Hamlet*, to Gielgud's 'rehearsal' *Hamlet* on a Broadway stage stripped of scenery, to the cavernous dark spaces of Richardson's Roundhouse *Hamlet*.

The great strength of the theatrical mode is that because the performance is conceived in terms of the theatre the text need not be heavily cut or rearranged. Shakespeare's tremendous range of verbal and dramatic styles from stark naturalism to metatheatrical playfulness need not be narrowed in the name of film convention and decorum. (It is the blatant *theatricality* of Olivier's *Hamlet* which permits him to instruct the players from off-camera in the simultaneous roles of film director, Prince of Denmark, and surrogate for Shakespeare, and allows us to enjoy the irony that the performances in 'The Murder of Gonzago' prove they weren't listening.) Its great weaknesses are that superficially it seems to be cheap and easy to capture the essence of a theatrical performance on film (in fact it is very time-consuming and difficult, for like anything else a great performance must be powerfully *seen* to be effective on film). On the screen as on the stage,

> the Deadly Theatre takes easily to Shakespeare. We see his plays done by good actors in what seems like the proper way – they look lively and colourful, there is music and everyone is all dressed up, just as they are supposed to be in the best classical theatres. Yet secretly we find it excruciatingly boring – and in our hearts we either blame Shakespeare, or theatre as such, or even ourselves.[3]

Most films in the theatrical mode fail because they were never good theatre in the first place.

The realistic mode takes advantage of 'the camera's unique ability to show us *things* – great, sweeping landscapes or the corner of a friar's cell, a teeming market-place or the intimacy of a boudoir, all in the flash of a moment'.[4] This is the most popular kind of Shakespeare film, not merely because filmmakers are most familiar with it and mass audiences enjoy the spectacle of historical recreations, but because everyone senses that at bottom Shakespeare is a realist. If realism in film implies something more than a visual style or authentic costumes and settings, it seems to many that this playwright – who filled his Globe with duels, battles, shipwrecks, tortures, assassinations, storms, coronations, trials, suicides, feasts, and funerals, who juxtaposed the ugly with the sublime, the base with the noble, everyday with holiday, who ruthlessly explored both the need for and the dangers of centralised power, the conflicts of young and old, the rocking of order and tradition by frightening, invigorating forces of change – virtually demands screen realism. The kind may be left up to the filmmaker. It may be Zeffirelli's decorative, spectacular, orchestrally accompanied variety, which is a descendant of the elaborate productions of the nineteenth century, or the harsh documentary style of Brook's *Lear*, or a mixed style, as in Polanski's gory, twilight

Macbeth, the fortress and tangled forest of Kurosawa's *Throne of Blood*, or the silences and wintery empty spaces of Welles's *Chimes at Midnight*.

One weakness of this mode is that since for many 'the poetic drama does not thrive on photographic realism ... [which] has the effect of making the poetry sound unnatural and self-conscious',[5] Shakespeare's poetic and rhetorical patterning, overtly formal structures, and emblematic scenes and objects must be disguised or cut. A playwright who juxtaposes several levels of illusion and creates highly subjective dramatic worlds often finds realist collaborators who can deal with but one level of illusion and do not always succeed in avoiding a neutral and unaffecting objectivity. Realistic settings are seldom suffused with emotions and ideas, with poetry, biography, and ideology as well as history. Their outer eloquence is not always matched by inner truth.

The second major weakness is that in shifting the emphasis from the actors to actors-in-a-setting, one risks loss of focus. In response to the declared quest for 'authenticity' in Cukor and Thalberg's *Romeo and Juliet*, John Feugi quite properly asks, 'does the wealth of physical detail (the life of a great epoch) illuminate the story or does it weigh the story down under a mass of intrusive detail? Does Shakespeare in his "pursuit of reality" actually seek to "present life in all its fullness"?'[6] Details must be given the proper emphasis, be powerful and significant yet also subordinated to an overall design, lest they obscure what is important.

The filmic mode is the mode of the film poet, whose works bear the same relation to the surfaces of reality that poems do to ordinary conversation. A filmic rendering of Shakespeare, says Kozintsev,

> shifts the stress from the aural to the visual. The problem is not one of finding means to speak the verse in front of the camera, in realistic circumstances ranging from long-shot to close-up. The aural has to be made visual. The poetic texture itself has to be transformed into a visual poetry, into the dynamic organisation of film imagery.[7]

Like the realist, the film poet uses many non-theatrical techniques – a great variety of angles and distances, camera movement. He substitutes for the classical style of playing *on* the lines, the modern style of playing *between* the lines.[8] But unlike the other modes, there is emphasis on the *artifice* of film, on the expressive possibilities of distorting the surfaces of reality. In Olivier's *Henry V* we find 'the frank admixture of the real (e.g., horses and the sea) and the unreal (painted backdrops, frank acknowledgement of the presence of an audience, stylised gesture, overtly symbolic settings)'. His films 'avoid a simple equation of film and realism, ... hover magnificently, as André Bazin has also observed, between "things" and "art", the very area in which the plays themselves have their life and being'.[9] In Welles's films we find strong graphic compositions; in Reinhardt and Dieterle's *Dream*, fluid, lyrical movements set to Mendelssohn's music; in Hall's *Dream*, abstract patterns of light and jump cuts. Each work uses antirealist techniques to express important aspects of the plays.

The great strength of the filmic mode is that it takes advantage of the film's power to tell a story 'by overcoming the forms of the outer world, namely space, time, and causality, and by adjusting the events to the forms of the inner world, namely attention, memory, imagination, and emotion'.[10] It acknowledges the importance of everything that is not literal in Shakespeare's plays by exploring through sounds and images what Stanislavsky called 'subtext',

> the manifest, the inwardly felt expression of a human being in a part which flows uninterruptedly beneath the words of the text, giving them life and a basis for existing ... a web of innumerable varied inner patterns inside a play and a part ... all sorts of figments of the imagination, inner movements, objects of attention, smaller and greater truths and a belief in them, adaptations, adjustments and other similar elements.[11]

Peter Brook has written,

> if you could extract the mental impression made by the Shakespearean strategy of images, you would get a piece of pop collage ... The background that Shakespeare can conjure in one line evaporates in the next and new images take over. ... The non-localised stage means that every single thing under the sun is possible, not only quick changes of location: a man can turn into twins, change sex, be his past, his present, his future, be a comic version of himself, and be none of them, *all at the same time*.[12]

To the extent that this is so, despite the dangers of dazzling technique for its own sake, wooden performances, and decimated texts, the filmic mode is truest to the effect of Shakespeare's dramatic verse.

Parallel but by no means congruent with the theatrical, realist, and filmic modes are three means of treatment which describe a film's relative distance from the original text – presentation, inter-pretation, and adaptation.[13] In a presentation, the artist attempts to convey the original with as little alteration and distortion as pos-sible. At its worst, presentation represents a fatal misunderstanding of the collaborative nature of dramatic art and a failure of intelli-gence, feeling, and imagination. Here the artist substitutes for the living work a blend of stale, unemphatic run-through and uncon-sciously retailed clichés. He only manages to prove that it is poss-ible for actors to speak every word of a Shakespeare play before an audience and be completely untrue to its spirit. On film, one thinks of the opening court scene in Hall's *Dream*, the scene in England between Malcolm and MacDuff in Welles's *Macbeth*, and scores of studio TV productions and pedagogical 'Scenes from the Bard'.

At its best, presentation is what John Russell Brown has called 'free Shakespeare',[14] where the work is allowed its archaic words, thoughts, and conventions, raw juxtapositions of formalism and realism, full length, contradictions, and welter of possible meanings. In tone and emphasis, the performance attempts to preserve the bal-ances and tensions of the original while in an open, improvisatory, exploratory way seeking to rediscover its fluid, chaotic Elizabethan essence. Above all, good presentation avoids explaining, experienc-ing, and digesting the work for the audience – it is a realisation of the play, not a set of footnotes to it or a critical essay upon it. Examples: the closet scene in Richardson's *Hamlet*; Brutus's and Cassius's quarrel in Mankiewicz's *Julius Caesar*; the King's wooing of Katherine in *Henry V*; and 'Pyramus and Thisby' in Hall's *Dream*.

Interpretation entails shaping and performing a play according to a definite 'view' of it. Proponents of interpretative directing note that 'interpretation is inevitable. ... The actor's figure, the way he enters the stage, the colour of his hair, etc., everything perceived by the audience is interpretation whether it is so intended or not'.[15] They argue that it is a fiction (though fictions may be useful) that theatre artists render a work without altering it, that performers, audiences, and critics can somehow escape the influence of the French Revolution, the Industrial Revolution, Freud, Darwin, Marx, and mass media. They ask whether it is desirable or even possible for a single performance of a dramatic work to realise *all* its possibilities. At its worst, interpretation in performance is like 'modernising' a noble work of architecture in Second-Rate Contemporary, or bringing 'progress' to a lush tropical island. At

its best, it involves imaginative collaborative creation, revelatory
and powerful emphases which so enrich and illuminate the play
that they challenge the stern admonition by Susan Sontag: 'to interpret is to impoverish'.[16]

Reductive interpretations on film are all too easily illustrated:
Olivier's cutting of Henry's vicious threats before the gates of
Harfleur, Reinhardt's excision of Titania's long description of
death, disease, and disorder in his *Dream*, and Czinner's heavy cen-
soring of Touchstone's earthy humour and Jaques's cynicism in his
As You Like It. One thinks of speeches uprooted from their contexts and used as 'explanatory' prologues (the Prince's 'vicious mole
of nature' speech in Olivier's *Hamlet*, and fawning Rosencrantz's
proclamation to Claudius that 'the cess of majesty/Dies not alone,
but like a gulf doth draw/What's near with it' in Wirth's *Hamlet*),
eccentric performances by actors, melodramatic scores, and bathetic
interpolated scenes. Yet there is truth in Boris Pasternak's advice to
Kozintsev, which locates the Shakespearean essence not in the
poetry but in the characters and action:

> I always regard half of the text of any play, of even the most immor-
> tal and classic work of genius, as a diffused remark that the author
> wrote in order to acquaint the actors as thoroughly as possible with
> the heart of the action to be played. As soon as a theatre has pene-
> trated his artistic intention, and mastered it, one can and should
> sacrifice the most vivid and profound lines (not to mention the pale
> and indifferent ones), provided that the actors have achieved an
> equally talented performance of an acted, mimed, silent, or laconic
> equivalent to these lines. ...[17]

In *Hamlet* Kozintsev repeatedly demonstrates how a collaborator can
be true to the original by altering it. When he divides Claudius's
opening speech among a rough soldier reading it perfunctorily and
threateningly to the peasants outside, smooth courtiers who mutter
snatches of it to one another in several foreign languages, and finally
Claudius himself to his councillors, he underscores the King's mixture
of crass power, flamboyance, and sophisticated statesmanship. By removing the 'words, words, words' between the wounding of Hamlet
and 'the rest is silence', he underscores Hamlet's transcendence of
the mundane order, which is at least one of the major truths told
in Shakespeare's conclusion. And on a larger scale, both Olivier's
Hamlet, which incorporates the Freud/Jones oedipal interpretation,
and Brook's *Lear*, which was shaped by Jan Kott's existential view,

are true enough to important dimensions of the original and powerful enough in their own right to be valued alongside good presentations of the same works.

Frequently the interpretative process of conceptualising, shaping, and reimaging shades off into adaptation in which, just as Plutarch and Holinshed served Shakespeare, Shakespeare's plays serve as source material for new but still related works of art. More than any other period since the Restoration, this is the period of Shakespeare recast in new forms: musicals, ballets, operas, political satires, avant-garde collages, animated films, dramatic films, plays, and everything else imaginable.[18] Many of these are so distant from the scope and intent of the originals, or so slight, that they do not merit critical attention. A few, however, which borrow elements directly from Shakespeare, alter others, and add still others, being as Welles put it 'variations on his themes',[19] are of very high quality indeed.

There are three critical frameworks which seem useful in dealing with such works as Kurosawa's *Throne of Blood* and Welles's *Chimes at Midnight*: source study, the study of translation, and comparative literature. In source study one peers over the shoulder of the artist and watches the way he works with his raw materials. The earlier work clarifies, enriches, and provides a lever for discussion of the later. We study a translation (and in a sense *all* Shakespeare films are translations) as a creative attempt to recast and reimage a work conceived in a different language and for a different culture. Any but the most mindless literal translation is part literal rendering, part figurative leap, and part record of the translator's own responses. ('Don't translate what I wrote', said Ezra Pound, 'translate what I meant to write'.[20]) Using a comparative approach, we place two works side by side so that they may mutually illuminate each other. Shared patterns, relations to tradition, and unique qualities stand out because of their treatments of similar situations, themes, characters, styles, and structures. With regard to Shakespeare films, it is accurate to say that the true test is 'not whether the filmmaker has respected his model, but whether he has respected his own vision'.[21] It is necessary to add further, however, that because the artist has chosen to work with Shakespeare and knows his audience will come to his new work with knowledge of the earlier one, there must be important points of contact between Shakespeare's vision and his own, some resonance when the two works are juxtaposed, lest adaptation become travesty.

Used sensibly, these categories are, as Algernon says in *The Importance of Being Earnest*, 'quite as true as any observation in civilised life ought to be'. But having gathered what honey we could from these abstract flowers, we should pause and consider their limitations. First, they are useful chiefly as descriptive and not as evaluative terms. 'There can no more be a set of rules for principles for filming Shakespeare than there can be a set of rules or principles for staging him.'[22] Reading through the criticism of Shakespeare films, one gets the uneasy feeling that a game has evolved in which works are automatically praised or blamed because they have been made in a particular style or mode. Critics crucify Welles's films for being atrocious presentations or overrate them because they are ostentatiously filmic. They contemptuously dismiss Burge and Dexter's *Othello* as 'anti-cinematic' or praise it for being free of 'film gimmicks'. They rate Castellani's *Romeo and Juliet* above Olivier's *Hamlet* because it creates a more believable world. Zeffirelli is now despised for treating Shakespeare like a hack scriptwriter, now hailed for avoiding a dry, respectfully dull academic style. But granting that there will always be differences in taste and that we must not forego the obligation to judge, it still seems wise to avoid elevating our particular sensitivities to the status of universal laws. We ought to remain open to as many different kinds of excellence in Shakespeare films as possible.

Second, like many divisions favoured by critics and theorists, these three conceal much more than they reveal, perpetuating as they do the largely artificial division between the disciplines of literature, theatre, and film. Good Shakespeare films often move fluidly between modes and styles, merge several simultaneously, so that it is not possible to make simple judgements.

Third, and most important, these categories do not penetrate very deeply into the process of re-creating Shakespeare on film, into the interrelations of style and meaning which lie at the heart of these visions and re-visions. For this we require different terms and a different approach.

II

The remarkable density of Shakespeare's plays results from a blend of strong 'horizontal' movements (good plots, developing characters) with powerful 'vertical' moments (resonant images, penetrating meditations, complex poetic patterns).[23] Part of the filmmaker's task is to preserve the balance of the two. The first is relatively easy, for strong narrative movement has always been important in conventional films. The second is a complex and delicate matter, for Shakespeare's poetic images function in many ways. If they were simply word-painting intended to fill in the scenery which the Elizabethan stage lacked, the interpreter could deal with them like descriptive passages in novels. But Shakespearean images function in all sorts of ways: as embodiments of ideas and conflicts (the flash of light in *Romeo and Juliet*, animals in *King Lear*), as symbols for things unseen (disease in *Hamlet*), as renderings of emotional states (darkness and choking in *Macbeth*). Images may sum up the essence of the action (a body on the rack in *King Lear*), may bind together themes ('sun' and 'son' in *Hamlet*, 'crown' in *Richard III*), and may reflect character (Othello's images of glorious war, exotic places, sweeping landscapes; Iago's images of rutting animals, poison, webs, snares). Furthermore, the poetic images do not function independently of the theatrical images. They are all part of the same pattern. The shocking scene of the blinding of Gloucester and Kent's defiant 'see better Lear' merge. When we say that Shakespeare, like a good filmmaker, *thought* in images, we mean not merely verbal images, but movements ('The weird sisters, hand in hand ... Thus do go about, about'; Lady Macbeth walking in her sleep), gestures (Titania embracing Bottom the ass), and objects (a throne, a bed, a handkerchief).

It is often argued that 'the literary greatness of Shakespeare's dialogue, and to an equivalent degree that of the dialogue of all the masters of dramatic literature from the Elizabethans to Shaw, is the obstacle to its success as film dialogue'.[24] We are told that 'the photographic images and the language inevitably neutralise each other'.[25] But on the contrary, many Shakespeare films successfully imitate or find analogies for his unions of the verbal and the visual. The richest moments in these films often derive from the expressive possibilities of shifting relations between words and images. In rare instances, for example, the visual image may *be* the words when, as at the beginning of Olivier's *Hamlet*, the director wishes us to focus solely on the abstract meaning of a speech. When a director wishes the words to function alone, he may throw the images on the screen out of focus (Brook's *King Lear*), or make them so uninteresting that they 'disappear' (Lysander's speech on 'the course of true love' in Hall's *Dream*). The camera may play over the actor who registers, disguises, or plays against the ideas and emotions in the lines – the speeches being spoken openly (Olivier's stirring appeals to his men in *Henry V*) or rendered voice-over, emphasising the isolation and disturbed nature of the hero (Welles's *Macbeth*). Then too the camera may show the impact of the words on other characters: Hamlet's face as the Player describes Pyrrus's sword sticking in the air, Claudius's response as Hamlet sardonically describes the progress of a king through the guts of a beggar.

Frequently the visual image will both show the speaker and in some way embody the form or content of the lines. A verbal figure may become visual. Oxymoron may leap to life in a shot of angry Capulet and Tybalt in the foreground and a pair of dancing lovers in the background. Hamlet's repetition 'except my life, except my life, except my life' may be underlined by two sharply pointed arches and repeating arcades.[26] Helena's contrasting pair of lines 'things base and vile, holding no quantity,/Love can transpose to form and dignity' may be wittily echoed when she appears from behind a bush, plucks off a leaf, turns her back, plucks another leaf, and disappears once more. Often there is some attempt at direct illustration as when Macbeth's bloody hand is stretched out by a wide-angle lens as he asks 'will all great Neptune's ocean wash this blood clean from my hand?', Othello speaks farewell to his occupation on a hillside filled with the tents of his troops, or Macbeth remarks 'so foul and fair a day I have not seen' as he and Banquo watch refugees flee Duncan's wars on the muddy road below.

The visual image may exclude the speaker and even more directly work to embody the lines, making the character a voice-over commentator. In Schaefer's *Macbeth* we dissolve from the tyrant vowing to make his bloody thoughts deeds to hanging bodies and a burning village. In Brook's *King Lear* we watch hunted Edgar and his blind father set out across a bleak wasteland littered with dead horses as Gloucester speaks chorically: 'as flies to wanton boys are we to the gods – they kill us for their sport.' In Olivier's *Henry V* the camera pans away from sad Burgundy to illustrate in painterly tableaux the havoc wreaked on France by the war. The illustrations need not always be so realistic or so literal, however. In moments of extreme disturbance, directors have often permitted themselves a great deal of freedom in seeking a Shakespearean effect with cinematic means, as in the striking clay idol in Welles's *Macbeth*, the eerie blue green willow swirling in the wind at Desdemona's death in Yutkevitch's *Othello*, blurred shots of drowned rats in Brook's *Lear*, heaps of skulls and bones in *Throne of Blood*, and a white

mask streaming with blood in Calpurnia's dream in David Bradley's
student film of *Julius Caesar*.

To avoid redundancy, the lines themselves may be cut, the visuals
replacing or expanding upon them. Like other techniques, this is
not always successful. Not only is the link between character and
imagery broken, but the effect is often very different. When
Zeffirelli substituted a rather pedestrian shot of an early morning
Italian countryside for the Friar's lines,

> The grey-eyed morn smiles on frowning night,
> Check-ring the eastern clouds with streaks of light;
> And flecked darkness like a drunkard reels
> From forth day's path and Titan's burning wheels,

he captured one essential point – the Friar's optimism – but the
personifications and ornamentation are given up for no appreciable
gain. The visuals must be *powerfully* visual as well as significant. In
Schaefer's *Macbeth* Birnam wood coming to Dunsinane regrettably
resembles bargain day at a Christmas tree lot. In Kurosawa's film it
becomes a superb poetic hallucinatory moment as swaying, disembodied branches move in slow motion through the fog to ominous
music. Shakespeare films achieve power not only by portraying the
action, the battles, say, in *Henry V* and in *Chimes at Midnight*, and
illustrating the lines directly. Free renderings are also sometimes
very effective. In Kozintsev's *King Lear*, 'Albany's closing quatrain
("The weight of this sad time"), for instance, is conveyed simply in
an image of a shattered Edgar, walking into the camera, leaving
behind him the devastations of the battlefield where the Fool sits
piping a crazy dirge.'[27]

A filmmaker can be quite literal, direct, and realistic in rendering
a Shakespearean theme and still be very effective. In his gory film of
a gory play, Polanski suggests through images all of the meanings of
'blood' in *Macbeth*: heredity, kinship, lust, guilt, cleansing sacrifice
(including the ritual link between blood and wine), and the hunter's
thirst for the lifeblood of his prey. But at times a freer translation is
in order, as in Reinhardt and Dieterle's *Dream*, where the central
conflict is expressed in terms of the natural polarity of monochro-
matic film: night (Satan, evil, the grotesque) versus moonlight (lyric-
ism, good, angelic beauty). And at other times, the image may not
illustrate or reinforce the lines at all, but may heighten their effect
through contrast. As Falstaff eulogises sack, Hal drops his cup and

joins the soldiers leaving the battlefield, and becomes smaller and smaller. In one film Mercutio dies howling 'a plague on both your houses' by the well which gives Verona life-giving water, in another, on the cathedral steps where, the Friar and his values being impotent to prevent disaster, the bodies of the young lovers later lie in state.

Part of the interest in seeing several different films of the same play is in seeing what choices the artist has made in 'imaging' Shakespeare on the screen. J. Blumenthal has argued, for instance, that unlike Macbeth, 'Hamlet would be untranslatable because of the verbality of his experience.'[28] But this is to assume that verbal experience is foreign to good cinema, and that the only acceptable translation is a direct one. Hamlet's soliloquy, 'To be or not to be', has been rendered in many ways. It has been done humorously by Fred Mogubgub in a short film called 'Enter Hamlet', where with brightly coloured cartoon figures he provides a separate image for each word: 'Whether [man and nude woman under umbrella in bloody rain] 'tis [voice comes out of a well] nobler [man lashed to train tracks, train coming] in [bearded prisoner in cell] the [pianist plinking "the" on piano and echoed by conductor and audience] mind [shout from skyscraper causing shouter to fall]', and so on. In more serious efforts, Olivier has spoken to elaborate music as he stares dizzily down at the sea from the walls of Elsinore; Schell, with eyes shut, his face framed by stairs; Smoktunovsky, as he wanders among boulders at the meeting of Denmark and the sea; and Williamson, as he lies indolent in a hammock. John Howard Lawson has suggested still another rendering:

> Since it is manifestly impossible to translate the verbal metaphors into visual terms, a film version of the soliloquy must find contrasting images which take advantage of the contradiction between sight and sound to interpret the poetry, emphasise its philosophy or underline its irony. The voice might be heard while Hamlet is engaged in the dull round of court activities, comparing the cloud castles of his thought to the painful routine at Elsinore. The moral intensity of his thought might be contrasted to the depravity of the royal household. There might be another contrast between the words and the slimy waters of a moat, with shadows and shapes and monstrous insects moving across the rippling reflection of the hero's face. Visual images would in some way comment on the changing rhythm of the speech. In the short passage quoted, the flow is broken abruptly by the two monosyllables, 'end them'. There would be a sudden shift of visual emphasis, and possibly a discordant clash of sound, on these words.[29]

Macbeth's immortal speech of despair, 'Tomorrow, and tomorrow, and tomorrow', has also been realised visually in many different ways. Schaefer shows a greying, weary man leaning against a huge stone wall and speaking aloud, Polanski a man 'thinking' in a monotone as he walks down emblematic stairs and looks without emotion on his wife's contorted corpse. Kurosawa cut the speech altogether, choosing to show Washizu's despair in less articulate ways (he stares into space, shouts 'Fool!', grimaces and moves violently), while Welles has Macbeth look down at swirling, chaotic fog which eventually fills the frame – a perfect symbol of the horror and formlessness of his vision of life. If we are concerned with the art of filming Shakespeare and not merely with the craft of photographing actors, we must be sensitive to such varied and often complex relations between words and images.

III

There is nothing more *un*-Shakespearean than a film which relies solely on the poetry for its power, unity, and meaning. The words are always important, for on film, as on stage, the actors are like musicians performing a verbal score – badly in the case of Reinhardt and Dieterle's *Dream*, superbly in the case of Hall's. Part of the interpretation will always rely upon the actors' readings – shifts in rhythm and emphasis, pitch and volume – as they mould their parts, build and release tension over the whole arc of the role. A simple pause can force us to anticipate, adjust, reconsider. An unexpected inflection can hint at a flow of emotions and ideas which reveal the meaning of their lines. The very quality of the voice – Marianne Faithfull's worldly, sophisticated Ophelia versus Jean Simmons's timid, innocent one; Burton's virile, authoritative Hamlet, Olivier's sighing, melancholy Prince, and Williamson's nasty, snarling nasal one – shapes our response to the character and hence to the play. We can never spend too much time and effort listening to the words – their patterns and meaning.

But in films, as in live performances, there is so much more. Plays 'mean' in hundreds of non-verbal ways not often stressed in criticism or the classroom. We perceive the words in the context of gestures, costumes, groupings, and movements. The meaning of the action is coloured by its setting and the object involved in it. On the screen, the way lines, shapes, colours, and textures are arranged affects our response, as do music and non-verbal sounds, montage, and the structuring of the action beat by beat, scene by scene. These things communicate 'the psychological, physical or sociological realities that lie behind, and not infrequently enrich or deny, the more conscious interchanges of speech'.[30] Much of the freedom, the creativity allowed collaborators with an 'open' playwright like Shakespeare lies precisely in this fleshing out and orchestration of the nuances of the language and dramatic action.

Shakespeare thought in terms of eloquent gestures as well as eloquent speeches: Macbeth shattering a festive banquet with shrieks and a drawn sword, Othello putting out the light, Lear kneeling mockingly before Regan for raiment and food and later in earnest before Cordelia for forgiveness, Romeo tossing off the poison as a toast to his love. But a sensitive director will always complement these with other gestures which illuminate a dramatic moment, reveal the meaning of the words, define relationships, or establish a contrast or parallel.[31] Olivier as Richard III locates the point at which his controlled energy becomes uncontrolled when, in an unnecessarily emphatic demonstration of what is to be done to the young Princes in the Tower, he nearly smothers the man who is to do it. In Richardson's *Hamlet* a passionate kiss between Laertes and Ophelia shows how the disease of incest has spread outward in the court from the King and Queen. In Bradley's *Julius Caesar* a close-up of flowers being trampled on the marble steps foreshadows the general destruction to follow. Even where Shakespeare has provided the gesture, the actor must articulate it: one Othello stares at the handkerchief in disbelief, another is tortured by its softness and sweet smell, still another tears it in his teeth like a wild animal.

Costume, an extension of the actor's body, is really another form of gesture. It communicates not only sex, age, social class, occupation, nationality, season of the year, and occasion, but subjective qualities – moods, tastes, values. Costumes speak to an audience through line, shape, colour, and texture. Often Shakespeare gives some direction – Hamlet's suit of mourning, Osric's foppish hat, Malvolio's yellow stockings – but again much is left to the performing artists. Welles makes great comic capital out of the incongruous sight of Falstaff drifting across the battlefield like a huge armoured blimp. It is not only his movement but his flowing robes that set Othello apart from the Venetians. Changes in character are often signalled by shifts in dress – Juliet or Ophelia appearing in mourning,

Hamlet in a travelling robe, Lear in rags, the young Athenian lovers in the *Dream* in muddy, torn parodies of the civilised, freshly laundered apparel of the opening.

Bergman once said 'our work in films begins with the human face'.[32] Despite the complaints of insensitive viewers about the boredom of 'talking faces', in many of the best Shakespeare films it is the expressiveness of those faces, controlled from within by the actors and from without by makeup and lighting artists, that generates much of their power: the ferocious mask-face of Washizu in *Throne of Blood*, the obscene grins of Polanski's witches, the immobile brutal faces of Goneril, Regan, and Cornwall in Brook's *Lear*. Recall too the fresh, innocent faces in Zeffirelli's *Romeo and Juliet*, Joe E. Brown's deadpan Flute, Mickey Rooney's Pan-like Puck, Welles's Father Christmas Falstaff, and various incarnations of Gertrude's beauty gone to seed. Quite apart from casting and facial expression, faces are photographed in a great variety of ways: from the front, the rear, or in profile, distorted by reflections and shadows, masked by bars, veils, flames, armour, and 'beetle brows'. Faces are rouged and powdered, glisten with sweat, are dirty or bloodied. They appear upside down, sway back and forth, are fragmented by the edges of the frame, and all of these things affect the meaning of the dramatic moment.

Spatial arrangements and relationships, on stage and on film, are metaphoric. To be spatially in between is to be caught in conflict – Gertrude between Claudius and Hamlet, Romeo between Mercutio and Tybalt, Desdemona between Othello and Brabantio. As Othello and Desdemona become estranged in Welles's film, the distances between them become huge. Movements away from one character and toward another often announce a shift in allegiance, as when the lords hastily abandon Hastings when they realise Richard intends to kill him. Rapid regroupings signal confusion, as in the mob in *Julius Caesar* or the lovers in *Dream* who do a kind of dance in which they constantly change partners. Film is capable of capturing larger movements, like the fine assassination scene in Mankiewicz's *Julius Caesar*, where after swimming from blow to blow and wiping the blood from his eyes, Caesar staggers down steps toward Brutus only to receive the fatal thrust. Film far surpasses the stage in portraying the charge and countercharge of battle scenes.

Despite the capacity of theatregoers to 'zoom in' on a detail, however, film also has more power to make small movements and relationships huge and important. On film, a glance or the nervous flutter of a fan may be as striking as a forty-foot leap. Motion in films is also complicated by the fact that the camera can move and the focal length of the lens can change, placing the characters, setting, objects, and camera in an intricate dance. Distance, perspective, and relationships can change with the fluidity and subtlety of a line of verse. Static theatrical space becomes dynamic. The rhetoric may be very strong, as when the camera races along with charging troops, wanders the halls of Elsinore, or rushes toward Hamlet as he spies the ghost in Kozintsev's film. Or it may be 'invisible' as we move with an actor, including or excluding elements of setting, light, or colour, shifting tempo to comment quietly on the action.

As in poetry and fiction, rooms, buildings, streets, and landscapes may be saturated with ideas, associations, and emotions in film. Realist or expressionist, settings may reinforce or counterpoint with action, character, themes, and verbal styles. The pastoral scene behind Orsino as he sighs out his melancholy to Viola underscores the distinctly forced, literary quality of his love in Fried's Russian *Twelfth Night*. The innocence of the young children playing outside the cathedral in Castellani's film contrasts with Juliet's new seriousness and maturity as she seeks the Friar.

Sometimes the worlds of Shakespeare's plays are single – Denmark in many films is a political, psychological, and philosophical prison, puzzling, unknowable, sinister. Brook's Lear inhabits a world of unrelieved darkness and primitiveness which may conflict with Shakespeare's renaissance language and court but which unquestionably contributes to the intensity of the work.[33] Castellani's *Romeo and Juliet* takes place in a beautiful but stifling Verona, emblematic of an old civilisation built on rivalry and materialism which imprisons and eventually destroys innocence and love.[34] The exterior of Macbeth's castle in Welles's film suggests Faustian aspiration, but inside it is a solipsistic world of dizzying heights, jagged rocks, moonscapes, gnarled dead trees, fog, and Rorschach-test floors from which there is no escape. Sometimes the plays have two worlds and the films elaborate the conflicts between the two: the kingdom of Falstaff versus the kingdom of Henry IV; the daylight world of Theseus and the nocturnal world of Oberon; Venice and Cyprus. In his lush colour imitation of Welles's *Othello*, Yutkevitch created a film which, from the splendid shots of the ghost ship under the titles to Othello's death on the ramparts of Cyprus, is saturated with images of the sea, demonstrating that a motif can work as powerfully in setting as it can in poetry.

In Shakespeare's plays, props often carry great symbolic weight, but once again it is up to his collaborators to articulate and complement what is indicated explicitly in the text. In Welles's *Macbeth*, the awkward, oversized, horned crown blends the Satanic theme with the poetic theme of ill-fitting clothes. In Schaefer's film there are two crowns: a crown of thorns mockingly given Macbeth by the prophetic witches, and the jewelled symbol of the power which Macbeth cannot keep from passing on to Banquo's sons. In Polanski's version, the crown is part of a circular motif which runs through the entire film, from the circle inscribed in the sand by the witches, to the iron collar around Cawdor's neck, to the huge shield at Macbeth's coronation, and the ring to which the baited bear is chained. In Brook's *Lear*, the throne is a coffinlike stone enclosure which isolates the King, makes his voice boom out at his subjects, and prefigures death. In Kozintsev's film, it is a huge chair which dwarfs the wispy, white-haired King, who sits on its edge like a child.

Occasionally such effects are obtrusive and unsubtle: Duncan riding through a herd of sheep as he goes to be sacrificed at Macbeth's castle, Othello wandering distracted among picturesque classical ruins which are an emblem of his own ruined grandeur. Often, however, they enrich our understanding. In Wirth's *Hamlet*, Polonius's monocle reveals both his pretentiousness and his figurative blindness. The flaring flame as Lady Macbeth burns Macbeth's letter reflects her inner fire in Schaefer's film, and the skull-like oil lamp on the table as Antony, Octavius, and Lepidus determine which of their enemies must die underscores the grisly nature of their work in Bradley's *Julius Caesar*.

Consider the various uses of the bed in Shakespeare films. In Olivier's *Hamlet* it is a rather abstract symbol, overstuffed, decorated with labial curtains, helping to emphasise the Oedipal nature of Hamlet's conflict. Richardson's film shows the bed as a 'nasty sty' where overweight Claudius and pallid Gertrude drink blood-red wine and feast with their dogs on greasy chicken and fruit. In films of *Macbeth*, beds connote sterility, brutality, perversion, in *Othello* altars for sacrifice, symbols for love covered with shadows or fragmented by the frame. While in Zeffirelli's *Shrew* the bed is a playful battleground, in *Romeo and Juliet* it is associated with the funeral bier. Not only do words and acts speak in Shakespeare films. *Things* speak.

From one perspective, the camera selects and records things in front of the lens, the most important variables being the apparent distance from the subject (are we involved or detached? do we see individual details or the larger pattern?) and the angle of view. From another perspective, film is a graphic art in which the artist composes images with light and shadow, colour and texture, shape and line, within a rectangle. Within shots we 'read' a hundred different variables which work on us more or less simultaneously and often carry conflicting messages. Welles makes us *see* the sound of the trumpets in *Othello* by creating a harmony of diagonal lines and bell-shaped mouths. When Richard III's shadow fills the frame or a lense distorts his face as he moves near the camera, we *see* his egotism and warped personality. The formal beauty of the shot in which Washizu kneels beside a rack of arrows before going to kill his lord in *Throne of Blood* suits the cool ironic tone of the film and contrasts vividly with the scene in which he is slain violently with arrows. In *Macbeth*,

> Welles uses silhouettes throughout the entire film. Characters and objects are very frequently shown with the source of light behind them, as if they had passed over to a realm beyond light with their dark side forward. A variation of this is seen in the partial lighting of people and things, the constant suggestion that only part of the truth can be seen, only part of the real nature of a person noticed.[35]

Olivier consistently associates Ophelia with light. And as with lighting, colours can clarify conflicts (Capulets against Montagues, English versus French), signal shifts in tone (the draining of colour from Zeffirelli's *Romeo and Juliet*), establish an overall atmosphere, or create associations.

Composition is a complex tool in film since it also involves creative use of *montage*, the juxtaposition of image with image. If *within* a shot Polanski may contrast the external beauty of Lady Macbeth, her red hair blowing against an intense blue sky, with her voice-over prayer for cruelty enough to kill Duncan, if Kozintsev may set Lear's royal commands ('Know that we ...') against a shot of Lear playing with the Fool by the fire, if Zeffirelli in *Taming of the Shrew* may place the wedding guests in the top half of the frame and dogs gnawing hungrily on bones in the bottom half, *between* shots the possibilities are infinite. Those who find the written word more expressive and subtle than the visual image might consider the number of meaningful contrasts possible between two shots – contrasts of one colour with another, stability with instability, a large pattern with a small detail, one rhythm with another, obscurity with clarity, light with dark, stasis with movement, and a hundred other such juxtapositions. Much of the explosiveness of Shakespeare's verse, Peter Brook has pointed out, results from montage. Words and images constitute many messages, 'often crowding, jostling, overlapping one another. The intelligence, the feelings, the memory are all stirred. ...' Using 'free verse on the open stage enabled him to cut the inessential detail and the irrelevant realistic action: in their place he could cram sounds and ideas, thoughts and images which make each instant a stunning mobile.'[36]

Entrances in Shakespeare often duplicate shock cuts: 'Enter Lear, with Cordelia in his arms'; (upon Duncan's expression of amazement at his complete trust of Cawdor) 'Enter Macbeth'. No wonder then that filmmakers use montage extensively. The filmmaker may seek a comic effect, as when in *As You Like It* Paul Czinner dissolves from the ludicrous, mustachioed, melodramatic villain, Oliver, to the wiggling posterior of a swan; or he may underscore the unity of a mood, as when Welles, in *Chimes at Midnight*, dissolves from rebels hanging motionless from gibbets to the solitary, sick king, and from sleepless Henry, hemmed in by huge stone columns and peering out through barred windows, to his melancholy son Hal before a stagnant, glassy pond. He may establish a parallel, as when Welles, in *Othello*, dissolves from jealous Bianca, clutching the handkerchief, to Desdemona, worried about its loss; or he may reveal unspoken thoughts, as when in Schaefer's version Macbeth registers the prophetic nature of his act as he hands the sceptre and crown to Banquo, who in turn hands them to a young boy.

Often scenes are punctuated by associative pairs of shots. Schaefer dissolves in successive shots from Macbeth's brutal kiss of Lady Macbeth to the murderers waiting for Banquo (one of them whittling a stick), linking sex and violence; from dead Banquo's bloody face to the roast pig brought in to the banquet being held in his honour; from Ross's whispers about armies on the way from England (cause) to Lady Macbeth staring out the window at the dawn and Macbeth guzzling wine (effect); from Macbeth resolving to execute each violent thought to the aftermath of such thoughts; and from the burning Scottish village strewn with bodies to England with its sunlight and green trees. But often, in much more subtle ways, such associations and comments are made within scenes as well.

From the days of so-called silent films, music has been used to underscore or counterpoint with the tempo and rhythms of physical motion. It has been used to clarify dramatic conflicts, create moods, give a sense of period, provide unity, bridge transitions, punctuate bits of business, and heighten meaning and effect in scores of less easily verbalised ways. Shakespeare himself often used music brilliantly in his plays – Iago's drinking song and Desdemona's willow song, Titania's lullaby, the gravedigger's song – and the filmmaker may simply follow the playwright's directions. Shakespeare has provided another kind of musical accompaniment in his plays however, the music of the words, which has not always received kind treatment in films. Subtle verbal harmonies are often obliterated by the heavy syrup of cliché movie music. Similarly, it sometimes seems that the director is striving with full orchestra to provide the emotional power which his actors cannot. Castellani's *Romeo and Juliet* and Yutkevitch's *Othello* serve quite well to illustrate both faults. They help us understand Brook's decision to strip *King Lear* of musical hyperbole, and help us appreciate critical pronouncements that 'additional music has more frequently proved a hindrance than a help in conveying the dramatic poetry'.[37]

Nevertheless, William Walton's music for *Henry V* is very successful in underscoring the film's great variety of visual styles. Nino Rota's boisterous 'Where is the life that late I led?' captures Petruchio's character and the dramatic moment perfectly. And Miklos Rosza's careful development of separate themes for each major character contributes much to Mankiewicz's *Julius Caesar*. There is no hindrance in the obscene rasping pipes which accompany the play within the play done in *commedia* style in Richardson's *Hamlet*, the festive ceremonial music by Walton which dies off in Olivier's *Hamlet* when the observers realise the duel is in earnest, and the ironic religious music of Olivier's *Richard III*. Even more powerfully ironic are the angelic chorus which is juxtaposed with the shrieks of wounded horses, clashes of iron, and cries of pain in the battle scene of *Chimes at Midnight*, the sour bagpipe music signalling the presence of the witches in Polanski's *Macbeth*, and the haunting chants of the chorus and forest spirit in *Throne of Blood*. And in at least two instances this side of opera and ballet – Reinhardt and Dieterle's *Dream* with Mendelssohn's music, and Kozintsev's *Hamlet* with

Shostakovich's score – films heavily saturated with music succeed in part because of it.

Finally, to round out our survey of non-verbal expressive means in realising Shakespeare on film, let us consider an element used less creatively than almost any other – non-musical sounds. It has been said that they 'have almost no place in the presentation of Shakespeare'.[38] Yet Shakespeare's own company used many acoustical 'props' – owls, clocks, cannon, tolling bells, battle sounds, crowing cocks, thunder, and so on.[39] Many of the most memorable moments in Shakespeare films are inextricably bound up with such sounds: the crackling of the flames as Lady Macduff stares in wordless horror at her slaughtered children in Polanski's *Macbeth*, the hollow thud of the gravedigger's hammer as he nails on the lid of Ophelia's coffin in Kozintsev's *Hamlet*, the slam of the massive door which seals in Othello and Desdemona in Welles's film. Welles is often acclaimed for his acoustic artistry because sound in his films is often highly subjective: the dripping noises in the cave in *Macbeth* which suddenly accelerate madly, the soft, slow, irregular ringing of the alarm bell which greets Macbeth's call to arms (Seyton's body is swaying from the bell rope). His *Othello* includes the fine aural collage of celestial chorus, thunder, pounding waves, mandolins, wind, a clanking alarm bell, shouts, barking dogs, and notes from a harpsichord which serve as a transition from Venice to Cyprus, and the blend of laughing soldiers and whores and the cries of gulls as Othello wakes from his fit and stares up at the ramparts.

The sheer power of discreetly heightened 'natural' sounds often creates meaning as well. There is a grim rightness in sensual Gertrude's horrible, panting death in Richardson's *Hamlet*. The battle which we hear but never see under the fog at the beginning of Polanski's *Macbeth* suggests a brutality and ferocity that literal images seldom achieve. Sounds in Castellani's *Romeo and Juliet* often articulate tomblike spaces eloquently, such as the echoing clank as Romeo smashes a huge iron candlestick on the cathedral altar, or the grinding sound of the tomb lid as Romeo pries it off, suggesting the weight of the forces working to separate the lovers. The birds shriek with laughter as the lovers make fools of themselves in Hall's *Dream*. Whether expressionist, as in the rush of water at the moment of Roderigo's death in Welles's *Othello*, or realist, as in the crunching sound of a knife piercing bone as Macbeth kills Duncan in Polanski's film, non-musical sounds are often important interpretative tools.

To speak with precision and understanding about style in Shakespeare films, we must go far beyond categories which divide films according to their relative distance from the language of poetry and the theatre or which measure in some simpleminded way the relative distance of the film from the original play. We must gauge the truth of the actors' performances and the power of the director's aural and visual images, which often must be thought of as free translations, cinematic equivalents, or re-creations rather than attempts at transparent presentations of Shakespeare's poetic and theatrical images. We should always seek the *why* of filmic techniques, ask how they are integrated into overall patterns which constitute a significant style appropriate both to the spirit of Shakespeare's work and to the collaborative artist's vision. (Clearly the same cinematic style could never suit both *As You Like It* and *Hamlet*.) Shunning pedantic fervour, we should ask how the re-structuring from play to film constitutes an interpretative act – inquire in such a manner that we learn about both play and film. (Is it true that all good films stress physical action and plays stress emotional and reflective reaction? Is it more effective on film to show the killing of Duncan, or to leave it to our horrible imaginings?) Style describes many things – acting style, the personal themes and techniques recurring in a particular filmmaker, the genre and period of the play, the proportion and relation of verbal to visual meaning, and much more.

In its largest sense, however, style deals with the integration of all expressive effects. Peter Brook praised Kozintsev's *Hamlet* precisely because his 'structure is inseparable from his meaning'. The film is 'a search for over-all meaning as opposed to the many and varied, sometimes dazzling, attempts to capture on the screen the actor-manager's view of the play as imagery, theatricality, passion, colour, effects'.[40] A unified style need not imply simplistic narrative clarity, reductive concepts, or a single level of dramatic illusion. The strength and truth of the play within the play in Richardson's *Hamlet* – a parodic event in which Claudius becomes a red-nosed clown, Elsinore a flimsy cardboard castle, the cuckolding of King Hamlet a game of sexual leapfrog between the Queen of Hearts and her two royal studs, and the murder as a festive dance around the Maypole turned grotesque as the King is strangled in the brightly coloured streamers and the self-crowned murderer leaps into the Queen's arms – its strength and truth is its duplicating in terms of visual style the insane discord in Hamlet's mind. Stylistic truth and unity come from the overall vision of the actors and the film artist. Said Orson Welles,

> With me the visual is a solution to what the poetical and musical form dictates. I don't begin with the visual and then try to find a poetry or music and try to stick it into the picture. The picture has to follow it. And again, people tend to think that my first preoccupation is with the simple plastic effects of the cinema. But to me they all come out of an interior rhythm, which is like the shape of music or the shape of poetry. I don't go around like a collector picking up beautiful images and pasting them together. … I believe in the film as a poetic medium … poetry should make your hair stand up on your skin, should suggest things, evoke more than you see. The danger in the cinema is that you see everything, because it's a camera. So what you have to do is to manage to evoke, to incant, to raise up things which are not really there.[41]

From Jack J. Jorgens, *Shakespeare on Film* (Bloomington, IN, 1977; rpt Washington, DC, 1994), pp. 7–35.

NOTES

[Jack Jorgens's book was the first full-length critical analysis of Shakespearean film, and has provided the point of departure for practically all subsequent discussion. In this extract, Jorgens sets out a pluralistic approach which departs from that of the majority of previous commentators in that it treats filmed Shakespeare in terms of the specific creative potentialities that the cinematic medium affords, rather than as an inferior adjunct to reading and/or stage performance. Jorgens offers a typology of Shakespearean film adaptation, the theatrical, the realist, and the filmic; and focuses upon the last of these to argue that the self-consciously, unapologetically cinematic mode is the most appropriate for Shakespeare. Ed.]

1. See Roger Manvell, *Shakespeare and the Film* (New York, 1971), p. 153; Donald Skoller, 'Problems of Transformation in the Adaptation of Shakespeare's Tragedies From Play-Script to Cinema', PhD dissertation, New York University, 1968; Peter Wollen, *Signs and Meaning in the Cinema* (Bloomington, IN, 1969), p. 137.

2. Susan Sontag, 'Film and Theatre', in *Film Theory and Criticism*, ed. Gerald Mast and Marshall Cohen (New York, 1974), p. 362.

3. Peter Brook, *The Empty Space* (New York, 1969), p. 10.

4. Arthur Knight, 'Three Problems in Film Adaptation', *Saturday Review*, 18 December 1954.

5. Roy Walker, 'Look Upon Caesar', *Twentieth Century*, 154 (1953), 470–1.

6. John Fuegi, 'Explorations in No Man's Land', *Shakespeare Quarterly*, 23 (1972), 41.

7. Clifford Leech and J. M. R. Margeson (eds), *Shakespeare 1971* (Toronto, 1972), p. 191.

8. Stanley Kauffmann, *Living Images* (New York, 1975), p. 358.

9. Fuegi, 'Explorations', p. 41.

10. Hugo Munsterberg, *The Film: A Psychological Study* (New York, 1970), p. 74.

11. Quoted in John Russell Brown, *Shakespeare's Plays in Performance* (New York, 1967), p. 53.

12. Peter Brook, 'Finding Shakespeare on Film', *Tulane Drama Review*, T33, 11 (1966), 118.

13. These categories resemble those used by Stanley Wells, 'Shakespeare's Text on the Modern Stage', *Shakespeare Jahrbuch* (West) (1967), pp. 180–1, and Thomas Clayton, 'Aristotle on the Shakespearean Film, or, Damn Thee, William, Thou Art Translated', *Literature/Film Quarterly*, 2 (1974), 185–6.

14. John Russell Brown, *Free Shakespeare* (London, 1974).

15. Roger Gross, *Understanding Playscripts* (Bowling Green, OH, 1974), pp. 17–18.

16. Susan Sontag, *Against Interpretation* (New York, 1969), p. 17.

17. Quoted in Grigori Kozintsev, *Shakespeare: Time and Conscience* (New York, 1966), p. 215.

18. Charles W. Eckert (ed.), *Focus on Shakespearean Films* (Englewood Cliffs, NJ, 1972), lists many of these which have wound up on film.

19. Quoted by Joseph McBride, *Orson Welles* (London, 1972), p. 109.

20. Quoted by Hugh Kenner, *The Pound Era* (Berkeley, CA, 1971), p. 150.

21. George Bluestone, *Novels Into Film* (Berkeley, CA, 1971), pp. 110–11.

22. Paul Dehn, 'The Filming of Shakespeare', in *Talking of Shakespeare*, ed. John Garrett (London, 1954), p. 49.

23. Maya Deren, 'Poetry and the Film: A Symposium', in *Film Culture Reader*, ed. P. Adams Sitney (New York, 1970), p. 174.

24. Stanley J. Solomon, *The Film Idea* (New York, 1972), p. 341.

25. Siegfried Kracauer, *Theory of Film* (New York, 1965), p. 106.

26. Eckert, *Focus on Shakespearean Films*, p. 17.

27. David Robinson, 'Majestic Lear', *Financial Times*, 7 July 1972.

28. John Blumenthal, '*Macbeth* into *Throne of Blood*', in *Film and the Liberal Arts*, ed. T. J. Ross (New York, 1970), p. 133.

29. John Howard Lawson, *Film: The Creative Process*, 2nd edn (New York, 1967), pp. 201–2.

30. Brown, *Shakespeare's Plays in Performance*, p. 41.

31. See Arthur Colby Sprague, *Shakespeare and the Actors* (Cambridge, MA, 1944) and subsequent books for much interesting information on the stage business of Shakespeare's plays, much of which carries over into films.

32. Quoted in Lawson, *Film: The Creative Process*, p. xxii.

33. See James Naremore, 'The Walking Shadow: Welles' Expressionist *Macbeth*', *Literature/Film Quarterly*, 1 (1973), 361.

34. See Paul A. Jorgenson, 'Castellani's *Romeo and Juliet*: Intention and Response', and Roy Walker, 'In Fair Verona', both reprinted in Eckert, *Focus on Shakespearean Films*.

35. Skoller, 'Problems of Transformation', p. 429.

36. Peter Brook, Introduction to Peter Weiss, *Marat/Sade* (New York, 1966), pp. 5–6.

37. Charles Hurtgen, 'The Operatic Character of Background Music in Film Adaptations of Shakespeare', *Shakespeare Quarterly*, 20 (1969), 53.

38. Ibid., 57.

39. See Frances Shirley, *Shakespeare's Use of Off-Stage Sounds* (Lincoln, IL, 1963), though of course all his non-verbal sounds were not off-stage.

40. Peter Brook, 'Finding Shakespeare on Film', in Eckert, *Focus on Shakespearean Films*, p. 37.

41. Juan Cobos and Miguel Rubio, 'Welles and Falstaff', *Sight and Sound*, 35 (Autumn 1966), 160.

2

Laurence Olivier's *Henry V*

ANTHONY DAVIES

In addition to being an adaptation of Shakespeare's play, a morale-boosting film for the Britain of 1944 and a fusion of historical event and myth and legend, Olivier's *Henry V* is also a cinematic treatise on the difference between cinema and theatre as media for the expression of drama. This last dimension of the film's complex stature is coming increasingly to be acknowledged as this adaptation's claim to enduring significance. More important than any scenic amplification which cinema is able to afford the original theatrical concept is the organic structure within which the elements of space and time are cinematically organised. This relation of space to time can be usefully examined on two levels: the external level (the reciprocity between the work of art and the historical moment of its creation) and the internal level (the way that spatial details within the film's visualisation signal time strata as artistic substance).

In two respects the immediate political and historical circumstances surrounding the film's creation give its spatial strategy a dynamic relevance. Firstly, the film clearly derives certain spatial manipulations from stage productions which preceded it and which established the play's particular theatrical tradition. Tableaux, trumpets, moving dioramas, rich medieval costuming, a prominent musical dimension, an elaborate coronation scene – and even a white horse for Henry – can all be traced back to productions of the eighteenth and nineteenth centuries, when the spectacular elaborations of McCready, Kean and Charles Calvert marked the play with a particular stamp of epic pageantry in performance.[1]

It was only to be expected that the film would in turn influence theatrical stagings which came after it. The productions of Joseph Papp and Terry Hands in the mid 1970s bear particular witness to the fact. Papp produced the play in New York's Central Park in 1975, and strove specifically to capture the exterior, realistic dimensions of the film by moving the action of the play from an austere stage to 'a naturalistic setting with realistic props; four cannons, pikes, poles, arrows, a promontory up which Henry [could] rush before Harfleur'. There were actual camp-fires lit in the darkness before the day of battle, and arrows were shot 'flying into the lake'.[2] Terry Hands's production for the Royal Shakespeare Company at Stratford in 1976 aimed to achieve spatial effects of the film in a different way. Hands followed the film's shift from theatrical performance to cinematic presentation by suggesting a movement from one level of reality to another within the theatre. The movement of the plane of action was implied by use of a great canopy which opened out, and by the costuming of the actors, who changed their dress from rehearsal track-suits (at the start of the play) to period costumes which were donned as the action developed. Only the Chorus retained his rehearsal clothing throughout, as he held the connection between the levels of action.

More recently, the staging of the play at Stratford, Connecticut, in 1981 made explicit its spatial derivations by effecting 'a playful crossing between the world of theatre and the world of illusion within the play'. In this production, Christopher Plummer played the parts of both Henry and the Chorus 'much as Olivier takes on the roles of the actor playing Henry (back-stage) and of Henry himself (on stage)'. The set too was adapted to incorporate a reminiscence of the Globe structure, and there was much deliberately similar detail in the staging of Henry's reaction to the Dauphin's gift. The cask and the arrangement of the tennis balls within it looked identical with those revealed in the film, and like Olivier, Plummer tossed his crown to hang on the back of the throne.[3]

The second respect in which external time affected the spatial strategy of the film lies in the film's special relevance to the wartime circumstances of Britain in 1943–4. Like the films of Eisenstein, Olivier's *Henry V* was directed partially towards social control. In its endeavour to project a romantic illusion, the film incorporates colour-plate illustrations from the original manuscript of *Les Très Riches Heures*. The text in that manuscript is accompanied by calendar pictures painted by Pol de Limbourg and Jean Colombe. The use of these pictures as a basis of set design gives the film a spatial delicacy and visual charm which justifies their own artistic validity. Yet, at the same time, the pictorial stylisation moves the film close to the realm of the fairytale, whose brightly coloured glamour and spectacle was highly appropriate for the aesthetic appetite of the time. Equally well suited to the susceptibilities of a war-time audience was the comic reduction of the scene in which the Archbishop of Canterbury and the Bishop of Ely explore the legal justification of Henry's claim to the French throne. The latter effect is especially important, for it raises weighty questions about artistic integrity in the interpretation of Shakespeare's play.

The most unyielding criticism on this score comes from Gorman Beauchamp who, in a powerfully argued essay written more than thirty years after the film's release, considers the entire issue of Olivier's studied distortion of the play. He points out that the intricate issues of legitimate succession are deliberately obscured by the presentation of the scene as 'farce ... which is fundamentally dishonest in that it directs attention away from, rather than toward, the central problem of war's justification'.[4] In a slim volume devoted wholly to a discussion of this film, Harry Geduld with more deference to Olivier's intention suggests that this scene is debased essentially by the fact that its 'buffoonery over the documents' is also designed to make an implicit statement about theatre. The strained artificiality of the theatrical conventions and the derisive interruptions of the groundlings, maintains Geduld, are designed to emphasise at the start of the play 'the shortcomings of theatre as a medium for presenting a dramatic epic like *Henry V*'.[5]

More subtle in its effect upon the dialogue's direct impact is Olivier's use of camera movement. In discussing the technique of filming moments of strong Shakespearean rhetoric, Olivier has pointed out that to accommodate the gestural and vocal expansiveness of 'Shakespearean climax', the camera must be pulled back to a distance from the actor.[6] This makes very good sense, and as a means of reconciling theatrical style with cinematic mobility it is employed to good effect in *Henry V*. Nevertheless, while it affords the actor's rhetorical projection its natural dramatic shape, the camera's withdrawal inevitably makes its own statement. One instance of this is the framing of Olivier in the stirring speech before the conquest of Harfleur. As Henry's rhetoric gathers force, the camera moves back and upwards so that at the speech's climax,

Henry is framed among his soldiers from a high-angled distant camera position in the upper rigging of a ship. In moving to this position, the camera's implicit statement is to stress Henry's relative smallness, 'that despite his obvious valour, he has begun his campaign as the underdog'.[7] The reduction of Henry's dominance in the frame and of his vertical advantage in relation to the camera conceals the savage explicitness of his war-like exhortation. The camera movement here gives the speech a 'colouration' of romantic and plucky resolution, an effect achieved through 'visual image working against verbal image [which] draws our attention and their context … toward … a romanticised, non-contextual image of the hero-king'.[8]

A second instance of the camera's making a high-angled reduction of Henry at a moment of triumph is the moment of his entrance through the gates of Harfleur. This shot further increases an audience sympathy for Henry, for it frames him as he gives instructions for the merciful treatment of the city's captive inhabitants. An expressive variation occurs at the climax of the St Crispin's Day speech immediately before the Battle of Agincourt. Here, the camera pulls directly back, keeping a horizontal level with Henry. In eschewing the high subtended angle, the movement of the camera no longer gives Henry a sympathetic diminution, for his cause is now fully established, and he can proclaim his intentions as an equal.

The inclusion of the Battle of Agincourt in Olivier's film has raised less critical comment than the textual cuts or the simplification of Henry's character. Yet it is, for modern sensibilities, a highly controversial addition of spectacle to Shakespeare's play, and before considering its value as cinema it is necessary to accept the different perspective which it gives the dramatic impact of the film. While it has been suggested that Shakespeare was prevented from developing spectacular realism as an extension of his dramatic material by the confining limits of the theatre, and that he would have welcomed the visual potential of cinema, a more perceptive view holds that Shakespeare's overtly theatrical presentation of battles is in itself a very pointed statement about war. As Beauchamp observes, the only encounter which is directly staged in the play *Henry V* is that between Pistol and M. le Fer, and by promoting Pistol's 'ridiculous exploit' to a position where it becomes 'the sole synecdoche for, the single dramatised episode in, this capstone of Henry's French Campaign', any military magnificence and heroism with which the romantic imagination might have invested Henry's victory is diminished by satire.[9]

Where Shakespeare's play presents military glamour and conquest as absurd by revealing the instincts which operate beneath its rationale, the promotional power behind the making of the film in 1943–4 would clearly have been more sympathetic with a depiction of Agincourt as a glorious legend, a romanticised presentation of a bloodless, chivalrous encounter in which brutality was made an abstraction and arrogant disdain, luxurious self-indulgence and aristocratic pride were made the casualties.

The relation of visual signals within the film's spatial manipulation to an internal stratification of time is at once more complex and more significant, for it reveals a dynamic interplay of levels of action within an apparently simple structure. Spatial signals in the film indicate three layers of time: Renaissance time, medieval time and what one might call 'universal time'. The first of these is signalled by the model of London and the occasion of performance filmed in the Globe Playhouse. The second covers the action related specifically to the estrangement, and reconciliation through marriage, of the realms of France and England, together with the campaign, major battle and the personal affinities and differences which give it particular dimensions – that is, the time of the central historical event. The third layer, universal time, is less easy to relate to specific aspects of the film, or indeed to define, for it is not historically objective. Universal time is a convenient term here for that imaginative reconstruction of time stimulated and reinforced by myth – in this case, the Agincourt myth. It is in essence romanticised, fluid and peopled with archetypes, for it is a removed epoch conceived of as unambiguous by the contemporary imagination. For all its elusiveness of definition, this level of universal time is artistically crucial, for the power of myth on the imagination makes possible the liberation of time from history (a phenomenon which surfaces, too, as a political manifestation in the emergence of nationalism).

The liberation of time from history is the primary dissociation on which that important genre the fairy tale is based, and, as suggested earlier, the fairy tale embodies a special relationship of nature to art which modifies our logic of space. Just as characters become archetypal, so space becomes ideal. Therein lies the major artistic achievement of Olivier's film, whereby the artistic representation of the French landscape styled on the plates from *Les Très Riches Heures* becomes aesthetically satisfying as cinematic space.

The interplay of the three layers of time so far considered is not only wrought in Olivier's film. The three layers are very much evident in a theatrical experience of the play in performance. It is the particular nature of their inter-relation and visual treatment which is intrinsic to the film. This is equally true of space. The play itself incorporates areas of action which can be isolated and identified. It is the special property of the film to bring its own dynamic to bear on these discrete elements – which the theatre accommodates on one stage – and so to create a unique cinematic structure within which entities of space sometimes coalesce, sometimes are sundered to make clear where one entry ends and another begins.

Like any play, Shakespeare's *Henry V* concerns itself initially with two areas of action: the microcosmic space of theatre, and the amorphous space of the imagination. Both of these spatial realms become constructs of the real space of events in history. Olivier exploits the cinematic potential of a Chorus whose monologues consciously explore the relationship between the spaces of history, theatre and imagination. But to these three areas of action, Olivier adds a fourth, the historical occasion of the play's own performance. Out of these four spatial entities is woven the structure which makes the film an organic whole.

There are two aspects to notice about the camera's treatment of its material. Firstly, there is a sustained ambivalence whereby the spatial detail in the frame seems to hover between theatrical stylisation and cinematic realism. Secondly, there is no simple progress, as the film proceeds, from theatrical fragmentation to cinematic flow. Rather there is a complex and subtle manipulation of the spatial elements, so that the visuals take on the credibility of cinema without losing the consciousness of theatre. The model of sixteenth-century London with which the opening shots of the film engage us does not pretend to be other than a model. Yet the camera's operation upon it, making it so clearly a photographic subject in a style we are accustomed to having cinema treat the real city, confers upon it an additional realistic dimension.

This is especially so when one considers that by 1944 newsreels had established, as regular fare on cinema screens, the aerial photography of cities as evidence of allied or enemy bombardment. What would seem to be an aerial approach over a London out of another age, with the Thames surface glassy and blue, constitutes a masterly and complex combination of convention with illusion. This suspended ambivalence of perspective prepares us for the idiom of the film's language and flow, for it is immediately followed by what is theatrical reconstruction of the whole social bustle of actors preparing to become the play's characters, and of the audience preparing to partici-pate in the experience of theatre. However, this is constructed so that it can be filmed in minute realistic detail. Once again, there is the am-bivalence of what we know to be artifice given realistic camera treat-ment, with actors acting as actors who are not yet characters.

The next major development in the spatial fabric of the film is its visual isolation of the staged play in the Globe theatre as filmed theatre presentation. The bumbling and protracted debate in which the bishops attempt to justify Henry's claim is deliberately made ridiculous, received as it is with jeers and derision by members of the theatre audience. Apart from the interpretative reasons for pre-senting this scene as burlesqued comedy – which are rightly ques-tionable – there are more acceptable justifications in terms of the requirements of media transposition which the film is, in this early stage, exploring. The comedy of incompetence being acted out on the stage carries with it Olivier's assertion that the film will not concern itself with the mere presentation of a photographed theatre performance. The brief moments of this scene, during which the camera is wholly focused on the stage action, are interspersed with sound-track signals which keep alive our consciousness of a dual role. We are members of both the Globe theatre audience and the cinema audience. We lose our awareness of our double-audience situation only when Henry is presented by the French ambassador with the Dauphin's gift of tennis balls.

We become wholly involved in the theatrical nature of this scene because the theatricality itself is operating on two levels. Firstly, it is a staged scene with the character of Henry established as believ-able. Secondly, the king's situation among the subjects in his imme-diate presence is necessarily theatrical. In an absorbing article for the Royal Shakespeare Company's production of *Richard II* in 1973, Anne Barton has pointed out that

> Only Shakespeare ... seems to have seized upon and explored the latent parallel between the king and that other twin-natured human-being, the Actor. Like kings, they are accustomed to perform before an audi-ence. Like kings, they are required to submerge their own individuality within a role, and for both the incarnation is temporary and perilous.[10]

Political theatre is encapsulated within scripted and staged theatre, and these in turn are both treated as cinematic presentation. Three audiences watch the king respond to the French jibe. It is as though the whole weight of the theatre's potential is consolidated at this point, and we are poised for cinema's move out of the Globe theatre and into the unconstrained areas of cinematic realism.

Our expectations are only partly met, for the move from the Globe coincides with the play's move to Southampton with preparation for Henry's embarkation for France. Even so, the move has about it unexpected intricacies, for it is no mere direct cut. It is a transition made and subtly integrated with the fabric of the play. The move from the Globe is made, but the theatrical presence of the Chorus is still with us. What does emerge is a significant shift in the relationship between the camera and the Chorus. In an unpublished thesis on Olivier's Shakespeare films submitted in 1978, Sandra Sugarman Singer has made some most helpfully detailed observations of the transitions in the film. She observes that the unity of 'physical Chorus and vocal Chorus [which] existed together and were seen as synchronic' dissolves at this point. The camera no longer shows a 'story of the Chorus telling a story' but, instead, it directly reveals 'a different story about which [the Chorus] speaks'.[11] The shift from narrative congruency to narrative co-operation between Chorus and camera indicates a major movement of the film's spatial concentration. The move in time and space is from the occasion of performance in the Globe playhouse in Shakespeare's London to the historical action and story of King Henry's campaign in medieval France.

The transition from Southampton, across the Channel to France, is made with a further development of the camera/Chorus relationship. With the lines

> Thus with imagin'd wing our swift scene flies
> In motion of no less celerity
> Than that of thought
>
> (III.i.1–3)

there is the start of accompanying music. The Chorus, filmed in close-up, is faded in against a black background, and then the camera tracks slowly back to leave the Chorus in the distance, in an extreme long-shot. The screen grows brighter and the Chorus appears to float in space as swirling mists begin to envelop him. He extends his arms, and then with the lines

Oh, do but think
You stand upon the shore and thence behold
A city on th' inconstant billows dancing
(III.i.13–15)

he turns his back on the camera and is 'completely blotted out by
the mist', while the camera tracks forward over the ships crossing
the Channel. In turning his face away from the camera, the Chorus
becomes 'a part of the audience, for he looks as we do, towards
what the camera will show'. The camera's image dissolves to a
long-shot, high-angle view of the French palace, and the Chorus,
now no longer visible, remains with us only in voice. He will reappear only when the film returns ultimately to the space and time of
the filmed performance in the Globe. For the intervening duration
he has, in Singer's words, 'gained the physical freedom of the
camera [and] lost his physical being'.[12]

The Chorus has kept alive the consciousness of theatre. With his
departure, another figure takes on that role with a less obvious theatrical effect. Apart from the Chorus, only Pistol in this film makes
direct eye-contact through the camera as he speaks to the cinema
audience – anticipating in this a major aspect of Olivier's strategy in
Richard III. Pistol is clearly the most prominent and important of
the comedy players and in his special relationship with the cinema
audience he carries forward the emphatic theatricality which has
distinguished the film's treatment of the comic scenes on the Globe
stage. Despite suggestions of realism achieved through the camera's
selection of expressive detail and the off-frame sound-track laughter
which presented cinematically a wider social situation than merely
that which is projected from the stage, Geduld is right in seeing the
performances of the comedians as 'more self-conscious, more in the
nature of theatrical "turns"'. In the same way that Robert Newton
(who plays the part of Pistol in the film) commanded affectionate
attention from cinema audiences, so Pistol appears to elicit a show
of accustomed pleasure from the groundlings who 'seem to be responding to a star comedian rather than to the role he is playing'.[13]

On the stage, furthermore, Pistol wears what looks like a leek with
the feathers in his hat. In his later appearances, after the film's move
out of the Globe, he continues to display this leek as a visual reminder of the theatrical dimension of the film. The leek is a specific
illustration of the subtle complexity of Olivier's spatial strategy.

It affords the action a multiplicity of occasions in time and space, and in so doing it introduces to the mind of the spectator an awareness of the film's narrative complexity. While for the other characters make-up and costuming has lost its theatrical emphasis, and while the major thrust of the film's spatial and temporal concern has clearly left the Globe occasion of performance, Pistol's leek achieves what Peter Brook believed (more than twenty years later) to be unattainable on film – simultaneous and multi-layered dramatic relevance.[14] The cinema audience is asked not to suspend disbelief, but rather to engage with the dramatic action in a new way.

The space of the Globe theatre and the space of the central historical action in medieval France are linked by two other significant strands: that of water imagery, and much more significantly that of music. The musical connection is especially complex, because while music accompanies both the action within the Globe theatre and the action in time and space outside it, its distinctive orchestral and choral textures make clear the division between *theatrical* and *cinematic* music.

Cinematic music is used to give atmosphere to dialogue or action and is an overlay to the structured action of the scene. Theatrical music, on the other hand, is part of the scene's intrinsic structure and reality. Its source is naturally accommodated within the locality of action photographed by the camera. Theatrical music is produced (and seen to be produced) by the theatre musicians who are part of the Globe theatre company. Some instances of cinematic music are the choral effects which accompany the camera's ranging over the model City of London and the *sforzando* which accompanies the Chorus' initial invocation of the audience's imagination, 'Suppose within these walls. ...' (I. Prologue. 19). This last instance displays a complexity which is almost of the order of Pistol's leek, for like the leek, the music transcends one single level of action and space. It is cinematic music, yet the camera and Chorus are still very much 'within these walls'. Clearly the texture and tone-colour of the music remove it from the music produced by the theatre musicians, and so its function must therefore be to establish a tension between an aural awareness of film while the eye is still engaged with the immediacies of the theatre.

Cinematic music achieves its most memorable stature in two sequences. One is the musical accompaniment to the Duke of Burgundy's speech of reconciliation where the Auvergne folk-theme gives the spoken verse an elegiac suggestion of song as the camera follows the gaze of the Duke to move outside the confines of the French palace. The other is the musical accompaniment to the action of the Battle of Agincourt. Certainly Walton's battle music in this film is among the finest cinematic music written in its sustained power of movement and the versatility of its comment on details of the preparatory action. The range of the music's function is impressive as it captures the English resolve and the French complacency, pointing with sparkling humour the cumbersome descent of the heavily armed French knights on to the saddles of their chargers, accompanying the reflections of the French horses as they step through puddles with a jagged tremolo on the strings, and giving a dramatic rhythmic development to the gathering pace of the French cavalry charge photographed with the camera moving forward in a sustained tracking shot from abreast of the formation.

Whatever criticism the inclusion of the battle provokes about the distortion of Shakespeare's play, there is no doubt that it is an outstanding piece of cinema. The sustained integration of musical and visual development is wrought through montage which juxtaposes the gathering momentum of the French charge with the poised stand of the English army as it waits for the French to come within the range of its archers. The dramatic visual emphasis arises from the opposite natures of the two armies: the movement of men, horses, flying pennants and the colour of the French battle-dress set against the tense stillness and functional austerity of the English; the vast line of French horsemen set against the mere handful of English; the sweeping speed of the cavalry and the tracking camera set against Henry's raised sword held against the sky and the line of English archers drawing back the arrows on their bows.

In his *Lectures on Dramatic Art and Literature* published in 1809, Schlegel observed that the staging of Shakespeare's battles raises an inevitable problem of dramatic perspective. On the one hand, there is an element of the absurd in the suggestion that 'the fate of mighty kingdoms' is decided, even on the theatre stage, by token warriors 'in mock armour'. On the other hand, realistic battle effects too readily displace 'that attention which a poetical work of art demands'.[15] It is an aesthetic problem for which the resources of cinema do manifestly offer a solution because cinema is capable of orchestrating a very wide spectrum of spatial suggestions and giving unity to diversity through music. Contrapuntal and convergent spatial strategies such as detail selection, montage, camera movement, variety of colour and movement in the frame can be given an overall aesthetic shape by an accompanying orchestral versatility of colour and rhythm. Cinema can then produce a fusion of visual and aural energy which sustains the engagement of the ear by balancing the spectacle with intelligent musical articulation.

The water imagery in the film is less complex. It provides a direct linking device for the various spatial levels of the action. The glassy Thames in the model of London, the thunderstorm which breaks over the Globe theatre, the ships crossing the Channel to France and the pools of water which reflect the French cavalry preparing to charge at Agincourt, constitute a unifying structural element in the spatial composition of the film. More particularly, the violent downpour which suddenly drenches both the players and the audience in the Globe switches concentration from theatrical involvement into the area of cinematic realism, both in its immediate visual effects and in subjecting the actors and the audience of the Globe to the same ordeal suffered by Henry's army, whose 'gayness' and whose 'gilt are all besmirch'd/With rainy marching in the painful field' (IV.iii.110–11). It also subtly qualifies the unclouded view of the past that might otherwise predominate, and so makes this an unromantic, recognisably English, wet day.

The return of the dramatic action to the Globe in the closing moments of the film is achieved once again through a series of transitions through non-defined distinctions between medieval France and Elizabethan England on the one hand, and between theatre and cinema on the other. The film's achievement in these shifts has gone largely unnoticed by critics who have written generally about the narrative potential of cinema. Jean-Luc Godard is more often credited with being the pioneer in the manipulation of diegetic space in the cinema. In an article written in 1972, Peter Wollen supported this latter claim:

> In Hollywood films, everything shown belongs to the same world and complex articulations within that world – such as flashbacks – are carefully signalled and located ... Traditionally, only one form of multiple diegesis is allowed – the play within the play – whereby the second, discontinuous diegetic space is embedded or bracketed within the first ... Godard uses film-within-a-film devices in a number of early films ... The first radical break with single diegesis, however, comes from *Weekend*, when characters from different epochs and from fiction are interpolated into the main narrative.[16]

The film *Weekend* was released in 1967. Olivier, with *Henry V*, had broken away from single diegesis more than twenty years before.

Two final points to be made by the spatial fabric of Olivier's *Henry V* are its pictorialism – a cinematic tendency that will surface again in our discussion of *Hamlet* – and its dominant colour motifs. The use of the *Book of Hours* plates as scenic design for many of the film sets establishes a profound relationship between painting, photography and poetry, which Singer identifies as 'a prevailing visual attitude' in Olivier's Shakespeare films.[17] Jack Jorgens points to the particularly static depiction of the French in the film, noting that 'save for the battle, there is very little movement in the French sequences', and he quotes part of Geduld's observation about the intention behind the film's pictorialism in the interior scenes of the French palace.[18]

Geduld maintains that the intentions behind Olivier's strategy are 'to reduce the incongruities between the stylised, two-dimensional set and his three-dimensional actors', and to ensure through reducing all movement to a minimum 'that the actors always seem to belong to the pictorial composition'.[19] While the pictorial function of the French court scenes is clear enough, Geduld's deduction of Olivier's motive is questionable. There is enough evidence elsewhere in the film to suggest (as has been shown above) that Olivier's intention is not simply 'to reduce incongruities' of dimension. Wherever possible, the directorial intention has been to allow the image to function on more than one level in order to keep alive the film's tension between what is spatially theatrical and spatially pictorial. The incongruities constitute a necessary ingredient. The film's respect for aesthetic ambiguity is corroborated by Jorgens when he notes the reminiscence of the Globe flag and trumpeter on the battle-field, and the elevation of Henry exhorting his troops as a reminder of Burbage on the Globe stage. He suggests, too, that 'the arch into which the banquet is crushed at the French court' recalls the arch over the inner stage of the Globe.[20]

The most noticeable of the colour motifs is the constantly recurring juxtaposition of blue and red. It is established in the opening shot of the film with the combination of sky and red roofs of Shakespeare's London carrying through to assume the final heraldic importance in the joining of the French and English kingdoms. The white horse (which, as noted earlier, had become traditional) gives the filmed Henry his allegorical stature.

While Olivier's *Henry V* is in many respects an innovatory film, it does also draw on other established genres. One of these is the Western genre. Geduld draws attention to the dimension of Olivier's characterisation of Henry, his 'likeable displays of casualness and sportsmanship' which give his dramatic destiny a special aura of inevitable success and which associate him peripherally with the image of heroic nonchalance cultivated by the RAF. The glimpses of his physical nimbleness (for instance, his athletic vault into the saddle in contrast to the French being lowered on derricks) also recall 'traditional heroes of Westerns whose rugged individualism and inevitable triumph over their adversaries have become clichés'.[21]

The affinity of Olivier's *Henry V* with the Western film genre is not, however, confined to Henry's 'particular quality of lyric and exuberant inevitability'.[22] In his essay on the Western film André Bazin points out that while the Western exists as literature, it has a very limited appeal as literary material. It is as film that the Western achieves its immense popular success, sustaining its power of attraction across a wide range of cultural diversity. The challenge that arises, then, is one of attempting to define the specific essence which ensures that this particular kind of fiction so clearly finds its expressive culmination as cinema. He identifies a number of narrative elements in the classic Western story which make it especially appropriate material for the screen:

1. The relation of action, conflict and spatial context to the formative process of romanticised history;
2. The epic nature of the genre arising out of simplicity of narrative concentration on archetypes rather than on complexity of character, and the consequent closeness to the establishment of myth;
3. A spatial strategy which relates man to close detail on the one hand and to natural terrain on the other;
4. The separate roles of men and women in society;
5. The relation of action to morality on the one hand, and to law on the other;
6. The early and unambiguous polarisation of moral categories;
7. The particular significance of the horse as a visual proclamation of man's alliance with nature.[23]

Though muted in expression, all these ingredients can be discerned in Olivier's film, contributing to its popularity as a romance of heroic spectacle. Of particular relevance to this discussion are those elements of the Western film which concern the treatment of space. Two sequences in *Henry V* justify examination in this light. The most obvious of these is the build-up to the battle climax at Agincourt, with its relation of men and horses to open space. 'The Western', writes Bazin, 'has virtually no use for close-up, even for the medium shot, preferring by contrast the travelling shot and the pan which refuse to be limited by the frameline and which restore to space its fullness.'[24] Henry's parleys with Montjoy and the gathering momentum of the cavalry charge are reminiscent of shots and sequences in battle scenes from John Ford Westerns.

The second sequence is very different and the parallel is less direct. Henry's ultimate conquest of Katherine, with its clear suggestions that rugged success on the field of battle does not in itself endear man to woman has a strong affinity with the classic Western resolution. Like the hero of the Western, Henry is faced with obstacles in his approach to Katherine, which are very different in nature from those he has overcome on the battle-field. He has finally to grope his awkward way through the unfamiliar territory of French courtly elegance, its manners of amorous propriety and the cultivated refinements of the French language as used by the women of the court. There is a subtle spatial suggestion of Henry's ordeal in the love scene with the Princess. After the realistic heroism of the battle with its spatial elements of earth, sky, pools of water and galloping horses, Henry has suddenly to contend with the ornamental pictorialism of the French palace interior, so that his approaches to Katherine take the visual form of intrusions into posed compositions framed by arches. The new territory of 'manners' which Henry has to conquer is thus spatially articulated in the shift from the realism of the battle ground to the composed balance of the French court with its pictorial groupings.

This is not to suggest that Olivier has made *Henry V* structurally congruent with the Western. Clearly there are complexities of dramatic development such as the traditional national rivalries among Henry's soldiers, the comic interplay of Pistol, Bardolph and Nym, and the relation of period costume to realistic space which the Western genre does not accommodate. The important point to emerge from the generic affinity is that both Olivier's *Henry V* and the classic Western find a focal register of origin in the medieval romance. The cowboy is, as Bazin observes, a reincarnation in the New World of 'a knight-at-arms'. His ordeal in winning the affections of the woman of his choice 'comes close to reminding us of the medieval courtly romances by virtue of the pre-eminence given to the woman and the trials that the finest of heroes must undergo in order to qualify for her love'.[25]

Olivier's *Henry V* is a remarkable Shakespearean adaptation, for despite the diversity of its constituent elements, the spatial strategy of the film engages both an emotional identification and an intellectual alertness without the imposition of an ostentatious intrusion of style. There is wrought a unique congruency of the film's movement with that of the imagination, a congruency which is prompted in the first place by the structure of the play. The film will stand against any criticism because of its organic structuring of space and time. Stephenson and Debrix consider the evolution of a 'time-space' entity to be a resource of cinema which is of major importance in investing film with its artistic distinction. Their comment on time and space in cinema, and the relation of the 'time-space' entity to the imagination might refer wholly to this film:

> While the spatialisation of time and the temporalisation of space are useful concepts, the two are finally inseparable. One of the achievements of cinema is that it can effect an ideal synthesis. It divests time and space of their everyday, commonsense (but not scientific) characteristics and, investing them conjointly with the immateriality of thought, associates them together in a new whole – cinematographic space-time. Despite appearances, this is a mental rather than a physical entity ... It is this which makes cinema truly an art and one of the richest and most developed of them all.[26]

From Anthony Davies, *Filming Shakespeare's Plays: The Adaptations of Laurence Olivier, Orson Welles, Peter Brook and Akira Kurosawa* (Cambridge, 1988), pp. 26–37.

NOTES

[Laurence Olivier's film of *Henry V* has attracted more sustained critical attention than any other Shakespeare film. In this chapter from his full-length study of four Shakespearean directors, Davies approaches the film on a number of levels: as an exploration of the relationship between theatre and film; as a hybrid text which synthesises disparate genres and pictorial forms, including historical epic, fairytale, and the Western; and as a sophisticated meditation upon the relations between historical and cinematic time and space. Although he makes a few references to the film's conditions of production and reception, Davies plays down its politics in favour of an appreciative (and, in that the ruling concern is the organic unity of the film, implicitly Leavisite) close reading which demonstrates its aesthetic richness and complexity. All quotations from *Henry V* in the essay are from *The Complete Works of William Shakespeare*, Oxford Standard Authors edition, ed. W. J. Craig (London, 1974). Ed.]

1. Marsha McCready, '*Henry V* on Stage and on Film', *Literature/Film Quarterly*, 5 (1977), 318.

2. Ibid., 318.

3. *Shakespeare on Film Newsletter*, 4 (1982), 1.

4. Gorman Beauchamp, '*Henry V*: Myth, Movie, Play', *College Literature*, 5 (1978), 230.

5. Harry Geduld, *Film Guide to Henry V* (Bloomington, IN, 1973), pp. 29, 27.

6. Roger Manvell, *Shakespeare and the Film* (London, 1971), p. 117.

7. Geduld, *Henry V*, p. 37.

8. Beauchamp, '*Henry V*', p. 232.

9. Ibid., p. 234.

10. Anne Barton, 'The King's Two Bodies', in Royal Shakespeare Company Programme for *Richard II* (1973).

11. Sandra Sugarman Singer, 'Laurence Olivier Directs Shakespeare: A Study in Film Authorship' (unpublished PhD dissertation, Northwestern University, 1978), p. 58.

12. Ibid., p. 60.

13. Geduld, *Henry V*, pp. 30–1.

14. Geoffrey Reeves, 'Finding Shakespeare on Film: from an Interview with Peter Brook', in *Focus on Shakespearean Films* (Englewood Cliffs, NJ, 1972), ed. Charles Eckert, pp. 38–9.

15. Schlegel, cited in Beauchamp, '*Henry V*', p. 236.

16. Peter Wollen, 'Counter-cinema: vent d'esté', *After Image*, 4 (1972), 4–5.

17. Singer, 'Laurence Olivier', p. 80.

18. Jack J. Jorgens, *Shakespeare on Film* (Bloomington, IN, 1977), p. 124.

19. Geduld, *Henry V*, pp. 54–5.

20. Jorgens, *Shakespeare on Film*, pp. 132–3.

21. Geduld, *Henry V*, pp. 54–5.

22. James E. Phillips, 'Adapted From a Play by Shakespeare', *Hollywood Quarterly*, 2 (1946), 87.

23. André Bazin, *What is Cinema?*, vol. II (Berkeley, CA, 1967), pp. 140–8.

24. Ibid., p. 147.

25. Ibid., p. 147.

26. Ralph Stephenson and J. R. Debrix, *The Cinema as Art*, 2nd edn (London, 1976), p. 156.

3

Shakespeare and Film: A Question of Perspective

CATHERINE BELSEY

The history of criticism seems to support the assumption that Shakespeare's texts are plural, or in other words, that any reading of a Shakespeare play which offers to define the play's single meaning is partial in both senses of the word. I also want to support this assumption, not in the interests of a happy pluralism in which anything goes and all readings contribute to our understanding of the full richness of the text's meaning, but on the contrary, on the basis that the history of criticism indicates that all readings are readings from specific positions, and that all readings have implications beyond our individual understanding of a particular play. I have discussed elsewhere the role of criticism in producing the meaning of the text,[1] but in the case of a dramatic text, there is yet another production process, the production of meaning in the course of producing (literally) the play. The play-in-performance necessarily interprets the text: the actor speaks the lines so that they make sense – a sense – and so narrows the plurality of the possible meanings. The history of Shakespearean production is thus in an obvious sense the history of the interpretation of Shakespeare, and this clearly does not exist in isolation from the history of ideas. Film, however, I want to suggest, tends to narrow plurality to a greater degree, to specify and fix a reading as its reading. Shakespeare on film may enhance our understanding of the text: it certainly offers us a way of grasping the ideological conditions of its own production. What it cannot do, however, is reproduce the conditions of Elizabethan staging which emphasise a specific kind of plurality. By offering itself as intelligible on two distinct planes simultaneously, a performance on the Elizabethan stage tends to bring into collision different orders of understanding, leaving its audience to ponder questions which the play itself does not resolve.

The *Julius Caesar* of Joseph L. Mankiewicz (1953), perhaps because of its distance from us in a number of ways, formal as well as ideological, may prove a persuasive instance. Mankiewicz's film is a direct descendant of the classic western, and its central conflict is between two individuals, Brutus, honest, liberal, possibly misled, and Antony, subtle, devious and self-seeking. Brutus' mission to clean up Rome misfires, and therein lies the tragedy of the noblest Roman of them all. The transformation from play to western culminates in the battle of Philippi. Brutus' men make their way through a narrow pass in the mountains and are ambushed by Antony's Indians who, at a signal, appear on a rise wearing animal skins and brandishing bows and arrows.

The focus on Brutus and Antony as individuals is to a high degree the result of the film's use of classic Hollywood cinematic modes. It is above all the close-up which is the source of the distance between film and stage. Brutus' inner conflict, his integrity and the intensity of his emotion, are registered in James Mason's face at least as much as in his words, and a series of close-ups show him sweating with the effort of doubt and concern for the ordinary people of Rome.[2] When Antony turns to the camera from his rhetorical triumph in the marketplace he fills the screen, while tiny citizens, insect-like, begin looting and wrecking the city behind him. The nineteenth-century liberal concept of the opposition between the individual and society is here sharply defined.

The unease of the film, evidence of the partiality of its reading, is registered in the problem of cinematic modes confronted by long (and 'great' because Shakespearean) speeches. Actors must not move while they speak Shakespeare. They therefore speak in close-up, and the static shots, not much enlivened by the statues introduced to signify Roman-ness, alternate with shots of life in Ancient Rome, where the narrow streets teem with bustling citizens. Again individual and society are sharply juxtaposed.

The film's triumph, however, is the certainty with which it clarifies an area left uncertain in the text. Antony pauses in his address to the Romans, overcome with emotion: 'Bear with me/My heart is in the coffin there with Caesar. ...' (III.ii.105–6). As he turns away, the camera swings round to show his calculating expression. The citizens, wrought to hysteria by his rhetoric, are seen as gullible victims of the demagogue.

This reading is clearly possible, if partial. But it would be harder to establish on the stage without the benefit of close-up, and virtually impossible at the Globe,[3] where Antony's expression would have had to be visible to an audience located on at least three sides of him, and possibly four. The effect of the close-up here is to produce ethical and political coherence, and in the process to close off many of the ethical and political questions left open by the text.

Julius Caesar can alternatively be seen as bringing into collision two antithetical political orders; one hierarchic, authoritarian, ritualistic and, if we take Antony's account of Caesar's will seriously, benevolent; the other deeply distrustful of despotism, convinced of the rationality of the people, a proto-liberalism as yet unauthorised in 1599, whose only mode of assertion is political assassination. This collision finds a focus in the juxtaposition at the centre of the play of the two speeches in the marketplace. The text's plurality – and its political significance in its own period – lies above all in its inability or unwillingness to choose decisively between absolutism and the right to resist. This issue became increasingly central in English politics during the next fifty years; it was a major area of political debate in Europe throughout the sixteenth and seventeenth centuries.[4]

Julius Caesar is an interrogative text in that it poses questions which are not answered within the play. The ethical uncertainty of tyrannicide is sharply rendered for the audience when Brutus emblematically defines the play's central contradiction:

> let us bathe our hands in Caesar's blood
> Up to the elbows, and besmear our swords.
> Then walk we forth, even to the market-place,
> And waving our red weapons o'er our heads,
> Let's all cry 'Peace, freedom, and liberty!'
> (III.i.107–11)

The possibility of peace and liberty through violence has again become a major political issue of the 1980s. Mankiewicz's film excises this speech. In the context of the Cold War such questions were not open to debate. What was known with certainty was that social disorder was produced by unscrupulous individuals in quest of personal power. The message of the film is that Romans (the costume and setting), Elizabethans (the play is by Shakespeare) and modern Americans (for whom the film paradoxically provides a mirror) are all instances of the universal, tragic and timeless truth that integrity, however heroic, is no match for political sophistication, and that the people are perpetually in danger, easily misled by demagogues pretending to have their interests at heart. The Lord Chamberlain's Men in 1599, wearing Elizabethan dress to perform a play by a contemporary author, must have offered a version which was no less politically 'relevant', but in which ideological closure was not sealed by the invocation of universal recognition of its trans-historical truth.

But if the film has a specific political context in the Cold War, it also has a more general one in the conventions of Shakespeare criticism. The Introduction to the authoritative Arden edition by T. S. Dorsch (1955) analyses the play under two headings, 'The Characters' (thirty-five pages) and 'Language and Imagery' (eight pages). Traditional literary criticism is ostensibly a-political, and the assumption in 1955 was presumably that the two categories specified exhausted the main critical possibilities. The film's overt focus on the psychology and motivation of the individual is in no sense surprising. In the Arden analysis there are four characters 'of absorbing interest', namely Caesar, Brutus, Cassius and Antony (p.xxvi), and the rest are minor characters, worth only six pages between them. Brutus, whose liberalism is viewed less sympathetically here than usual, is nonetheless an entirely honourable man (p.xlii), a good husband and kind to children, 'most sympathetic in his intimate personal relationships' (p.xliii). He is the private man who mistakenly dabbles in politics, an unscrupulous business which he does not understand.

Shakespeare's achievement in the play, according to Dorsch, is the convincing analysis of individual psychology in language which displays 'fine poetic or rhetorical qualities' (p.lxi). The discursive framework of both this analysis and Mankiewicz's film is itself ideological. It is the framework of assumptions of nineteenth-century liberal humanism, which posits individual subjectivity as the origin of thought and action, which poses a radical distinction between personal and political, with a high premium on the former, and which culminates, as far as Shakespeare criticism is concerned, in Bradley's masterly analysis of character (challenged by events) as destiny. It is also the theoretical framework of a mode of history which seeks the origin and meaning of the English revolution in the personalities of Charles I and Cromwell, or a politics which finds the sources of debate between right and left in psychological differences.

These nineteenth-century assumptions, 'obvious' to Bradley and still, perhaps, 'obvious' in the 1950s were not, I believe, at all obvious in the 1590s, though the fact that they begin to be glimpsed as possibilities in the Elizabethan period is one of the sources of the plurality of Shakespeare's texts. The plays are, I suggest, poised at the intersection of two distinct discursive frameworks, the product of an ideological crisis which is manifest in the theatre as well as outside it. If two political orders are brought into collision in *Julius Caesar*, two radically distinct kinds of staging, one medieval, one modern, are brought into collision to produce the Elizabethan theatre. Film is the apotheosis of the modern, and it is in this sense that it inevitably narrows the plurality of an Elizabethan text.

The morality drama, the main native influence, through the Tudor interludes, on the Elizabethan stage, was performed, whether in the open air or in a hall, in the round. All the evidence indicates that the action of the play takes place on the ground, at the level of the audience. With spectators on all sides, the action is offered to no specific viewpoint, though we may probably assume that in the hall steps were taken to ensure that it was fully intelligible from the high table. In certain plays (most notably Medwall's *Fulgens and Lucres*, c. 1500) the boundary between players and spectators is seen as indeterminate: the world of the fiction is not radically differentiated from the world of the audience. Props, if any, are emblematic (symbolic castles, hell mouths). Lighting effects are natural in the open air or minimal in the hall. The author is typically anonymous. The main project of the morality drama is to show that things are not what they seem, that behind the veil of experience Mankind is caught up in a cosmic struggle between vice and virtue, in which it is the role of evil to blind its human victim to what is truly at stake. Since experience is no guide to the real nature of the world, illusionism – photographic realism – is not valued, nor is the author's subjective experience of the world thought to be important as a guarantee of the play's truth.

When in 1605 Inigo Jones presented *The Masque of Blackness* at court with a perspective backdrop, he introduced a form of staging radically new in England. It was not until after the Restoration that the proscenium arch and the use of perspective became normal in the commercial theatre, and not until the early nineteenth century that the diminution of the forestage caused the whole world of the fiction to retreat behind the frame of the proscenium. Until the late nineteenth century, lighting tended to be uniform throughout the theatre. Nonetheless, the early seventeenth century witnessed the emergence of a form of staging which culminates in film, where a lighted, framed, rectangular space presents to a single position, the fixed position of the spectator in front of the screen, a fictional world which offers a replica of the real world of the spectator's experience.

The project of the perspective system, developed by Brunelleschi in Florence in the early fifteenth century, was the faithful reproduction in painting of what the eye sees. Although in detail it is not visually correct, Renaissance artists took it to be true, precisely as Euclidean geometry was true.[5] Perspective staging offers to reproduce, through illusion, the spectator's experience of the world. In illusionist drama certain coherences of spatial relationship are taken for granted. Objects defined on the painted backdrop are in proportion to the size of the actors; props are realistic and are in proportion to both; but proportion is defined from the point of view of an optimum position in front of the stage from which the fictional world is intelligible and recognisable.

Photography is the culmination of this reproduction of the recognisable, the 'true', and film is the final realisation of the project of perspective staging.[6] Depth of field, the vanishing point holding and closing off the spectator's gaze, offers the possibility of an illusion of balance between the world of the audience and the fictional work offered as a replica of it (see Fig. 1).

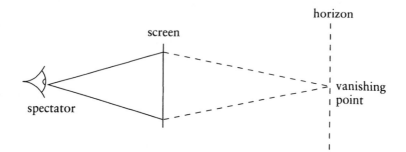

Fig. 1

The two worlds are isolated from each other by the dividing screen. Meanwhile the spectator, immobilised in a private space, the individual seat in a darkened auditorium, is involved in a personal and private response to the experience of the fiction,[7] intelligible to the degree that it seems to replicate experience in the non-fictional world. The coherence of spatial (and narrative) relationships in the film is the source of the audience's mastery of its meaning and recognition of its 'truth'. The modern liberal humanist spectator understands, on the basis of experience, the meaning of a text which is seen as the expression of the author's experience. This (single) meaning is guaranteed by the transcendent subjectivity of the author, source and origin of the fiction itself. When the author is Shakespeare, this transcendence is known in advance and ensures the 'truth' of the fiction. In penetrating the depths of the fictional world, the spectator thus meets the gaze of Shakespeare himself (see Fig. 2).

The two triangles of the diagram thus come to represent the worlds of experience of two subjectivities, the one replicating the other and thus guaranteeing its truth. Small wonder, then, that film and literary criticism converge on the analysis of subjectivity as the origin of thought and action, dwelling on the personal and experiential at the expense of the public, abstract and political issues also raised in the play.

That such a reading is possible, if partial, is a product of the ideological collision of which the Elizabethan stage is one effect. Poised between two modes, the Renaissance stage is raised, sometimes fenced, isolating the world of the fiction. But there is no framing proscenium arch, no backdrop, no perspective. The audience may surround the stage. The relationship between the world of the narrative, the canopy of 'the heavens' and the trap door to 'hell' below the stage creates an emblematic representation of the macrocosm. Within this context the microcosmic human figures conduct and re-conduct the cosmic struggles of which they are part, and with which they are

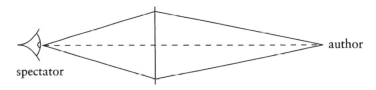

Fig. 2

continuous. At the same time, they are no longer identifiable as morality abstractions. Named, individualised characters in a specific narrative, they have internalised the *psychomachia* of Mankind in what begins to be perceived as the private world of personal experience (Brutus' stoicism at Portia's death implies the existence of an inner, *unspoken* suffering inconceivable on the morality stage).

The Elizabethan stage is thus the site of conflicting dramatic modes, one emblematic and the other illusionist, one challenging the audience to interpret a pattern of abstract meanings, the other specifying a fixed and 'obvious' relationship between the audience and the world simulated on the stage. The gap between these contradictory modes decentralises the plays of the period and insists on the specific form of plurality which tends towards the interrogative text.

It does not follow, of course, from what I have suggested, that all filmed Shakespeare is confined to character-analysis. Conventions are there to be broken and Peter Brook, for example, in his *King Lear* (1970) breaks a good many of them. But here again the plurality of the text is inevitably narrowed in consequence of the form. The film presents its brilliant rectangle filled with meaning to a single place from which its world is intelligible as coherent and recognisable.

Lear, if not so obviously as *Julius Caesar* an interrogative text, can nonetheless be seen to raise questions about power – its origin in property, its right use, its value – and about identity – its uncertainties and discontinuities ('Who is it that can tell me who I am?' I.iv.229). Poor Tom and Lear's shadow move in a world of dispossession and madness marginalised by the rationality of possessive individualism. The challenge of *Lear* lies in the fact that this world is not presented as a pastoral retreat, and that no purged or untainted ruler steps forward at the end of the play to heal the gored state. The questions finally left open include the issue of rule itself – who wants it, and why.

Peter Brook's film eliminates most of these questions in favour of a single certainty: that all law, justice and morality are ultimately illusory. The relationship between property and power is virtually obliterated: in these desolate landscapes, what property? The formal subtlety of the film obscures the complexities and contradictions of the text. The treatment is experimental and cinematically exciting. The grainy black-and-white photography, out-of-focus shots, montage sequences, and black spacing reach a climax in the storm scene, where the camera breaks the 180-degree rule, showing Lear in profile at the edges of the screen, in line-by-line alternation from the right and from the left. This film uses almost exclusively close-ups or, more rarely, long shots, but relatively stylised acting (lack of facial movement) distracts attention from the individual psychology. Since the close-up is the dominant technique and since, therefore, all the actors are shown in this way, foregrounding of specific characters is minimised.

The settings are illusionist and primitive – rudimentary castles, animal skins, Viking ships, battle-axes, snowy, uncultivated heathland. Most touches of optimism in the text are cut (notably Edmund's 'Some good I mean to do. ...' V.iii. 243), and the effect is of primaeval struggle for survival against the bleak, unyielding landscape, the elements, and, supremely, the menace of human indifference or ferocity. The evocation of the primitive (through the techniques of filming as well as the settings) naturalises this struggle, makes it eternal and inevitable. A sequence of shots in the hovel evokes Poor Tom as Christ Crucified. The grotesque is emphasised: humanity preying on itself without the trappings of civilisation is pathetic, degraded, ineffectual.

The immediate and direct critical influence is Jan Kott's comparison of *King Lear* and *Endgame*, but the context in which this book became influential was, as Kott makes clear, the Theatre of Cruelty and the Theatre of the Absurd.[8] More broadly, the context of its success in the West was the Vietnam War and the aftermath of May 1968. The film is luxuriously, excitingly nihilistic. It proclaims the eternal triumph of desolation. This is a powerful reading, and one which the text will readily bear, but it is not plural, and it closes off all questions in its single vision of a world of bland, relentless cruelty.

Illusionist film cannot be contradictory because the camera shows the 'truth'. Much that is left undefined on the emblematic Elizabethan stage is inevitably specified on the screen. It is possible, however, to break with illusionism itself, to withhold the 'truth', the coherence which guarantees intelligibility from a single position. That, I think, is the project of Derek Jarman's *The Tempest* (1979). The blue filter, the use of distorting lenses, mirrors, firelight, foreground the film's own devices. The rearrangement of the narrative produces formal discontinuities which repudiate coherence in favour of a series of brilliant visual moments. The consequence is a fragmentation of meaning which enhances plurality – the film is closer to the 'writable' text as Barthes defines it in *S/Z*.[9] But it does so at the expense of that specific form of plurality which I have defined as interrogative, and which, I have suggested, is characteristically produced by a specific moment in the history of the theatre.

From *Literature/Film Quarterly*, 11 (1983), 152–7.

NOTES

[Applying poststructuralist literary theory to the study of film and theatrical performance, Belsey proposes that the cinematic medium completes the project of the proscenium arch illusionist stage, in that it reduces the multiplicity of meanings and perspectives generated on the Elizabethan stage to a single, determinate point of view. Realist film, she argues, is inherently conservative, and closely implicated within the ideology of liberal humanism. Drawing upon Roland Barthes' distinction between 'readable' (*lisible*) and 'writable' (*scriptible*) texts, Belsey draws a distinction between the openness and interrogative plurality of the Shakespearean text in the context of the Elizabethan theatre (and within poststructuralist reading), and the closed form of the illusionist film. Quotations from *Julius Caesar* and *King Lear* in the essay are from the Collins Tudor Shakespeare edition, ed. Peter Alexander (London, 1951). Ed.]

1. Catherine Belsey, *Critical Practice* (London, 1980), pp. 125–46.

2. Roland Barthes, *Mythologies*, trans. Annette Lavers (London, 1972), p. 27.

3. The play was probably performed at the new Globe. See *Julius Caesar*, ed. T. S. Dorsch (London, 1955), p. vii.

4. Quentin Skinner, *The Foundations of Modern Political Thought*, 2 vols (Cambridge, 1978).

5. Morris Kline, *Mathematics in Western Culture* (Harmondsworth, 1972), pp. 163–5.

6. Stephen Heath, 'Narrative Space', *Screen*, 17 (1976–7), 68–112.

7. Keir Elam, *The Semiotics of Theatre and Drama* (London, 1980), pp. 64–5.

8. Jan Kott, *Shakespeare Our Contemporary*, trans. Boleslaw Taborski (London, 1967), pp. 100–33.

9. Roland Barthes, *S/Z*, trans. Richard Miller (New York, 1974). The translator unhelpfully offers 'writerly'.

4

Radical Potentiality and Institutional Closure

GRAHAM HOLDERNESS

I

Whereas the BBC TV Shakespeare series could be regarded as a characteristic expression of the cultural policies of the producing corporation, cinematic reproduction of Shakespeare constitutes at best a marginal dimension of film history. The primary function of cinema as a cultural industry in a bourgeois economy is to reproduce and naturalise dominant ideologies; and by contrast with the theatre, the plays of Shakespeare seem to have offered few opportunities for the prosecution of that function. The relation between 'Shakespeare' and 'film' is very much that ... [of] the exchange of cultural authority between institutions in a reciprocal process. The repute of cinema art and of the film industry can be enhanced by their capacity to incorporate Shakespeare; the institution of Shakespeare itself benefits from that transaction by a confirmation of its persistent universality. Shakespeare films exist on that important but peripheral fringe of cinematic production, where the values of high art can be held to justify or compensate for the lack of commercial success (they are probably screened more often and witnessed by more spectators in the form of 16 mm prints hired by institutions of education than in the commercial cinemas), and they can scarcely be regarded as central to the mainstream practice and development of the cinema.

This essay has no space to attempt a general survey of Shakespeare films (which can in any case be found in some excellent full-length studies); but will instead confine itself to two basic problems: the position of Shakespeare films within what has been defined as the ideological function of the cinema in society; and the existing status and potential value of films within the dominant practices of literary education.

Writing from within the embattled domain of 'Literature' teaching and criticism, we are likely to assume that any translation of a Shakespeare text into a 'live' dramatic form – theatrical performance, film adaptation, television production – will automatically constitute a progressive act. Such translation seems inevitably to entail a liberation of the *play*, a text for reproduction or recreation in performance, from the fetished holy writ of the *text*; and any move to challenge the hegemony of that dominant form of ideological oppression must, surely, be welcomed.

Theatrical, film and television productions have always been accorded a place and a potential value within the broad conspectus of a literary education: the question is what place, and what value? Are such things ancillary to the essential critical labour, marginal diversions to the study of texts? Traditional 'Literature' must keep them peripheral, since when they become a central focus they tend to displace the text from its central role in constituting the nature of the subject; tend to render the discipline itself unstable, open to question, vulnerable to change. Useful evidence of the tension created when film is introduced into the institution of Literature can be found in GCE O level examiners' reports (I offer a few instances from many examples):

> Imaginative interpretations of texts can be misleading. The visual impact of films and productions of plays was often stronger than the impact of Shakespeare's or Hardy's words.[1]

> Films and stage-productions are not always entirely helpful. Lady Macduff bathing her son, Macbeth's soldiers attacking her maids, Lady Macbeth leaping from the battlements, Macbeth's mutilated body scattered across the stage, were so commonplace that it seemed fortunate that productions of *The Crucible* were less easily available.
>
> (1973, p. 9)

> ... most candidates appeared to know *Macbeth* well. Some, however, were handicapped by having seen a film version ... candidates should remember that it is Shakespeare's text which is being examined.
>
> (1977, p. 9)

'Literature' here encounters 'Film' as a subversive influence to be resisted, marginalised or suppressed. Is the adoption of Shakespeare by the cinematic medium in educational practice, if not in the commercial cinema, inherently radical?

Catherine Belsey, in a very interesting article,[2] proposes exactly the opposite: in her argument, both the literary text and a theatrical production under Elizabethan stage conditions are potentially productive of plurality of meaning: whereas films operate to close the plural work into a single dimension of significance. [...]

This [...] represents a body of opinion which forms, to my original thesis, the antithesis: that film is an inherently *conservative* medium, which inevitably exercises a despotic ideological control over the spectator's responses, closing off the work's potentiality for multiplicity of significance, depriving the audience of an opportunity to participate in a collaborative construction of meaning. 'Film', in the words of another writer, 'overwhelms the mind with a relentless progression of visual and auditory impulses ... all other arts liberate the imagination, film entraps it.'[3]

In terms of this latter view, the medium of film itself can only be an invisible, apparently innocent communicator of ideology. Like the naturalist stage, it purports to provide the spectator with a transparent window on to experience: isolated in the darkness of an auditorium she or he is overwhelmed with an enormous concentration of visual imagery insistently signifying its irreducible reality. Belsey offers as illustrations two films, both of which are said to offer ideology a free, unhampered passage: Joseph L. Mankiewicz's *Julius Caesar* (1953) transmits the liberal dilemma of a bourgeois-democratic society; while the *King Lear* (1970) of Peter Brook communicates a 'theoretical nihilism': '... like *Julius Caesar*, this film also makes a political statement: that the struggle for change, however heroic, is doomed in a world where all law, morality and justice are finally illusory'. Mankiewicz's film is of course a piece of thoroughgoing film naturalism, alternating close-ups of the main characters with long-shots of crowd scenes, all played against a 'realistic' Roman background. Belsey acknowledges, in an enthusiastic critique, that the cinematic techniques of *King Lear* are stylistically very different: she lists the grainy black-and-white photography, stylised acting, direct addresses to camera, lightning changes of focus, rapid superimpositions, violations of screen direction.[4] She could have added the Brechtian titles, the absence of music, the distorted images, zoom-fades, blurred visions, surreal apparitions; the 'disjointed and staccato quality, elliptic camera-work, and violent mannerist cutting';[5] all devices which estrange the film's techniques from naturalism and from familiar screen conventions. Can a film constructed from such alienating, deconstructive devices really be a vehicle for the smooth and uninterrupted passage of ideology; can such discordant techniques really operate to naturalise ideology, obediently miming its chosen language?

Consider Brook's handling of a particularly complex dramatic moment, Gloucester's attempted suicide. Grigori Kozintsev in his film of the play felt that this scene was essentially a theatrical gesture, and avoided it by cutting. Brook, with Beckett and Jan Kott in the background, embraced the moment as a central thematic and dramatic focus of the work.

> The director duplicates in cinematic terms Shakespeare's blend of blatant stage artifice and imaginative reality ... a long shot shows Edgar and Gloucester struggling along a flat plain. But then, in a series of tight, low-angle close-ups, Edgar and Gloucester seem to climb. The sound of the waves in the distance accords with Edgar's description, and following film convention it makes us imagine an off-screen reality. Set on 'the extremest verge', Gloucester bids farewell to poor Tom, and his final speech of despair is filmed in low-angle close-up ... as he falls forward, however, Brook jolts us with an illusion-shattering cut to an extreme overhead long-shot. From this godlike perspective, we watch a tiny old man take a silent pratfall on a barren stretch of sand.[6]

The complex effects of this filmic montage can't adequately be summarised either in terms of Belsey's 'political statement', or of Jorgens's 'absurdist pantomime'. The director has certainly composed and edited his shots to expose the distinction between Gloucester's physical tumble and his psychological fall down mountains of the mind; and the final perspective is that of a god dispassionately watching a wanton boy killing flies. But the effect of, for example, the low-angle close-up of Gloucester's face (described by Jorgens as 'one of the most savagely beautiful shots of a human face ever put on film'[7]), a frame from which the character towers over the spectator in the tragic dignity of suffering, is *complicated* but not *negated* by the jump-cut to an overhead long-shot of his pathetic fall. Moreover the fracturing of naturalist conventions increases the spectator's awareness of the camera as a constructive device, not a window opening on reality, but a mobile and changing point-of-view which can choose to record in a spirit of empathy or of alienation. The primary function of alienating devices, in this film or any other, is to intensify the viewer's awareness of the mechanisms by which this simulated reality is being produced; to impede the free transmission of ideology by discouraging unconscious, empathetic involvement and encouraging a vigilant and self-conscious curiosity, both about the object of the medium, and about the medium itself.

Belsey's identification of film with naturalist staging, though suggestive, is potentially misleading. Though the proscenium-arch perspective stage is very obviously a *selector* of reality, it can only *appear* to be an innocent *constitutor* of the reality: the spectator's point of vision is fixed, the access to the stage's simulated reality circumscribed, the window on to experience absolutely static. The film camera, by contrast, can do either: it can, like the proscenium arch, efface itself in a privileging of its object, constituting reality as objective in the illusionistic manner of naturalism; or it can, by violating those naturalist conventions, by emphasising and exploiting its mobility, call the spectator's attention to the mechanisms of its own perception. Without employing alienation devices, the naturalist stage can *only* offer itself as the *premise* of a simulated reality; the film can be seen to operate as a moving *commentary* on its object, releasing the viewer from the tyranny of empathetic illusion to a freer consideration of reality and of the artifice which produces it.

Considering Shakespeare films in the light of this most fundamental distinction in the whole of film theory – between naturalistic, illusionist cinema and its opposite – we can conclude that certain filmed adaptations of the plays operate simply as vehicles for the transmissions of ideology. Other films block, deflect or otherwise 'work on' ideology in order partially to disclose its mechanisms. The same method of evaluation will reveal which films are potentially more valuable for mobilisation in the educational context; and which can only work to reinforce and familiarise conventional attitudes to Shakespeare. Again, the object of this essay is not to attempt such evaluation across a wide range of films, but rather to suggest, with the help of particular illustrations, methods of procedure and analysis appropriate to such investigation.

In addition to describing the formal characteristics of the medium, some account must be taken, in however abstract a fashion, of the audience itself: which is not, after all, entirely created by the particular work of art it happens to be witnessing. A film of Shakespeare is never experienced in total vacuum, because

of the ubiquity, the universality of Shakespeare as a cultural phenomenon. A film's 'arrested play of meanings' will enter into
conflictual or co-operative relationship with certain ideological
premises, certain cultural assumptions, certain definite levels of
knowledge. The school students rebuked by the JMB examiners
were witnessing a film *in the light of* some knowledge of the play as
literary text. The film may be experienced in a context of other encounters with the play – a TV or theatrical production perhaps, or
another film (most of the 'great' Shakespeare plays have been filmed
several times). Or the film may simply reinforce or subvert an inherited cultural concept of 'Shakespeare' – the familiar associations of
costume drama, perspective staging, unintelligible plots, projected
delivery. It is this body of assumptions that an effective film translit-
eration is likely to subvert: clashing with the spectator's preconcep-
tions to produce a liberating dialectic, to foster that very 'play of
meanings' which art can press ideology to deliver.

I have chosen to concentrate my analysis on two examples of ideol-
ogy-resistant Shakespeare film treatment: Akira Kurosawa's *Throne
of Blood* (1957), and Peter Hall's 1969 production of *A Midsummer
Night's Dream*. Hall's own conception of how a Shakespeare play
should be filmed was expounded in an interview with Roger Manvell:

> The greatest influence on me, or my generation, was Leavis, who be-
> lieved above everything in a critical examination of the text, the
> search for meaning and metaphor ... Too much normal film art con-
> tradicts the techniques of the plays, at least as far as their most im-
> portant element, the text, is concerned. But the medium of film can
> certainly be used to communicate the text most effectively, even to
> the extent of making its meaning clearer than is sometimes possible
> in the theatre ... This is not a film *from* a stage production or a film
> *based* on the play. It attempts to bend the medium of the film to
> reveal the full quality of the text.[8]

Hall insists that the film should be a visual embodiment of the text,
fleshing the verbal structure with the concrete reality it signifies, but
subordinated absolutely to the authoritative structure and rhythm
of the text. In practice, the experiment produced something entirely
different. Hall thought the film was probably 'not a film at all', but
an incarnation of literary language; in fact the director's 'textualist'
ideology enters into sharp and disruptive conflict with the film
medium to produce one of the most inventive and valuable of all
the Shakespeare films.

The film opens with a deliberate disruption of naturalist film convention: superimposed on an English neo-classical country house,
surrounded by images of order and authority, appears the title
'Athens'. The assurance customarily guaranteed by film techniques
which confirm our normal habits of perception, is subverted: what
we see on the screen may well be deceptive. The 'Athenian' court is
set in a chaste, barren and colourless environment, shot with a tele-
photo lens to make the images two-dimensional. The movement
away from the court towards the forest is signalled by further disruptive devices, as the narrative rhythm of the text clashes against
the essentially cinematic technique of *montage*: 'Momentum,
regular rhythm and continuity are provided by the text while jump
cuts disrupt our sense of realistic space. A tension is established
between what sounds like a conventional, clearly articulated stage
performance and visuals which whisk the star-crossed lovers from
the grey interior to a flat boat pond ...'[9] These sequences were
filmed with hand-held camera: the slight movement imparted to the
shots calls attention to the camera as a recorder of these simulated
events. The actors address the camera directly, demolishing the naturalistic 'fourth wall'. In the wood itself, the conjuring tricks of the
photography and editing emulate Oberon's magic: Puck appears
and disappears, disjunctive editing confuses the reality of time and
space. Puck's concluding invitation to the audience to

> Think but this, and all is mended,
> That you have but slumbered here
> While these visions did appear.
> And this weak and idle theme
> No more yielding but a dream
> (V.i.410–14)

is spoken in darkness. Puck snaps his fingers, and it is morning.
Which is the reality, which the illusion: daylight and the solid
facade of Theseus' rationalistic Athens, or the 'magic' of the forest
conjured by the film's 'radical cinematography'? In this way the film
foregrounds its constructive devices, offering the spectator an open
awareness of the medium as a conjuring and simulating power
which makes 'reality', yet renders itself visible in the act of making.

Ultimately, however, the film is pulled back into an ideological
resolution. When Hall's 'rustics' present their play, the courtly
audience is thoroughly involved in a shared experience of festive

celebration. Despite his reverence for the text, the director cut the courtiers' condescending comments, and filmed a scene which suggests that the lovers have benefited by their flirtation with the occult, and can take their places in a society united into community by the combined magic of supernatural agency, enthusiastic popular theatricals and *avant-garde* film: a liberal resolution which almost reconstructs Leavis's 'organic community'. Finally the film's subversive and self-reflexive experiment is pulled towards a resolution expressing the well-balanced harmony of the formalist's literary text.

Akira Kurosawa's *Throne of Blood* (1957) is the most complete translation of Shakespeare into film. The text is abandoned altogether, not even translated; the action shifted from medieval Scotland to feudal Japan; a western Renaissance tragedy becomes an Oriental samurai epic. This most celebrated of all Shakespeare films has been praised particularly for the completeness of its transformation of drama into cinema: 'the great masterpiece' (Peter Brook), 'the finest of the Shakespeare movies' (Grigori Kozintsev). Critics have stressed the *independence* of play and film: Frank Kermode called it 'an allusion to *Macbeth*', and Peter Brook asserted that it 'doesn't come into the Shakespeare question at all'. J. Blumenthal calls it 'a masterpiece in its own right', wholly liberated from 'the dreaded literary media'.[10] Clearly, if play and film occupy entirely different spaces and cannot even be compared, much less evaluated, against one another: not only do the separate 'masterpieces' enjoy their independent prestige, but the film is rendered incapable of violating the integrity of 'Shakespeare', unable to interrogate or subvert the play's immortal and immanent identity. If this proposition were accepted, *Throne of Blood* would disappear from 'the Shakespeare question' altogether and would offer the possibility of meaning only in relation to Kurosawa's other work and to Japanese culture, ideology and society.[11]

The most substantial critical objection made against the film is that it robs Shakespeare's play of its tragic form and style: 'Kurosawa's Macbeth is not grand',[12] 'His crime is not against God but against Society';[13] 'Kurosawa has betrayed the power of the play'.[14] In fact this is clearly a fundamental aesthetic strategy of the film, which begins in a style more epic than tragic, with a chorus commenting on the images of a ruined castle and a grave: 'Behold within this place now desolate stood once a mighty fortress,/Lived a proud warrior murdered by ambition, his spirit walking still./Vain pride, then as now, will lead ambition to the kill.' The film's narrative is thus framed by an artistic device which contains the story in an explicit moral meaning offered for consideration, to an epic rather than a dramatic audience. Epic detachment is also characteristic of the film's visual style, which is largely structured by the conventions of Japanese Noh drama. Acting and *mise-en-scène* are conventionalised rather than naturalistic; 'Noh is ritual drama, and the world of the Noh is both closed and artificial.'[15] The camerawork, as Kurosawa himself declared, entailed a deliberate avoidance of close-ups.[16] The effect of this technique is detachment: 'the camera and chorus maintain an aesthetic distance from the action';[17] or as Donald Richie terms it, 'alienation': '... alienation is one of the effects of moving the camera back just as moving it forward suggests empathy. The full-shot reveals everything, ... it disengages the viewer and allows him to see cause and effect'.[18]

What can this cinematic interpretation tell us about Shakespeare's *Macbeth*? To begin with, it locates the problem of regicide (*ge-koku-jo*) into a very specific historical and social context, parallel with Duncan's feudal Scotland but radically unlike Shakespeare's England or the modern world. The film displays a militaristic society with an elaborate code of loyalty, expressed in conventionalised social rituals: the intensely-stylised social intercourse of samurai and lord seeks to control the power and violence by which such a society exists. 'Ambition' in this society is not some eccentric personality-disorder, but a central historical contradiction: a natural extension of the militaristic violence which is both liberated and restrained by the feudal pattern of authority. 'What samurai does not want to be lord of a castle?' Washizu (Macbeth) asks Miki (Banquo). The question cannot be explained away in psychological terms, nor collapsed into a universalist moral system. It has meaning only within the historical world of the film. To adopt a similar perspective on *Macbeth* would entail a focus on the play's reconstruction of a distant society, observed not as a shadowy presage of the present, nor as a universal, providentially-established natural kingdom of the past. *Macbeth* opens with a startling contradiction: between the ugly, violent butchery described by the captain, in his account of Macbeth's killing of Macdonwald; and the elaborate rhetoric of chivalry and courtesy used by Duncan to control that power. Macbeth is bound to Duncan by that language of trust, loyalty, honour; but also by a social relationship which depends on a vulnerable and unstable division of authority and power. When Duncan declares Malcolm his successor (a declaration which indicates that this is *not* a hereditary dynasty) he is simultaneously creating a hierarchy and rendering it open to assault by suppressing the very power, vested in the thanes, which sustains his authority.

Critics have complained at the film's understanding of tragic 'inevitability' as social rather than psychological or supernatural: 'Washizu is given social and biological excuses for what can only be put down to unfathomable greed in Shakespeare's Macbeth'.[19] But it is evident that *both* Kurosawa's film *and* Shakespeare's play can be seen primarily as *social* tragedies, set within a distanced historical context in which social problems and contradictions can be rendered visible and fully intelligible to the audience's *curiosity*. Furthermore, tragedy narrated with such aesthetic detachment becomes 'epic'. The *tragedy* of Macbeth involves some degree of empathetic involvement by the spectator in the protagonist's experience; like Malcolm, we identify with Macbeth in order to live imaginatively through the knowledge of evil in a cathartic purgation. *Throne of Blood* denies the spectator that experience, and offers in its place, in the epic style, a detached scrutiny of certain actions and events within a certain social context. The choreographed artifice of Noh drama can certainly express a sense of constraint and predetermined destiny: but the artifice is visible, self-evident and self-conscious; the actors are acting out a stylised performance, not miming an inevitable process of psychological development. Again, it is valid to see *Macbeth* itself as an epic rather than a tragic drama. A performance of the play in Elizabethan stage conditions would have possessed certain qualities evident in the film (excluding of course the film's location sequences): bare sets, conventionalised acting, certain possibilities for detachment and alienation (consider Macbeth's self-reflexive characterisation of himself as a 'poor player'), and the acting-out of a well-known story the outcome of which is known beforehand. Even the soliloquies, so highly privileged by modern psychological interpretations, would not have been played as intense self-communings but as colloquies, dialogues between actor and audience. This is no mere academic speculation: Trevor Nunn's 1976 television production of *Macbeth* brings out these qualities of the play with startling distinctness: using a bare studio, actors visible *as* actors, nondescript costume, direct addresses to camera; all techniques which foreground the 'epic' rather than the 'tragic' dimension of the play.

I am not attempting to argue that Kurosawa has discovered and expressed the *true meaning* of Shakespeare's play: that would be to

acknowledge that the text has an authentic, immanent meaning released by a particular act of interpretation. *Throne of Blood* is self-
evidently *not* Shakespeare; and therein lies its incomparable value for
strategic use in a radical exploration of the play. If the text can be reproduced in a virtually unrecognisable form, then the plurality of the
text is proved beyond reasonable doubt. This bastard offspring, the
play's *alter ego*, can then be brought back into conjunction with
the text, to liberate some of its more radical possibilities of meaning.

I have offered reasons why some films should be regarded as possessing deeper radical possibilities than others. Ultimately, though,
the *political* potentiality of these film adaptations depends on their
strategic mobilisation in the educational rather than the general
cultural context.

[...]

Film and television reproductions of Shakespeare are in essence
no different from other forms of reproduction, in theatre or education: they have specific commercial and cultural functions within
the economic and ideological apparatus of a bourgeois-democratic
society. Spaces are created within that cultural apparatus for radical
intervention, and such opportunities have to a limited extent been
seized. The most promising space for cultural intervention remains,
despite systematic attacks on the system, that of education; where
film and television productions can be introduced into literature
courses, posing fundamental cultural questions, liberating radical
possibilities of meaning, and contributing to the much needed
politicisation of the 'Shakespeare' institution.

From *Political Shakespeare: New Essays in Cultural Materialism*,
ed. Jonathan Dollimore and Alan Sinfield (Manchester, 1985),
pp. 182–92, 199–200.

NOTES

[Holderness's essay utilises a historical materialist approach to
Shakespearean film, both as a mode of cultural production and as material
for (potentially progressive) appropriation within the educational context.
Grounding his methodology firmly and explicitly in educational praxis,
Holderness takes issue with Belsey's argument that film is an inherently
conservative medium effect, by emphasising elements of Shakespearean
cinema which interrogate the conventions of illusionism – and hence, potentially, the ideologies which underpin it as a form. The quotation from *A*

Midsummer Night's Dream in the essay is from The New Arden
Shakespeare edition, ed. Harold F. Brooks (London, 1979). Ed.]

1. Joint Matriculation Board *Examiners' Reports*, vol. 1. *Arts and Social Sciences* (1974), p. 9.

2. [Reprinted above, see pp. 61–70 – Ed.]

3. S. D. Lawder, 'Film: Art of the Twentieth Century', *Yale Alumni Magazine* (May 1968), 33.

4. [See p. 68 above – Ed.]

5. David Robinson, *Financial Times*, 23 July 1971, quoted by Jack Jorgens, *Shakespeare on Film* (Bloomington, IN, 1977), p. 240.

6. Jorgens, *Shakespeare on Film*, p. 240.

7. Ibid.

8. Quoted by Roger Manvell, *Shakespeare and the Film* (New York, 1979), pp. 121–6.

9. Jorgens, *Shakespeare on Film*, p. 55.

10. Peter Brook, 'Shakespeare on Three Screens', *Sight and Sound*, 34 (1965), pp. 68; Grigori Kozintsev, *Shakespeare, Time and Conscience* (New York, 1966), p. 29; Frank Kermode, 'Shakespeare in the Movies', *New York Review of Books*, 10 October 1972; John Blumenthal, '*Macbeth* into *Throne of Blood*', *Sight and Sound*, 34 (1965), 191.

11. The film has been very usefully discussed in this latter context by Ana Laura Zambrano, '*Throne of Blood*: Kurosawa's *Macbeth*', *Literature/Film Quarterly*, 2 (1974).

12. Donald Richie, *The Films of Akira Kurosawa* (Berkeley, CA, 1965), p. 117.

13. Zambrano, '*Throne of Blood*', p. 269.

14. John Gerlach, 'Shakespeare, Kurosawa and *Macbeth*', *Literature/Film Quarterly*, 1 (1973), 352.

15. Richie, *Akira Kurosawa*, p. 117.

16. Ibid., p. 121.

17. Zambrano, '*Throne of Blood*', p. 16.

18. Richie, *Akira Kurosawa*, p. 121.

19. Gerlach, 'Shakespeare, Kurosawa and *Macbeth*', p. 357.

5

Symbolism in Shakespeare Film

I

Warner Brothers' film of *A Midsummer Night's Dream* was released towards the end of 1935. It was ostensibly a movie of the theatre production that Max Reinhardt had presented in the United States the previous year. According to official publicity the movie was co-directed by Reinhardt and William Dieterle. In actual fact most of the on-set direction was done by Dieterle.

In film criticism the movie has often been examined via the *auteur* theory. There are political advantages to this strategy, which is used in the work of Jorgens and Manvell. For a critical heritage that places the author (i.e. Shakespeare) at the centre of creative meaning it is logical to approach cinema from the assumption that a film, like a play, book or poem, is really the product of one individual's efforts. Once this has been established then a film of a play can be reduced to the safe and simple level of one person's interpretation of another person's text. Secondly, in the case of Warner Brothers' film, it enables the movie, and Reinhardt's involvement in it, to be partly redeemed as serious literary work. At the same time the populist, Hollywood influences can be relegated to the background as, at best, intrusive commercialism.

For those convinced that Shakespeare is the province of high drama the interpretation of a European stage director renowned for his evocative and symbolist productions is far more palatable than that of a Warner Brothers' movie maker. At close quarters this theoretical division, between simplistic Hollywood commercialism and the more profound demonology of Reinhardt's Expressionist theatre, doesn't coincide with either the historical evidence or the evidence in the film itself. Rather it suggests that the analysis is, in fact, a re-appropriation of the film, embodying a strategy commonly applied to works that appear radical or which challenge orthodox critical belief in some way.

In the case of the Warner Brothers' film the existence of two directors is used to support the belief that *A Midsummer Night's Dream* displays a tension between two largely exclusive methodologies, i.e. the Hollywood production values used by Dieterle and the Romantic and mystical theatre of Reinhardt. Behind this separation is a strong current of elitism, with which the North American entertainment industry is derided in favour of European theatre. When this demarcation of different elements of a Shakespeare film is used, in an attempt to re-integrate it into a standard, orthodox interpretation, the movie is dehistoricised. In other words this process of appropriation tends to obscure or exclude the real relationships between its diverse structures and their historical context. Yet in the case of the Warner Brothers' film the differentiation is illuminating simply because the actual production, and the finished product, acknowledged and played on the demarcation of its different elements (a demarcation very different to that between high and low art).

A Midsummer Night's Dream was made as a prestige picture, a lavish production that was intended to establish Warner Brothers' reputation as an enlightened company dedicated to culture. Not only was it perceived of as a duet between a renowned movie business and a famous director but it was also used as a showcase for the studio's technical skills and acting talent. In the same way that the British silent films combined the imagery of painting, spectacular theatre and historical narrative, so *A Midsummer Night's Dream* consciously acknowledged a diversity of genres: musical revues; romantic comedies; classic silent films and cartoons.

Warner Brothers' film made explicit the method of production of many other Shakespeare movies. It showed that a film of Shakespeare is not so much the reproduction of a text as a specific point in cultural production where varied concepts and methodologies are brought together within the economic framework of a country's film industry. What is interesting about this particular film is that it was produced in circumstances that led it to reveal an ambiguous tension between the self-defined needs of aesthetic intellectualism and the ideology of entertainment controlled by business. It was made using production methods culled from the 'theatre of light' designed to evoke a mystical atmosphere. This was achieved using contemporary technology, music and precise choreography; the ingredients that Appia felt were essential if Wagner's *gesamtkunstwerk* was ever to be realised. At the same time the film was created in a tightly scheduled studio. It was intended as a celebration of the economic and technological power of large industry and America's ability to emerge from a crippling depression. As a result the 'tension' between Reinhardt and Hollywood is actually a demonstration of the alliance between the Expressionist stage and the economic and cultural edifice of capitalism.

The Warner family had been involved in the film business since before World War I but their company only emerged as a fully fledged part of the North American movie industry in 1923. At the turn of the century Edison's patenting of film technology in the United States meant that production was the only area of the film industry that wasn't subject to a rigid monopoly. So many distributors, Warners included, began to make their own films in an attempt to exploit this part of the market. In 1925 Warner Brothers bought the studios and distribution chain of Vitagraph. A similar deal brought them the production facilities of another silent company, First National, and a major competitive role in the movies. From early on Warner Brothers committed themselves to the development of an effective sound system for film. Their initial period of technical and economic expansion from the mid to late 1920s was heavily geared towards this. Their experiments culminated in the release of the first 'talkie'; *The Jazz Singer* in 1927.

Nick Roddick suggests in *A New Deal in Entertainment: Warner Brothers in the 1930s*, that the company's production methods were a classic example of the Hollywood studio system. This is fundamentally an economic classification; Warners' approach to materials, personnel and products was organised along the lines of an advanced, management-based, mass production line. The film technique that Warners used for the majority of their movies stemmed from a methodology typical of the 'Hollywood codes of editing'. The key features were: a character-centred, closed narrative and a coherent and self-contained world portrayed as unmediated reality. The style and structure of the finished movies, from *The Jazz Singer* to *The Adventures of Robin Hood* (1938), marshalled cinema in

support of an apparently uncontradictory and authoritative perception of reality; a world centred on, and manipulated by, the actions,
motives and fortunes of the bourgeois individual. Roddick goes on
to point out that the economy of making films using the studio
system was chiefly responsible for this style. In fact the aesthetic
nature of the finished product was determined, in a very immediate
and concrete sense, by the economic demands of a studio-based
production method designed to make films quickly and efficiently.

The 1930s represented, for Warners, a decade of growth and con-
solidation after a drop in profits following the Wall Street Crash.
The rapid turnover of the studio system allowed them to make
movies covering a wide range of subjects, with the financial loss accompanying occasional prestige pictures like *A Midsummer Night's
Dream* (or the failures of bad movies) compensated for by returns
from a steady flow of contemporary dramas. Warner Brothers made
realistic crime films and social conscience documentaries, their repertoire included the successful musical revues of Busby Berkely,
biographical films of famous historical figures, swashbuckling adventures starring Errol Flynn, romantic comedies and cartoons.

Superficially *A Midsummer Night's Dream* seems atypical: it has
no immediate relationship with any of the above. The movie was
produced as a conscious exercise in prestige building, not necessarily
with any cynical motives but rather as an attempt to consolidate
Warners' reputation as a socially responsible company with both the
public and the Hays Office. Yet when we look at the economic and
cultural relations that shaped the film's production and reception we
see that it, like the movies before it, was a forcing ground for many
of the social tensions and contradictions that companies like
Warners had already addressed and attempted to work through in
other products. At the same time the nascent theories of the 'theatre
of light' filtered into *A Midsummer Night's Dream* through the
work of the two directors: Reinhardt and his ex-pupil Dieterle. Thus
the finished film also illuminates the uneasy alliance between the
mystic, symbolist stagecraft and the commercial production of art.

One of Warner Brothers' most famous films, *The Jazz Singer*, was
a musical. Warners sank a vast amount of capital into film sound, a
long-term approach to investment typical of large, advanced North
American businesses. That most of the big budget films that they,
and others, produced to herald the end of the silent era were revues
or musicals is significant. It shows that the transition from a silent
film idiom was neither easy or automatic. Because of the expense

sound producers simply couldn't afford to create the epic narrative scope of films like Abel Gance's *Napoleon*. Also there was no sound equivalent to the subtle and intricate codes of representation used in silent film to transmit meaning. Yet there were ways in which the economic and technical significance of sound, as perceived by the producers, could be impressed upon the movie-going public. The most direct was by making the means of production explicit in as lavish and spectacular a way as possible. *The Jazz Singer* had little pretensions towards a realistic film with a coherent self-contained narrative world. It consisted of a loose story wrapped around a number of songs which, more often than not, Jolson sang directly to the camera. MGM's response to *The Jazz Singer*, *Hollywood Revue of 1927*, was instrumental in starting the genre of the musical or musical revue; episodic cabarets in which a film company would demonstrate its capacity for spectacular sound production and its own particular stable of artists.

The genre of the musical waned briefly in the early 1930s before picking up again halfway through the decade, largely owing to the work that Busby Berkely did with Warners. This reflects contemporary attitudes to the Depression and subsequent recovery as well as the financial constraints imposed upon studios who were pushed to afford a continual round of spectacle. The re-appearance of the revue coincides with the beginning of the nation's slow climb out of hardship towards economic recovery. The films, deliberately encompassing the whole production capacity of the company, iterated a positive, expansionist theme. Roddick characterises it as that of a corporate group pulling together.

Berkely's *Gold Diggers of 1933* and *42nd Street* were lavish cabarets that interspersed singing and dancing with comedy and vast, spectacular dance routines. Berkely was famed for his escapist, fantastic stage shows in which chorus lines of women were marshalled into hymns to conspicuous consumerism. Reflecting a perception of an economy that is impersonal and, on occasion, dangerously soulless, these films echo the ambiguity of Craig and Appia's dictatorial theatre of marionettes: 'Berkely's attitude towards individuals is that of a silent film director, iconographic and symmetric. The community of the Berkely girls is cold and anonymous, like Lang's workers, a community created by a non-participating choreographer-director.'[1]

Yet during the mid 1930s, when Roosevelt's New Deal began to provide a way of restructuring the economy, this wish fulfilment was especially popular. It showed, to a public short of work and money, the liberating power of the capitalist dream as formulated by a company that dedicated itself to producing socially worthy films. At the same time it hinted at the darker, more alienating aspects of society in its portrayal of a perfect, almost clinical fantasy world. In *A Midsummer Night's Dream* this ambiguity would be more explicitly acknowledged – in the dark, fantasy sequences in the forest and in the treatment of the rustics – and then partly redeemed through the inclusion of the liberal, apparently egalitarian structure of romantic comedy.

The main way in which the romantic comedies of the mid 1930s differed from either the Berkely musicals or the earlier comedies of the Marx Brothers or W. C. Fields was in their positive affirmation of individual equality. These films, nicknamed 'screwball' comedies, often mirrored the reduction of social issues to the personal, intimate family level in the Warner crime or social conscience movies; and similarly cast corrupt urban institutions as the villains of the piece. Andrew Bergman, in his analysis of the films directed for Columbia by Frank Capra, pinpoints the ideological purpose of such films as 'a means of unifying what had been splintered and divided. The "whackiness" cemented social classes and broken marriages; personal relations were smoothed and social discontent quieted.'[2] 'Screwball' comedy celebrated the supposed egalitarianism of liberal America. It placed class difference firmly within the personalities of individuals, thereby perpetuating the myth that America was fundamentally classless and that any social inequalities were just the result of bad attitudes.

The humour of the earlier, more socially aware silent comedies was, at Warners, separated from the realistic medium of film photography and relocated in the cartoons which the company produced after 1932. Little radical work has been done on the animated films of the 1930s: the orthodox belief that cartoons are inconsequential entertainment for children is one that movie criticism is loath to dispel. Yet, in a sense, this making 'safe' of animation, removing it from the arena of theoretical debate, reiterates the process whereby the cartoons of the 1930s produced by Warners sought to neutralise the grotesque humour of the earlier comedy films. Certainly, as far as *A Midsummer Night's Dream* is concerned, animation in the 1930s needs to be examined more closely. Warners' film, with its strong fantasy elements, reincorporated into 'realistic' live action film many of the transgressive and grotesque structures which early animation had, in turn, picked up from the work of producers like Melies.

The animation produced during the late 1920s and 1930s echoes the contradiction in Symbolist aesthetics between the celebration of a transcendent Romanticism (their short cartoon *The Blue Danube* points to a link between *A Midsummer Night's Dream* and the pastoral sequence in Walt Disney's *Fantasia*) and frightening grotesques. In the early 1930s, animation imitated the alarming and absurd worlds of Melies; both Warner Brothers and Walt Disney used a rapid, very fluid style that often led to horrific results (some censors thought that the transformation scene in Disney's full-length feature *Snow White* (1937) was too frightening for children).

Alongside the more fantastic and innocent fairy tale cartoons there existed a sub-genre of nightmarish animation; of which the Betty Boop and early Popeye cartoons are good examples. In many of these, lovable, cute animals or anthropomorphic objects with childish personalities were victimised or tortured by mad scientists and monsters. These cartoons were often set in the world of dreams, nightmares, nursery rhymes or fairy tales; but the images, references and storylines were contemporary. Some even contained veiled references to underground culture: a send up of Disney's *The Old Water Mill*, *The Old Mill Pond*, was not only a cartoon tribute to famous jazz singers of the era, but was also liberally sprinkled with references to drugs.

The destruction, fragmentation and extreme distortions of form that occur in early animated films are similar to the displacement processes identified in the Freudian dreamwork. These cartoons operate like dreams, transferring childish fears and desires into a fantastic world. By and large the humour of later animation re-established the status quo. The situations in cartoons like the *Tom and Jerry* series are replayed time and time again without any resolution of the conflict. In the cartoons of the early 1930s this resolution is usually missing. The sense of unease is perpetuated by the frequent acknowledgement that the character's experiences were part of a vision over which it had no control.

In *The Dish Ran Away With the Spoon* (1932), a cartoon produced by Hugh Harman as part of the 'Silly symphonies' series, kitchen utensils are brought to life and sing excerpts from contemporary love songs. The cartoon becomes horrific when a lump of dough turns into a monster. The humour is far more grotesque than in later cartoons: the monster is seemingly castrated by cheesegraters as they fly between its legs, then it is flattened with a roller, minced and cooked. The film is unreal, violent, colourful and only partially successful in concealing Freudian fears of castration and dismemberment. Instead of isolating the dream-process within a real world and making it safe, the cartoon reveals its own processes as that of a dream work. Thus the mechanism of censorship becomes obvious. Warners' *A Midsummer Night's Dream* also replays the tension between the comforting, liberal world of the screwball comedy and the far more vicious and nightmarish childhood world of the early animated film.

Before concentrating on *A Midsummer Night's Dream* it is worth looking briefly at the other movies that made up Warners' output in the early 1930s. Roddick characterises the company's attitudes towards subject matter as, on the whole, liberal. The studio courted an image of itself as the producer of social conscience films, movies that were made as an attempt to address contemporary issues: courtroom dramas; anti-racist and anti-fascist movies and crime films. Understandably both the interpretation of the issues and the resolution were far from radical or revolutionary. 'Even the most apparently uncompromising of the socially conscious films ... are, in the end, reassuring about the ability of America's institutions to protect its citizens.'[3] In the early 1930s, when the economy stabilised, Warners' output began with a markedly liberal interrogation of the problems of the individual in an often corrupt society. This stance became increasingly problematic as the decade progressed. The 'Dead end' cycle of films (from *Dead End* in 1937 to *Angels with Dirty Faces* [1938]) had its stylistic roots in earlier films about the rehabilitation of juvenile offenders, but instead of saving the criminals through the benevolent power of the state the later movies have, as their reforming heroes, anarchic wise-guys like James Cagney's Rocky. Cagney's perceived role in Warners' films and its importance for *A Midsummer Night's Dream* will be examined in the next section.

II

When Kenneth MacGowan set out to describe the development of the new Expressionist stage in his book *The Theatre of Tomorrow* (1921) he cited Reinhardt as one of the leading exponents of the wholly integrated, spatially plastic drama. For much of his career

Reinhardt experimented with the use of light to create dramatic atmospheres, both on the vast sets of the Berlin theatre and amid the more intimate confines of his Kammerspiele theatre. While impressive, his ideas weren't especially revolutionary: Meyerhold thought his productions too derivative of Gordon Craig's and the acting styles excessively realistic. Between 1927 and 1928 Reinhardt used the theories of Appia and Craig in his first productions of *A Midsummer Night's Dream*. His version of the play was essentially a Romantic fantasy constructed around the fairy sequences. In 1934 Reinhardt had the play staged at the Hollywood Bowl.

When Warners filmed the play the following year they were imitating the process initiated by film makers like William Barker in Britain during the silent era. They were creating a prestige movie by shooting a successful stage production directed by an internationally renowned director. However, in America in 1935 the economic and political forces that shaped movie making were vastly different. While it's true that Warners were searching for prestige, their methods of mass production meant that film making already had a rigidly controlled methodology. Unlike Barker they were not searching for any potential new markets or attempting to shore up an indigenous culture against foreign influence. Instead they were seeking to confirm the company's economic and artistic position in a long-established cinema industry. They did this by demonstrating their capacity for ostentatious spectacle and by deliberately drawing attention to the financial and production capacity that had been used to create it. This was the framework into which the Reinhardt production was inserted.

Both the film and Reinhardt's original production of the play operated within the ideological structure of advanced bourgeois capitalism. Nevertheless there are huge historical and material differences between Germany in 1927 and Hollywood eight years later. It's important to realise that Warners' *A Midsummer Night's Dream* is not just a movie interpreting a stage production which is, in turn, interpreting a text. The process is one of appropriation made more emphatic by the fact that Reinhardt's play is being received in the context of an American stage and film industry that has a very rigidly coded perception of spectacle and a very efficient production process. What is remarkable is that elements of this visual and very positive affirmation of conspicuous consumerism imitated many of the images and structures that Reinhardt culled from Symbolist and Romantic stagecraft.

The film copies established Victorian perceptions of the play by setting it in Athens during classical times. The standards for North American portrayals of antiquity had been established in the silent films of Cecil B. DeMille and D. W. Griffith. They drew their inspiration from the precisely realised paintings of Alma-Tadema and tended to imitate the fussiness of Victorian genre art in general. The vision of Babylon that Griffith inserted into *Intolerance* was dominated by the legendary set; a vast and spectacular piece of architecture which, on film, appeared as an indiscriminated vista of monoliths and tiny people. Both film makers were also influenced by the Biblical illustrator John Martin; a nineteenth-century Romantic artist who painted apocalyptic Old Testament scenes. His huge canvases, in which minute figures struggled beneath disintegrating cities and mountains, transformed scripture into vast tributes to the theories of catastrophic Victorian geology.

After the credits *A Midsummer Night's Dream* begins with the pomp and splendour of an epic film about ancient history. Theseus, his army and their captives return triumphant from the wars and the population of Athens sing a victory hymn. Yet the compositional techniques used in *A Midsummer Night's Dream* are very different from those of DeMille, and can't simply be explained away by the increased costs of making an epic sound film. After all, Warner Brothers didn't skimp on the movie. In their publicity they emphasised its expensive production and were even prepared to accept a loss in exchange for the stamp of cultural respectability. Yet the crowds at the triumph cluster together in sets dominated by claustrophobic verticals and blocks of architecture arranged in abstractly 'Greek' patterns. Similarly footage taken out of doors for Theseus' hunt shows a minimalist approach to landscape, with a few Greek temples dotted about an otherwise empty wilderness. This chic, surrealist depiction of arcadian landscapes not only crops up in *Fantasia*, but also in contemporary advertising. There is a strong suggestion that what is being replicated is a conscious connection made between American culture in the 1930s and idealised classicism. The association was strong enough for it to be parodied in a number of films in which comedians like Eddie Cantor found themselves in an ancient Rome that had the customs and dialogue of 1930s New York.

At the beginning of Warners' film the camera switches between an establishing long shot and close-ups of the main characters in full or three-quarter profile. The overall impression is of tiers of people intermingling with a set composed of classical pillars, archi-traves, cloaks and plumes. Instead of an Alma-Tadema or a Martin the strongest impression is of a light and airy Craig set design; a sunnier version of his plan for the court of Elsinore in which the entire Danish court was shrouded by Claudius' gold cloak.

While the setting of Warners' film suggests the ancient splendour of the flashbacks in *Intolerance*, the smaller sets and rigidly deter-mined choreography of the characters and the camera point to a closer and more direct link with the company's successful musical revues. Like any revue sketch the musical number is perfectly har-monised and its use shows Warners' economical approach to film narrative. In turn the camera focuses on the main human protago-nists. It shows the four lovers who, through mime, indicate their relationships. The camera also picks out the group of rustics; the two most prominent members are, not surprisingly, James Cagney (Bottom) and Joe E. Brown (Flute).

At first glance the rest of the film seems like Olivier's *Henry V*; a patchwork of styles, images and motifs. In the first sequence the techniques, staging and camerawork have established that *A Midsummer Night's Dream* is outwardly a spectacular review in-tended as a showcase for Warners' in-house talent. Like many musi-cals it uses a fantasy setting to give narrative coherence to what are, in effect, a series of turns, cameo performances and musical se-quences. Thus, rather than disrupt the continuity of the film by chopping and changing from one 'turn' to another the overwhelm-ing dream-fantasy atmosphere ensures that the different styles merge without any significant disruption. Within the dream ratio-nale it is possible to combine the ballet sequences and the musical comedy routines with the Arabian changeling, the fairies, the goblin orchestra and the antics of the four lovers and the rustics.

Yet to categorise *A Midsummer Night's Dream* as a product of the Hollywood dream factory is not to invest it with glib escapism. Its exposition of the mechanism of fantastic cinema, and the various images and structures it culls from its many cultural sources, are far from innocent. Warners' Shakespeare film, like many of their musical revues and cartoons, uses the ability of the camera to ape the symbolism and techniques of Surrealism to mystify the taboos of sexuality and death. In the case of *A Midsummer Night's Dream* both these hazy and forbidden areas are drawn together, within the dream framework, using the images and motifs of childhood and childhood perception. It is here that the uneasy connection between the ideology of a big industrial economy and the self-definition of the Expressionist artist becomes apparent.

The first sequence set in the forest has visual links with the animated cartoons of the 'Silly symphony' genre. Like these it uses semi-grotesque imagery. The changeling prince romps through the gloomy wood in the company of fairies and goblins. At one point he chases after the fairies and they escape by flying over a pond. While he flaps his hands in a vain attempt to fly after them a goblin sticks its head out of the water and sprays him with a jet of water. The sequence is serenaded by a goblin orchestra (which plays with the enthusiastic mannerisms of a stereotypical Dixie band). It's dangerous to draw conclusions by identifying Freudian symbols in this scene. Flying, a spray of water and a monster lurking in a pool all had their place in popular perceptions of Freudian psychoanalysis but there is little evidence of any conscious coherence in the manipulation of these images. What the film does evoke is the structure of a generalised Freudian concept of the knowledgeable child experiencing the desires and fears of a dream. This, in turn, partially reiterates the duality of the mystical and the grotesque in Symbolist stagecraft. In this scene the disturbing elements of early animation and the uneasy mythology in Reinhardt's own understanding of the play overlap. Surreal and psychological symbols occur throughout the movie. The duel between Moonlight and Night, fought out in the form of a ballet, has strong sexual overtones. Oberon's appearance is remarkable in that it evokes a number of different associations. His pale face and black costume suggest an imitation of the references to fascism in *The Cabinet of Dr Caligari*. At one point in the film he appears in the hollow stump of a tree, shrouded with cobwebs. Not only is this juxtaposition nightmarish but it also alludes to the fashionable surrealist imagery beloved of 1930s magazine illustrators.

To a certain extent *A Midsummer Night's Dream* does try to work through the relationship between the individual and an oppressive, alien, adult world. It takes the mysticism of Reinhardt's production and translates it into positive and cathartic comedy through the characters of the lovers, the rustics and Puck. The arguments between the lovers follow the simple, knockabout pattern of the 'Screwball' comedies. The roles of Mickey Rooney and James Cagney are more significant because it is through them that the alienated childhood consciousness is articulated in the film. 'The basis of Cagney's star persona ... was his ordinariness – better able to handle himself than many of his contemporaries perhaps, and consistently funnier, but distinctly recognisable.'[4] Cagney was, with Edward G. Robinson, most famous for his portrayal of ruthless gangsters. He appeared in a host of films during the decade including *The Roaring Twenties* (Warner, 1939), *Angels with Dirty Faces* and *White Heat* (1949). These last two films showed crime and evil as being inextricably linked with the development of children and psychological instability. In *Angels with Dirty Faces* the gangster Cagney becomes the idol of a gang of youths. In *White Heat* Cody Jarrett is a rogue 'child' who worships his mother. This obsession brings him to the brink of psychosis; his behaviour is arbitrary and laced with sadistic humour. His dying words, which he screams from the top of a blazing fuel tanker, are 'Made it ma, top of the world!' These are extreme cases but they illustrate the equation of deviant behaviour with childhood. The resolution of a film like *Angels with Dirty Faces* showed how the taming of children was synonymous with the protection of society. Likewise it demonstrated the need for society to take responsibility for their 'redemption'.

If Cagney was an actor supposed to be an emblem of urban working-class man who played his characters as big, fast talking, comic kids then his appearance as Bottom is perfectly understandable. His transformation, like that in Kafka's *Metamorphosis*, is a grotesque experience that draws him into the mystical dream-like fairy realm. However his encounter with Titania is played largely as a romantic comedy with the atmosphere of a musical sketch. In a film that plays heavily on psychological imagery this passage, which should be disturbing, is leeched of any disruptive elements. Cagney's victimised child is hardly a victim, and his transformation back to normality works as a weaker, gentler version of the reconciliation between the Dead End Kids and society.

Cagney, the bluff, simple working man with the gaucheness and enthusiasm of a big kid is the opposite of Mickey Rooney's Puck. By the mid 1930s Rooney was a well-established child actor who specialised in playing infants in roles or situations that parodied adulthood. In Warners' film Puck is the knowing child who dogs the steps of the lovers through the forest. Mickey Rooney's portrayal of the character is energetic, although the continual shouting and face pulling tend to grate in comparison to the other, subtler, performances. Nevertheless his uncontrollability and contempt for the lovers reverses the power relationship between child and adult. The mortals, unaware of the true nature of the dream world, are innocent and stupid. Puck, the magic child, continually flaunts his power. The last shot of the film demonstrates this in an unusually frank way. Theseus and Hippolyta have retired to bed after watching the performance of the rustics. Standing outside the door of their chamber, Puck bids the audience farewell and then slips quietly through into the room, closing the door behind him. The connection between Puck and the bedroom is blatantly obvious and was picked up again (albeit in a much coyer, voyeuristic form) at the end of the *Pastoral Symphony* sequence in *Fantasia* when a cherub peeps furtively through curtains at a centaur and centauress.

The fact that *A Midsummer Night's Dream* belongs to a strong tradition of musical fantasy in the American cinema allows the various different styles and techniques in the film to work with little disjunction. Despite the orthodox insistence that a distinction should be made between high and low culture within the film, between Reinhardt and Hollywood, between Busby Berkely and Shakespeare, there is little internal evidence to support it. What the film does do is point out how the mystical imagery and dream symbolism developed in the Expressionist theatre stem from attempts to define culture, and a cultural role for the artist, in an industrial mass-producing economy.

Reinhardt embraced the Romantic elements of the Symbolist theatre. Because of this the links between Warner Brothers' musicals and cartoons and the ethereal world of his dream-like film are straightforward. A large company, devoted to churning out liberal entertainment for an American market, used structures and images that were very similar to those of the 'new stagecraft' in its everyday production. As a result, when it combined elements from its repertoire with Reinhardt's production to create its version of Shakespeare's play, the two styles merged easily.

The mystical aspects of the 'theatre of light', especially the individual's search for an ideal symbolic truth in the world of dreams, echo the uneasy relationship between the isolated artist and a world that is apparently controlled by the arbitrary forces of production. The fact that Warners had no worries about the benefits of market forces, other than the felt need to demonstrate their own adopted liberal position, meant that their film was a celebration of corporate wealth. Thus the angst of the individual's childish perspective was resolved, through the characters of Bottom and Puck, in a very gentle and humorous way. The sheer spectacle of the film also shows the importance of technology (specifically lighting) and labour control (people as marionettes in a 'factory' of the theatre) for the 'new stagecraft'. In this way it demonstrates a direct dialectical relationship between the theories of the Expressionist stage and the development of Western capitalism.

III

Orson Welles's Shakespeare movies, particularly *Othello*, show another aspect of the process whereby Shakespeare cinema production is used to work through the relationship between the artist and the state. In *A Midsummer Night's Dream* the theories of the nascent 'theatre of light' were, because of their very nature, effortlessly institutionalised within the commercial apparatus of Warner Brothers. Welles's *Othello*, made by an independent and self-styled bohemian director, tried to recreate the perception of the alienated intellectual while simultaneously trying to fulfil the otherworldly idealism of Wagner's *gesamtkunstwerk*. Instead of affirming the ostentatious production values of a large movie company, *Othello* reflects the negative aspect of Symbolist Shakespeare. It portrays the relationship between the artist and the state using the imagery of the grotesque.

In his early career Welles courted the image of a politically aware artist. Productions like the 'Voodoo' *Macbeth* and the 1937 *Julius Caesar* seemed, at the time, to be direct (if somewhat tendentious) political statements about colonialism and fascism. However, Welles's aura of radicalism was due more to his deliberate courting of left-wing political groups than to the plays themselves. Despite the fact that *Macbeth* was produced through the WPA Negro Theatre Project Welles's play was full of racist undertones. One of the main themes of the production was the duality between the tenuous oasis of civilisation inside Macbeth's castle and the primitive jungle beyond. This equation of voodoo savagery with the landscape was perpetuated by the performance of a whip-cracking Hecate and the use of hidden tribal drums to signify the encroaching evil of Macbeth's treachery. Similarly, for the 'fascist' *Julius Caesar* Welles made deliberate and obvious connections between Shakespeare's play and the situation in Mussolini's Italy and Hitler's Germany, even to the point of picking a Mussolini lookalike to play Caesar. While evoking liberal fears about totalitarianism he failed to acknowledge the political nature or origins of fascism, aiming instead for impressive lighting effects and choreo-graphed references to Nuremberg.

Despite his overt association with radicalism Welles appears to have had little personal commitment to politics. His interest lay in achieving the same unified, personal expressiveness that Craig was aiming for. He directed the people on his stage movement by move-ment, trying to control their bodies and counting out their steps as if they were the marionettes of Craig's ideal theatre. Yet, while *A Midsummer Night's Dream* was made following the rigid schedules of Warner Brothers, *Othello*, like many of Welles's films, was errat-ically produced. On many occasions shooting was suspended due to lack of money. This fragmentation is reflected both in the movie's structure and its strong atmosphere of disorientation. It also contributes to the cultural myth of the erratic, renegade artist victimised by economic circumstances.

In *Othello* the grotesque perspective manifests itself in many ways. Throughout the film coherent space is broken into a multi-faceted series of collages. The funeral at the beginning, which imi-tates the montage of Eisenstein's *Alexander Nevsky*, is shot in a way that prepares the viewer for a movie that interrogates and de-stroys any coherent and unified point of view, substituting a labyrinth of images. Tiny figures are swamped by massive architec-ture, a crenellated wall is dwarfed by the immense profile of the dead Desdemona as her bier is carried past the camera. After the credits (which are spoken by Welles) we are subjected to a number of fragmented pictures of Venice; figures tussling in empty court-yards, forests of ship masts, a cat watching a bird on a roof, and glimpses of Iago, the Moor and Desdemona. Iago leans against a balcony and his image is immediately dissolved in a rippling pool; when Roderigo is killed the screen is filled with an abstract combin-ation of wooden slats, racing past in all directions. Superimposed on this, the image of Iago's sword appears and disappears like a lightning bolt. The skies are broken by a framework of ships' rigging and the characters pursue each other through a maze of canals, streets and corridors. Welles set out to create a unified world for *Othello* and he succeeded; but this world is a world of piecemeal images and absurd logic.

In the films of Welles a diluted sense of political and historical movement becomes a deeply personal study of the individual vic-timised by a heartless and absurd universe. There are no concrete political structures, little sense of any context other than that offered by the costumes and settings. Instead the world is suffused with the nightmarish logic of Kafka's nightmares. This translation of political necessity into psychological angst accords with Welles's self-defined status as an isolated, maverick bohemian. Certainly it comes as no surprise to learn that he was interested in the absurdist worlds of Kafka's fiction. Many of the films he directed evoked the fragmented and illogical landscapes of a war-time and post-war world. They dwelt upon the characters and psychology of villainous or victimised 'children'. 'Rosebud', the great enigma of *Citizen Kane*, is nothing but a boy's sledge; and emblem of the childhood memories that the millionaire clings to at the point of death. In *The Trial* Joseph K has to stand on tiptoe like a small boy to reach the handle of the door that leads to the Law.

Welles's Othello is one of these infants, the innocent 'natural man' whose uncontrollable urges and insecurity are preyed upon by Iago. Welles came from a privileged and indulgent family of 'free thinkers'. His childish eccentricities, including the 'painting' trip to Ireland where he met Michael MacLiammoir and Hilton Edwards (who played Iago and Brabantio in *Othello*), were freely encouraged and funded. Thus he was able to turn his own, very muted sense of artistic alienation into extravagant bohemianism. Welles took on the lead role in most of his films. He was interested in the evocation of evil as childish aberration or adult cynicism. He was also extremely suspicious of women and his films often display a noticeable wish to return to a mythical childhood innocence. The protracted search for an actress to play Desdemona hints at an indecisiveness on Welles's part and an inability to come to terms with the sexual implications of the Othello–Desdemona relationship in the film. On the contrary sexuality is translated into commercial, political and military power in this and virtually all of Welles's movies. Welles's characters seek to overcome their oppression, both sexual and psychological, through the acquisition of money and power. Kane achieves this, ultimately hollow, control through wealth and Macbeth uses violence. Othello's nemesis is the childish impulse of sexual jealousy.

Othello, like *The Trial* and *Citizen Kane*, is a film in which Welles evokes the sense of a chaotic, absurdist and uncontrollable world. Othello falls as much victim to circumstance as to the calculated wickedness of Iago or the uncontrollable urges of his tragic fault. The camerawork of the film is very stylised. Even in the exterior shots, which offer the greatest potential depth, the lack of strong

diagonals compresses space and volume into two dimensions. When Cassio and Iago await Othello at Cyprus we see soldiers and artillery arranged along the sea defences. The firing of the cannon is punctuated by sudden and abrupt shot changes. The effect deliberately disrupts the visual and temporal continuity. In some of the more spectacular compositions the waiting soldiers are dwarfed by what appear to be the enormous waves of a raging sea. Even those settings that seem to demand an acknowledgement of perspective, the mighty battlements of Cyprus and the long colonnades of Venice, are usually photographed as flat, abstract compositions of light and shadow. Most of the exterior scenes in Cyprus have the same arid inhumanity as a landscape painting by de Chirico.

Perhaps one of the most remarkable sources of *Othello*'s unrealistic and dream-like atmosphere is the quality of the soundtrack. This seems to be very poor; the dubbing is obvious and often out of synchronisation with the character's lip movements. People speaking close to the camera sound far away and vice versa. In fact much of the text is delivered when the speakers have their back to the camera or are off-screen entirely. This technique makes dubbing for the international market easier and Welles repeated it in *Chimes at Midnight*. Yet *Othello* is not just a film with a badly put together soundtrack. Sound is all important in the movie: Welles places great emphasis on its use as an expressive medium. The powerful score and spoken credits echo the techniques used in the radio productions of the Mercury Theatre. Why then does the use of the spoken word appear so clumsy? It is very reminiscent of the use of sound in Dreyer's *Vampyr*. In this the disembodied voices and conversations that accompany the images are used to disrupt any sense of reality and to evoke the uncertain, shifting perspectives of a nightmarish Kafka novel. *Othello* regularly achieves a similar effect; the text often sounds more like a commentary than spoken exchanges and when it is combined with ambiguously defined scenery it evokes the atmosphere of a dream.

Othello is possibly the most austere and intellectual of the Shakespeare films made within the tradition of the 'theatre of light'. Although it uses the imagery and codes of representation evolved in Eisenstein's Constructivist films, Welles's overall approach owes more to Craig's work. Welles sets out to achieve the *gesamtkunstwerk* as an expression of his own genius. His position in society, and privileged background, enabled him to cultivate a strong sense of alienated individualism. Thus he conceived of the role of the intellectual in terms of aesthetic expression and personal angst. The motifs of abstraction and absurdity that run through *Othello* perpetuate the director's fascination with the mechanisms of commerce and politics as channels for adolescent revenge. The film deals with power expressed in psychological terms, as the control exercised by adults over children. Iago exploits this relationship for the sake of sheer intellectual and clinical malevolence. *Othello* has the texture of a nightmare and, in its treatment, structure and composition, is closest to Welles's film of Kafka's *The Trial*. Like Joseph K, Othello is the most unsuccessful of Welles's primitive infants. Unlike Macbeth, whose method of self-expression is unrelenting butchery, Othello has no control over the characters or world around him. Ultimately *Othello* translates the social impotence of the intellectual and artists into an undefined sexual and psychological angst in the face of an absurd universe.

[...]

The Symbolist and Expressionist stage designers working at the turn of the century sought to escape the vulgar materialism of the industrial society by discovering a mystical world of transcendent truth. In doing so they produced a theoretical framework for art which supported, rather than challenged, the accepted role of culture. Symbolism echoed its ideological roots by obscuring the real economic relationships in society. Therefore the relationship of its advocates with the means of production in the late nineteenth century European and American culture didn't undergo any major change.

This continuing separation of the intellectual from the mechanisms of social change was addressed in two ways. On the one hand film makers like Welles adopted the mechanisms of the Freudian grotesque to articulate their position. They transformed their own feeling of alienation into a fragmented recreation of the perspectives of childhood, trapped in an absurd universe and victimised by unreasoning and authoritarian 'adults'. Although this position allowed them to adopt a maverick and often adolescent bohemianism it is, ultimately, a negative and introspective response to the alienation of the intellectual.

The other approach to the relationship between art and industrialism, within capitalism, occurs in Warners' film. Appia's theory of the *gesamtkunstwerk* was dependent on the acknowledgement and use of advanced technology. This appropriation of practical science was accompanied by the evolution of an aesthetics that adopted many of the values of industrial society: specifically the supremacy of artifice over the natural world and the use of a single, guiding artistic genius. It's not surprising that Reinhardt's production of *A Midsummer Night's Dream* and the theories of the 'theatre of light' should be so easily absorbed into the milieu of a large production company like Warner Brothers.

From John Collick, *Shakespeare, Cinema and Society* (Manchester, 1989), pp. 80–98, 105–6.

NOTES

[Collick's book employs a cultural materialist approach to present a wide-ranging historical and theoretical analysis of Shakespearean film in its diverse cultural, institutional and commercial contexts. In this essay the focus is upon Max Reinhardt's *A Midsummer Night's Dream* and Orson Welles's *Othello* as instances of Symbolist and Expressionist Shakespeare, paying close attention to the economic determinants of genre, style and form. Placing both texts within the context of the Hollywood studio system, Collick argues that *A Midsummer Night's Dream* draws upon a range of popular genres to effect an adroit synthesis of surrealism and ro-mantic fantasy, while *Othello* self-consciously flaunts its anti-realist 'artistry' as a means of allegorising the absurd and alienated condition of the *auteur* under capitalism. Ed.]

1. Leo Braudy, 'Genre: the Conventions of Connection', in *Film Theory and Criticism: Introductory Readings*, 2nd edn, ed. Gerald Mast and Marshall Cohen (Oxford, 1979), p. 454.

2. Andrew Bergman, 'Frank Capra and Screwball Comedy, 1931–1941', in Mast and Cohen, *Film Theory and Criticism*, p. 762.

3. Nick Roddick, *A New Deal in Entertainment: Warner Brothers in the 1930s* (London, 1983), pp. 23–4.

4. Ibid., p. 105.

6

Olivier, Hamlet, and Freud

PETER S. DONALDSON

Laurence Olivier's film of *Hamlet* (1947) announces itself as a psychoanalytic, Oedipal text. The phallic symbolism of rapier and dagger, the repeated dolly-in down the long corridor to the queen's immense, enigmatic, and vaginally hooded bed, the erotic treatment of the scenes between Olivier and Eileen Herlie as Gertrude all bespeak a robust and readily identifiable, if naïve, Freudianism.[1]

Although Freud himself had written only briefly on *Hamlet*,[2] the play was central to his formulation of the Oedipus complex. Ernest Jones, a prominent British psychoanalyst, had expanded Freud's suggestions into a full-scale interpretation of the play in an article first published in 1910 which was to undergo numerous revisions and republication, finally appearing in 1949 as *Hamlet and Oedipus*.[3] It was through Jones that Olivier first learned of the Freudian approach to *Hamlet*. As part of their planning for the Old Vic production of 1937 director Tyrone Guthrie and Olivier, who played the lead, made a weekend visit to Jones.

> He had made an exhaustive study of Hamlet from his own profes-
> sional point of view and was wonderfully enlightening. I have never
> ceased to think about Hamlet at odd moments, and ever since that
> meeting I have believed that Hamlet was a prime sufferer from the
> Oedipus complex – quite unconsciously, of course, as the professor
> was anxious to stress. He offered an impressive array of symptoms:
> spectacular mood-swings, cruel treatment of his love, and above all a
> hopeless inability to pursue the course required of him. The Oedipus
> complex, therefore, can claim responsibility for a formidable share of
> all that is wrong with him. There is great pathos in his determined

efforts to bring himself to the required boiling point, and in the excuses he finds to shed this responsibility.[4]

Olivier never mentions Freud here or elsewhere in his autobiography, though of course Jones's 'own professional point of view' was that of Freudian psychoanalysis.

[...]

But the film's psychological explorations are also informed by autobiographical pressures and do not wholly conform to the orthodox Freudian interpretation Olivier learned from Jones. In the reading of the film I propose here, the Freud/Jones interpretation of *Hamlet* is a central, structuring presence the contours of which may be clearly discerned. At the same time, the Oedipus complex, so evident and even intentional in Olivier's *Hamlet*, serves partly as a mask or screen for other, perhaps even deeper issues. First, Oedipal conflict, especially as it is manifested in Hamlet's interactions with the ghost of his father, often has a passive or submissive character in the film. Although Freud had elaborated a theory of the negative Oedipus complex, in which conflict is resolved through a 'feminine' or passive attitude toward the father,[5] neither Freud nor Jones applied this theory to *Hamlet*. In addition, Olivier's film portrays, beneath the drama of Oedipal guilt and self-punishment, the narcissistic injury of Oedipal *success*. This Hamlet's relationship with his mother is too stimulating, and his interactions with his father are too tenuous and violent, for him to have internalised a realistic and stable sense of self-worth, so that he oscillates between grandiose aloofness and empty depression, plagued by persistent doubts about the worth and coherence of the self.

[...]

Describing his adolescent experience at St Edward's school, where he 'very soon caught the attention, rapidly followed by the attentions, of a few of the older boys', Olivier explains that unwelcome sexual advances had plagued him since his first day at his previous school:

> I did not in any way welcome such attentions; I knew well enough what they spelt. My first experience of that had been a somewhat frightening one. Calling at the All Saints church house one day before I joined the choir, I was stopped by a large boy, an old choirboy, who offered to show me the stage upstairs where the choir school plays were performed. I was dressed in my kilt, Kerr tartan (my second name, as was my father's, is Kerr; no one has ever found the

Scottish connection), with the velvet jacket and silver buttons, a customary Sunday outfit inherited from my brother. This boy flung me
down on an upper landing, threw himself on top of me and made me
repeat again and again, 'No, no, let me go, I don't want it.' This I did
willingly enough, but it only increased his ardour. His 'exercises'
were getting more powerful when to my relief he thought he heard
someone coming up the stone stairs. He pushed me down these steps
and himself disappeared farther up towards the top of the building.
I rushed down, tearful and trembling, in search of my mother, into
whose arms I gratefully flung myself. On the way home she asked me
the lad's name, which she recognised; a year or two back he had
come to a birthday party for me to which Mummy had invited all
fourteen boys. She made me promise to tell her if anything of the
kind should ever happen again.[6]

The kilt here is a dangerous inheritance: supposedly conferring a
masculine tribal identity and offering connection to brother, father,
and distant Scottish kinfolk, it looks much like a skirt, feminising
its wearer and exposing him to rape. Interest in acting, Olivier's
childhood sphere of grandiosity, sponsored to this point principally
by his mother, also exposed him to deflation and assault.

Olivier began work on the film of *Hamlet* a year after his remarkable, even glorious success in that other great Freudian part,
Sophocles' Oedipus. His love affair with Vivien Leigh had been reg-
ularised by marriage in 1940. His father had died in 1939. He was
a successful film actor, and his *Henry V* had gained the first un-
grudging critical success accorded any Shakespeare film. He was at
a plateau of success and respect. Yet the *Hamlet* film was in some
ways the boldest of his enterprises, for in addition to playing the
lead and directing the film, he drastically cut Shakespeare's text and
imposed on it a powerful interpretation, partly Jonesian and partly
his own. His daring was not without its doubts, hesitations, and
denials of the significance of the enterprise. Apologising for the
extent to which the text had been reworked, Olivier preferred to
call the film 'an essay in *Hamlet*'.[7] He describes his playing the lead
in terms that are simultaneously self-effacing and grandiose: he
would have preferred another actor 'of sufficient standing to carry
the role, or one upon whom I could have imposed my interpretation
without resenting it'; his own gifts were for 'the stronger character
roles'. In the end he found it 'simpler' to play Hamlet himself.

> But one reason why I dyed my hair was so as to avoid the possibility
> of Hamlet later being identified with me. I wanted audiences seeing

the film to say, not, 'There is Laurence Olivier dressed as', but 'that is Hamlet'.[8]

The wish to distance himself from the role may have been partly a result of the Freudian interpretation he intended to give it. Another instance of such distancing may be the choice of Eileen Herlie (who was twenty-seven) as Gertrude. Although her youth helps to bring out the sexuality of the part *for the audience*, it might also work to undo or reverse the generational direction of the incestuous subtext for the forty-year-old actor who played her son (like Olivier's flight from Thebes to Corinth the year before). In addition, Olivier was concerned about too close an identification with Hamlet's irresolution, passivity, and failure:

> Perhaps he was the first pacifist, perhaps Dr Jones is sound in his di-agnosis of the Oedipus complex, perhaps there is justification in the many complexes that have been foisted on to him – perhaps he just thought too much, that is, if a man can think too much. ... I prefer to think of him as a nearly great man – damned by lack of resolution, as all but one in a hundred are.[9]

Such a description, while conveying the author's wish to be res-olute where Hamlet had wavered, inscribes irresolution in its own interpretation, backing away from the Freudian theory while proposing alternatives that on examination are merely restatements of the question. The film itself pursues a similarly self-cancelling strategy, offering an undeniably Freudian reading while proclaiming that 'this is the tragedy of a man who could not make up his mind' – as if such a pronouncement were itself an interpretation rather than that which for centuries has seemed to require interpretation. Oedipal interpretation, like the Oedipal fantasies it explains, tends to generate itself as one of its own consequences, proposing polysemy and ambiguity as meaning; disguising decisions as eva-sions; blurring distinctions between fathers and sons, texts and their interpretations.

It is interesting that although Olivier could be somewhat evasive in what he said about interpretation and character in the film, he was much more direct about the genesis of its visual structure: 'Quite suddenly, one day, I visualised the final shot of "Hamlet". And from this glimpse, I saw how the whole conception of the film could be built up.'[10] This shot is a long shot of Hamlet's funeral procession ascending a steep staircase to the top of a bare tower.

The film begins with a closely related shot, a high-angle view of this tower, the bearers having reached the top. The human figures then dissolve out of the image as the action of the film begins in flashback. The narrative is thus framed by this ascent, by the elevation of Hamlet in death to the highest place in the castle, a place from which there is nowhere to go, even to complete the funeral. The procession vanishes from the screen at the end as it had in the opening sequence. One of the ways this complex symbol functions in the film, therefore, is to intimate the futility of Hamlet's 'success' in his grandiose mission: he accomplishes the revenge his father's ghost had charged him with, re-establishes an intense connection to his mother, and even momentarily takes possession of the throne. With this solemn funeral Hamlet's completion of his task is acknowledged in a way that reminds us that it is achieved at the cost of annihilation.

The final shot of the film does more than give this frame to the story. As Olivier said, it is the generating image for the film as a whole, the last of a long series of staircase shots and sequences that occur throughout. These are consistently associated with Hamlet's meeting with his father and his attempts to fulfil his father's commandment to revenge. Staircases are often the setting for violence, the locus of a repeated pattern in which someone is thrown down on the steps and the attacker flees upward, leaving the victim in an ambivalent state in which elements of reproach and pain are mingled with feelings of loss. Thematically this motif points to the well-studied problematics of revenge in *Hamlet*, whereby the revenger takes on the moral taint of his victim in a compulsive and cyclical pattern. Psychologically it is used to explore Hamlet's passivity, his oscillation between grandiosity and depression, and the blurring of his own identity in a partial fusion with the ghost. As I discuss its use, it will be seen that various aspects of the staircase motif as it is used in the film evoke, with surprising literalness, the traumatic incident the director suffered at All Saints in 1916 and first made public in 1982.

The towers and external staircases of Elsinore are introduced at the start of the film. The castle first appears directly after the credits, which are shown on a background of crashing surf. It has two towers, one in the middle of the castle and one, at the near corner, overlooking the sea. As in the opening shots of *Henry V*, there is some confusion between these two architectural features. The camera moves in on the corner tower from a high angle and stops. There is a fade to mist as Olivier in voice-over recites, 'So oft it chances in particular men ...' while the text of this speech is displayed on the screen. After Olivier's somewhat reductive addition, pointing the moral ('This is the tragedy of a man who could not make up his mind'), the central tower reappears, filling most of the image, and the camera moves in, as if continuing the movement begun before the speech, on four soldiers carrying Hamlet's body, his sword laid on his chest and face invisible as his unsupported head droops back, the body appearing almost headless from the spectator's point of view. The procession then dissolves from the image while the tower remains, and in a rapid series of cuts we are shown parts of the exterior of the castle, emphasising the steep external staircases that give access to the ramparts and the towers.

It is on these staircases that the sentries challenge one another as the guard changes and on which Hamlet is soon to ascend for his colloquy with the ghost. The ghost appears on the ramparts as Bernardo narrates to Horatio the story of its prior visit, and his first appearance establishes him as a numinous and intimately invasive presence. The camera moves in from a high angle to the terrified face of Marcellus (Anthony Quayle) in a disturbing stop-start rhythm, losing focus and regaining it as we hear an exaggeratedly loud pounding heartbeat in accompaniment. Because we cannot assign with certainty the beating of the heart and the loss of focus either to the ghost or to Marcellus, this treatment effects a blurring of the boundaries between the apparition and the human self to whom it appears. When the camera securely assumes Marcellus's point of view again, we see the ghost as a helmeted figure, his hollow-eyed face half shrouded in mist. It will not speak to the guards and disappears with a cut to the roaring surf.

The ghost is ponderously slow, dignified, sorrowful, and stately, but his effect on others is violent. The heartbeat, the blur of focus, and the insistent, pulsing downward movement of the camera are repeated when the ghost makes his second appearance, this time to Hamlet, whose response is to fling himself violently backward into his companions' arms. A low-angle shot follows from behind the human group, looking up several low steps to the ghost. As Hamlet questions it, the ghost begins to ascend, and Hamlet, reaching out his hand to it, begins to follow in a long, slow climb lasting nearly two minutes of screen time, punctuated by dissolves as we pass from one landing to the next. At the top of the central tower Hamlet, his sword hilt held before him, stops and declares he'll 'go no further', but this limit-setting gesture is ironic here because there is nowhere further to go.

Hamlet kneels as the ghost speaks, and the revelation of the murder, partly spoken by the ghost and partly rendered visually in a flashback to the murder scene, is shot from behind him looking toward his father. As the queen's infidelity is revealed the ghost fades out and, in the ambient mist, the royal couch fades in briefly, so that Hamlet's gesture (hand outstretched to the apparition) becomes ambiguous, as his longing for his father becomes confused with the question of his relation to the incestuous bed his father's discourse evokes. Such a treatment derives from Jones, but the connection between the poignant absence of the father and the Oedipal impulse is Olivier's own.

His charge to his son complete, the ghost fades in the morning air as Hamlet reaches forward to touch him. The camera pulls high above him as he stands and falls full length backward, overcome with what he has seen and heard. As he revives, his rage against his uncle and vows to revenge his father are delivered in a manic tone: the depressed and affectless mourner of the opening sequences becomes the precipitate revenger his father wants him to be – yet even in his assertions of murderous anger there are elements of passivity. Shakespeare's text suggests at this point that becoming a revenger entails a kind of self-obliteration for Hamlet: he offers to wipe clean the tables of his memory, leaving a blank page for the word of the father to be written upon. Olivier develops this, making his commitment to revenge with his eyes blazing and sword brandished, while still on his knees. At the climax of the vow 'Yes, *by Heaven*', he throws his rapier down upon the stones, a gesture that registers his anger but also, like similar actions later in the film, leaves him without a weapon at the very moment when the idea of using one is strongest.

In a way what the reappearance of the father visits on Hamlet in both film and text is a kind of abuse. Hamlet's potential for independent life is compromised and he becomes a mere agent of paternal aims, important himself only insofar as he is able to 'do what is required of him'. Even though Hamlet loves his father and accepts his 'commandment' to the point of self-obliteration, he is flung back, hurled down, and invaded while the ghost, inaccessible to Hamlet's longing reach for contact, ascends higher up the steps and finally disappears. The abusive character of the interaction becomes even clearer when one notices how closely the main features of the imagery in which Olivier renders the visit of the ghost resemble the incident of sexual assault the director had suffered as a nine-year-old on the staircase of All Saints. Not only the actual assault on the stairs but also the curious detail about the attacker fleeing further up are reprised in the film. Like the childhood memory, this sequence is presented as a kind of feminisation: the ghost does to Hamlet what he has just done to a woman; the symbolic casting down of the sword replaces the kilt as the emblem of castration; the suggestion that Hamlet has been invaded by the ghost replaces the near-rape; the father replaces the older boy as the abuser.

This pattern – assault on a staircase followed by flight upward – is repeated in the scene in which Ophelia is rejected by Hamlet. Ophelia has been set by the king and her father as 'bait' to discover whether or not Hamlet's madness is a result of love. Polonius and Claudius observe from behind an arras while Ophelia returns Hamlet's love tokens. Following Dover Wilson's *What Happens in Hamlet*,[11] Olivier has Hamlet overhear the plan to spy on him and feels betrayed by Ophelia's complicity in it. But there is also an earlier sequence, purely visual and invented for the film, that establishes a background for the rejection. In the Council chamber Hamlet customarily sits in a chair at the foot of the table, a special chair marked by distinctive decoration, pulled back from the others in distance and distaste. It is the chair in which he sits in sullen rejection of the court and its endorsement of his mother's marriage, and in which he remembers and mourns for his father. But it is also strategically placed in relation to Ophelia's chamber: by looking over his shoulder he commands a view of a long corridor leading to her room. After Polonius warns Ophelia not to accept Hamlet's love, Olivier, using the resources of deep-focus photography to the full, staged what he was to call, somewhat inappropriately, the 'longest distance love-scene on record'.[12] Ophelia, in distress, looks down the corridor to see Hamlet seated in his chair some one hundred feet away. Hamlet cannot see Polonius and registers Ophelia's refusal to come to him as a rejection. Thus even before he learns of the plot, he has begun to feel that Ophelia has turned away from him. This sequence links the failure of trust between the lovers to something already present in Hamlet's character. He is paralysed not only by grief but by the opportunity the empty chamber affords for imaginary sovereignty. His inability to rise and approach Ophelia manifests the power of his Oedipal resentments and grandiose fantasies. Because he cannot leave the empty chamber, he mistakes Ophelia's reluctant giving in to paternal command for rejection.

This Hamlet comes to the scene in which Ophelia returns his tokens with realistic suspicions as well as fettered emotions. He is moody, wary, and in distress; yet he also tries to establish a basis for trust by speaking to Ophelia about his low opinion of himself:

> I am myself indifferent honest; but yet I could accuse me of such things that it were better my mother had not borne me: I am very proud, revengeful, ambitious, with more offences at my beck than I have thoughts to put them in, imagination to give them shape, or time to act them in. What should such fellows as I do crawling between earth and heaven?

This is spoken in a quiet, reflective tone, partly to preserve the possibility of an intimate exchange despite the spying of the king and Polonius behind the arras, and partly because he recognises that his own low self-esteem and guilt feelings constitute a barrier to intimacy. He glances frequently at the arras and back to Ophelia, as if to see whether she will lie to him or accept his offered confidence. She does lie, and the tone and pace of the scene shift:

> ... crawling between earth and heaven. We are arrant knaves all; believe none of us. Go thy ways to a nunnery. Where's your father? [*still in a quiet tone*] **Ophelia:** At home, my lord. **Hamlet:** [*now loudly and in anger*] Let the doors be shut upon him, that he may play the fool no where but in's own house.

Here he shoves her away violently and his discourse shifts from disesteem of himself to condemnation of women. When she attempts to embrace him, he throws her down on the steps to sob and then flees up them. The camera, in a series of backtrackings and vertical cranes approximating the point of view Hamlet would have if he were looking back down the stairs, pulls back and up from the prostrate figure of Ophelia, her hand still extended after Hamlet, as his own hand was after the fading apparition of his father. As the camera cranes upward with Hamlet, Ophelia disappears then briefly reappears in longer shot as the backward and upward ascent of the camera reaches another landing.

The circling ascent of the camera continues as if following Hamlet to the top of the castle until, suddenly, there is a cut to a shot of the cloudy sky above the castle which fills the screen, and then a rapid crane down so that Hamlet's form rises abruptly into the image. He is seated on the parapet of the tower that overlooks the sea, his back to us. The camera moves in to an extreme close-up of the whorl at the top of his head, and, as if entering his skull, the inward movement continues with a dissolve to the rocks and crashing surf he is contemplating.

This is Olivier's introduction to the 'To be or not to be' soliloquy, which he has repositioned to follow the encounter with Ophelia, making it a reaction to the failure of that meeting to re-establish trust. In the text the scene comes earlier, just before Ophelia enters to him (III.i.90), and is a more diffusely motivated meditation. Olivier's delivery of the speech offers a sharp contrast to his fury at Ophelia's betrayal that immediately precedes it; in fact the moment at which the camera movement reverses its upward ascent marks a transition from rage to depression, from a grandiose and 'noble' anger to deflation. Here he is at his most languid and limp, dangling his 'bodkin' above his breast with a weak, three-fingered grasp while half reclining. At the end he proves too enervated or distracted to hold on to it and watches bemusedly as the tiny dagger falls into the sea far below. In this interpretation the meditation on suicide has no heroic quality but is played as an escapist revery, marking Hamlet's return to impotence and passivity.

In some sense Hamlet takes the place of the ghost in this sequence: it is he who casts down and ascends and is finally inaccessible, reached after in fear and longing. Yet at the top of the stairs, when the cut to the heavens likens him most closely to his father's ascending spirit, there is a sudden reversal to passivity and depression. The summit of the tower marks his mortal limits. Beyond is the air into which the ghost had vanished and the rocky surf is below. Retracing his father's path brings him to the prospect of self-annihilation.

The analogy between the ghost's treatment of Hamlet earlier and Hamlet's treatment of Ophelia here also suggests a reason, different from that of Freud and Jones, for Hamlet's condemnation of sex. For this Hamlet erotic response and abuse are closely linked. One is either abuser or abused, with little room for erotic shadings of activity and passivity that do not tend to extremes. One is either the mad figure who attacks and runs away or the figure left alone and hurt on the stairs. What the ghost does to Hamlet, which is in part a re-enactment of a key incident of abuse the director suffered as a child, is the cause of what he does to Ophelia. He cannot break the cycle of abuse the ghost's visit initiated.

The staircase motif is again used in a thematically significant way after the 'mousetrap' scene, when Hamlet makes a long ascent to his mother's chamber. Midway he comes upon the king in prayer and raises his sword for revenge ('now might I do it') but hesitates as the thought of sending his father's murderer to heaven detains him. Here the visual treatment of the scene again intimates a close relationship between the victims of violence and its perpetrators. As Claudius meditates on his guilty hand, he turns it over slowly, palm up, in extreme close-up, just as in the flashback to the murder, old Hamlet's hand slowly turned over and opened at the moment of his death. When his prayer fails, Claudius slumps from the altar, sliding to the floor in the posture in which King Hamlet had fallen from his bench in the orchard. Hamlet continues upward to his mother's bedroom in a slow, menacing ascent, his dark figure outlined against the jagged shadow of the overhanging steps, while his mother makes plans with Polonius to spy on him.

The bedchamber scene takes place after a climb, not during one, but is in other ways related to the scenes of abuse we have been examining. The scene is markedly violent and erotic, with the ghost's appearance dividing it into two sections, converting Hamlet's murderous threats into incestuous tenderness. In the opening exchange the play text calls for an unfilial degree of roughness: 'Come, come and sit you down; you shall not budge/You go not till I set you up a glass/Where you may see the inmost part of you.' Modern audiences may miss the insistent impropriety of the repeated plural pronoun, but the verbal affront is otherwise clear and is intensified in the film as Olivier flings the queen backward on her bed and, in close-up, presses his dagger to her throat across her ample bosom. As she cries for help and Polonius answers, Hamlet looks up with a maniacally rigid smile, runs to the arras, stabs through it, and delivers his next lines with the point stuck in the still standing body of his victim behind the curtain. He lets the body and his dagger fall, returns to his mother, and resumes his reproaches and attempts to force his mother to terms with her complicity in the murder of the king. As he compares Claudius with his father, he works up to a rage again and throws her down upon the bed, as simultaneously he hears the heartbeat that signals the approach of the ghost.

Eileen Herlie's performance during the threats and revelations of this scene is important to its meaning. Early in the film she had established Gertrude as a seductive mother willing to use a passionate, lover's kiss as part of her plea that Hamlet remain in Elsinore.

This creates a triangle that Claudius registers by angrily pulling her away and dissolving the council. Here, as she struggles with the mix of emotions Hamlet's wild discourse evokes (fear, remorse, confusion), her expression returns repeatedly to erotic appeal. We see how she could have remained ignorant of the murder and the moral implications of her remarriage: her response to ethical difficulty is to seek the comfort of a sexual response, even from her son.

As Hamlet casts her down and looks up to find the ghost, the camera repeats a movement from the ramparts scene, moving to a high-angle close-up of Hamlet as he half swoons and falls to the ground. He hears the admonition of the ghost from the floor, propped on one arm while reaching toward the vision with the other, a posture precisely that of Ophelia as she looks after the fleeing Hamlet, who has cast her down on the stairs. This shot, with its evocation of that parallel, is repeated four times, intercut with Gertrude's wonder and incomprehension as she sees her son gazing upon a presence she cannot perceive. It is the ghost who asks Hamlet to return to Gertrude:

> But look – amazement on thy mother sits:
> O step between her and her fighting soul;
> Speak to her, Hamlet.

As this point Hamlet's violence toward Gertrude, symbolically phallic all the while, becomes openly erotic as his appeal to her to abstain from intercourse with Claudius succeeds, and mother and son seal their union against the usurper with a fiercely passionate embrace and kiss accompanied by a romantic, circling movement of the camera in keeping with a cinematic convention reserved for lovers.

The influence of Jones is strongest here, for we see Gertrude trying to evoke an erotic response, which she ultimately gets, and we see how closely intertwined are the violence expected of Hamlet and the desire for his mother from which he cannot dissociate that violence. For him, to approach his revenge is also somehow to approach his mother's bed; being loyal to his father somehow entails flinging her down upon it. But also central to Olivier's conception of the scene are elements that derive not from Jones but from his own engagement with the issue of passivity and the compulsively cyclical character of abuse. As he had taken the place of the ghost in certain ways in the rejection of Ophelia, so here, at the point of a violent assault on his mother upon her own bed, he is himself cast down by the apparition of his father, on whom he gazes with a mixture of dread and longing evocative of Ophelia's response to his abuse earlier. In addition, the ghost's intervention does not put an end to the Oedipal energy of the scene but, rather, is the signal for its conversion from violence to tenderness. In fact the ghost seems actually to sponsor the merger of mother and son enacted here. 'But look – amazement on thy mother sits:/O step between her and her fighting soul' effectively annuls the earlier commandment to 'leave her to heaven', and permits Hamlet to recover the quasi-romantic, spiritual union with his mother that had been breached by her re-marriage. From this point she rejects Claudius's offers of intimacy and acts as Hamlet's ally, even to the point of knowingly joining him in death by drinking from the poisoned cup.

[...]

If the staircases of the set are important to Olivier's complex ap-proach to the Oedipal dynamics of *Hamlet*, so is another central feature of the set design: the persistent use of vacant chairs and empty rooms. This aspect of the film's style, the frequent absence of human figures from the image, is related to Olivier's interest in Hamlet's self-absorption and in the special way in which, for him, Oedipal confusion manifests itself in an irresolution of roles and meanings. As early as our first introduction to its interior, Elsinore is presented as a series of spaces empty of people and yet pregnant with significances we cannot yet fully grasp. After the first visit of the ghost, who is himself an absence and a silence that portends significance but does not yet announce it, Marcellus speculates that his appearance is linked to 'something rotten' in the state of Denmark. He glances offscreen and the camera begins to move slowly, following his glance, as if in response to the enigma he has proposed. In a series of invisible cuts intended to be read as a single long take, the camera explores Elsinore for the source of corruption, descending the winding staircases of the castle and pausing at several locations to dolly in for a closer look. The royal bedchamber, a room later identified as Ophelia's, and the empty council chamber are visited in turn. In this last location the camera lingers on an ornate empty chair, perhaps left vacant by the death of old King Hamlet. This sequence, with its slowly moving and tentatively in-quiring camera, ends abruptly and definitively with a tight close-up of the new king intemperately swilling wine from a large goblet. He tosses the emptied cup to an obsequious attendant, and a close-up of the smoking cannon's mouth 'respeaking earthly thunder' suggests that the rottenness in Denmark centres in the king, his appetites, and his sanctimonious court.

The sites visited on the way – each a possible, though cryptic indication of the kind of corruption Marcellus had in mind – are not definitive; they provoke us to interpret or guess. At each site we hear a musical motif that will later have meaning in the narrative. As yet we do not know that the smaller chamber is Ophelia's, the sunny musical passage her theme, or that the chair is Hamlet's. Most viewers guess that it is the empty chair of the murdered king; and though it is later identified as the chair Hamlet uses, it retains a fluidity of association and is often shown empty.

We know whose the bed is; and this symbol, in proximity to the phallic cannonade, is a kind of declaration of the film's Freudian intentions. The large chamber seems almost certainly the set for the scene to come. The chair, the bed, and the chamber are presented as if they pointed to some further significance: their literal vacancy suggests an as yet unspecified symbolic function. In the course of the film we come to understand them more fully, but they remain, at least partly, private symbols charged with meaning for Hamlet and not always for others. The queen's bed, with its 'incestuous sheets', is on Hamlet's mind during the first soliloquy, even before the ghost has appeared, and it never becomes an object of special attention for anyone except Hamlet and the film audience. The symbols one learns to interpret are Hamlet's symbols, and therefore through much of the narrative the spectator shares with him not only a dramatic point of view but an orientation toward the significances of the world of Elsinore that is privileged and private.

After the close shot of the king, the vacancy discovered by the travelling camera gives way to busy plenitude. Now cutting and camera movement function more conventionally to support narrative, following the dynamics of the king's interaction with the court. In a series of shots of increasing distance, the council chamber is reintroduced as the sphere of Claudius's power. The brooding, solitary, and symbolic mode of Hamlet associated with the long take, the vertical movement of the camera, and the empty room is contrasted with the political, interpersonal mode of the king, whose central importance in the busy court is emphasised by horizontal camera movement and cross-cutting.

Most of the scene is shot from the foot of the long council table looking toward the raised thrones of the king and queen at its head.

Hamlet's armchair, distinguished from the others by ball-and-point ornamentation, is at the right foot, pushed some distance away from the council table and at right angles to the thrones and to the screen. This is the empty chair of the earlier sequence, but it does not appear in the image until the council scene is well under way. In contrast to theatrical productions, in which Hamlet must be present from the start, the film stresses his absence: he is the reason for the king's anxious manipulations, but he is not present in the image until Claudius expresses his affection for Laertes: 'Take thy fair hour, Laertes; time be thine,/And thy best graces spend it at thy will!'

'Time be thine' is the cue for the discovery of Hamlet, sitting in his distinctive chair in a passive and sullen mourning posture as, with a cut, the camera pulls back to a shot of the full room. Claudius is on the throne with Polonius at his right hand and Laertes standing stage left in the foreground. Hamlet is excluded from the complex father-son-king affiliations implied by the *mise-en-scène*, yet he dominates the scene by his foregrounded position, clothes, posture, and striking blond hair. In some sense time will belong to Laertes, and never to Hamlet, in the film. The contrast between them as sons is one of the film's most successful exploitations of the implications of the Oedipal theme. Time (and timing) can only be mastered by a young man who finds his place in a temporal succession from father to son.

Space, on the other hand, seems to belong to Hamlet. If Old Hamlet haunts the ramparts, Young Hamlet is the ghost of Elsinore's interior. The freedom of the camera to explore at will is often associated with him. He stalks Elsinore's corridors overhearing, as Dover Wilson thought he should, the plan to use Ophelia to unravel the cause of his madness. And whereas the spying of others is always prepared for by elaborate and explicit conspirings, Hamlet seems to be there precisely when something is to be overheard. In fact even when he is not there we expect him, as when, during the plotting of the death of Hamlet by Claudius and Laertes, three times the camera cranes far above the speakers to privileged nooks above the chamber, where we have learned to expect the prince. But on this fatal occasion the camera's access to the secret is *not* matched by Hamlet's, and he enters in the background after Claudius and Laertes depart, unaware of his fate. In the council scene he remains nearly motionless and passive until the court departs and then reveals in voice-over soliloquy how much the empty room is his domain and how much its emptiness is the condition for his access to his feelings and inner life. Vacant, the thrones can evoke the imagined happy union of his parents, as they do when he stands between and links them with his hands, leaning on them for support against his sorrow; or they can stand for the present, detested union of his mother and uncle; or they can intimate his hopes for succession, and his fantasy of a closeness to his mother impeded by Claudius's intrusion.

One function of the film's emphasis on emptiness, then, is to suggest the narcissistic dimension of Hamlet's Oedipal difficulties. He is often the sole inhabitant of a large, unpeopled space, isolated and grandiose but unable to sustain the conflicts that might lead to his finding a place in the sequence of generations. The empty furniture so prominent in the film also intimates that there is a way, though one closed to Hamlet, by which Oedipal tensions can be and normally are resolved. Because the roles in the Oedipal situation are shifting, with sons becoming fathers in their turn, the Oedipus complex is normally terminated by identification with the father and deferral of the wish for primacy until it can be satisfied in adulthood by a substitute love object of one's own generation. Such a resolution requires, however, that empty chairs be occupied, vacant rooms possessed, ambiguous meanings clarified. The vacancy of space in Elsinore, like the ambiguity of its symbols, is congenial to Hamlet, but it prevents his succession to his father's rights. A symbolism that invests its signs with a meaning that is private, numinous, and unique may be the expression of a sensibility that cannot relinquish claims of uniqueness and transcendent value in the family.

A consideration of the player scene and its failure to resolve Hamlet's dilemma may make this relation between Olivier's stylistic choices and his Oedipal theme clearer, for it too offers us a vacancy or emptiness that seems pregnant with significance and yet proves impotent and self-enclosed. The sequence begins after the 'To be or not to be' soliloquy, Hamlet in his chair in a medium shot, his back to us, in a depressive, hand-in-chin posture. As Polonius announces to him the arrival of the players, he takes on his most joyous and elated mood, held until after his 'mousetrap' plot is fully laid, when he pirouettes wildly in the empty chamber – the council chamber which will now become the theatre for the 'Murder of Gonzago', in the confidence that 'the play's the thing'. In his joyous, animated, and highly professional direction of the players, Hamlet's special chair shifts significance once again, becoming a metacinematic figure standing for the director's chair, which it resembles in its bare, cross-legged wooden outline. Hamlet coaches the players on dramatic theory and technique from this chair, leaving it to impart specific instructions and retiring back to it to address the whole company as its temporary leader. Hamlet has been an actor; now he is also a director, and in being one he doubles for Olivier himself, directing and starring in his own *Hamlet*.

Other metatheatrical possibilities of the set are developed during the player sequence. One end of the immense council room is taken over as a theatrical space even before the play is staged: as Hamlet completes his instructions, the props and costumes are moved behind the arras – now not the place behind which Hamlet is spied on but a tiring-house curtain or even, anachronistically, a theatrical curtain before which Hamlet stands in confident mastery, as if ready to deliver a prologue to the play that will unkennel his uncle's guilt. This composition is the climax of the sequence between Hamlet and the players, and significantly this moment of mastery is presented with Hamlet alone in the empty chamber. During the preceding sequence, as Hamlet gains confidence that his theatrical ploy contains the solution to his real-life difficulties, the camera has almost ignored the double thrones that symbolise Claudius's status in the family and in the state. Hamlet's chair dominates the set. But at the moment of his greatest poise, when he seems to have subsumed the powers of the stage in his own person and confidently awaits the arrival of the court, there is a dramatic cut to a reverse, low-angle shot from behind him. The juxtaposition of the two shots shows us that if from one point of view he is master of the revels, from the other he is still the hieratic son standing humbly below the looming empty thrones that dominate the room even in Claudius's absence.

As in Olivier's life, the theatrical solution to the Oedipal dilemma is a dubious one in which real mastery and narcissistic refuge are hard to distinguish. The visual treatment shows us that despite its energy and liveliness, Hamlet's theatrical experiment is another attempt to people the empty spaces of Elsinore with a cast of his own devising.

In contrast, the use of the empty room by King Claudius represents, even though it is wholly rooted in evil intentions, a mature and powerful appreciation of the relativity and contingency of power and its dependence on the establishing of bonds of trust and alliance between fathers and sons. Basil Sydney's Claudius, an uneasy yet powerful monarch in the early scenes and an affecting failed penitent after the mousetrap, comes into his own as a character in the scenes with Laertes in the last half of the film, converting Laertes's rebellion into loyal alliance. The groundwork of this alliance is laid before Hamlet returns from his sea voyage, when Claudius is able, solely by the force of his personal authority, to deflect Laertes's rebellious threats. This encounter is filmed in extreme long-shot so that Laertes's murderous rage seems little more than a minor personal quarrel taking place in one corner of the castle, while the mad Ophelia – the real focus of our concern at this point – wanders poignantly distracted in another. By the time Laertes sees her his anger against the king has already been defused. The opportunity for Claudius not merely to placate but to use Laertes comes in the graveyard scene, when he assists Laertes in converting grief for a dead father into a commitment to revenge, succeeding where the ghost had so far failed.

As in the council scene in the beginning of the film, so here the figure of Hamlet dominates the foreground; meanwhile, the real nexus of power occupies a more modest part of the screen. As Hamlet realises that Ophelia is to be buried in the fresh grave, he challenges Laertes: 'What is he whose grief bears such an emphasis?/It is I, Hamlet the Dane.' Here Hamlet, his back to us, immense in our foreground perspective, with arms spread looks sharply down from a hillock on the tiny figures of Laertes and the king grouped around a stone cross at the grave. After the tumult of Hamlet's mad challenge and his leap into the grave have subsided, the significance of the king's quiet placement of himself in relation to the cross and in relation to Laertes becomes clear. Left alone on screen, Laertes kneels in mourning while the king stands before the cross so that he insinuates himself in the place from which mourning is sanctified – an assertion of paternal power by *mise-en-scène* far more effective than his verbal attempts to occupy the same place for Hamlet in the first scene. Laertes's submission to his grief becomes, through this placement, an implicit submission to the king, to whom he also seems to kneel, so that when Claudius places a comforting hand on his shoulder and gestures him to rise, grief for the dead is replaced by acceptance of the law as embodied in the king. 'Laertes, was your father dear to you, or are you like the painting of a sorrow, a face without a heart?' The funeral, of course, is that of Ophelia, not Polonius, but it is the death of the father that is the motive for a revenge directed against Hamlet, and the basis for the symbolic bond of sonship to Claudius. It is this bond which, despite the many ironic parallels between Laertes and Hamlet, distinguishes Laertes, who can 'do what is required of him', and Hamlet, who cannot.

Claudius, with fatherly concern, leads Laertes into the council chamber, on the way revealing candidly his own weaknesses and limitations; his dependence on the queen, his fear of an uprising in favour of the more popular Hamlet. The king acknowledges, in short, his need for Laertes's assistance in a project he cannot accomplish alone. In the council chamber, exploring the possibilities of an attempt on Hamlet, he seats Laertes in Polonius's chair, while he himself takes one of the armless benches farther down the table. In the symbolic tableau Olivier has provided the potential double meanings in the king's speech reveal not merely an ironic relation to Hamlet but a complex and troubled self-understanding on the part of Claudius: 'That we would do we should do when we would, for this "would" changes, and hath abatements and delays' is delivered with the king in medium shot, his hand knowingly laid upon Hamlet's empty chair. This advice to Laertes not only brings to mind Hamlet's temperamental incapacity for action but also invokes (for us, though not Laertes) the king's own decisive but guilty act in pursuing his desires, an act to whose consequences he is still unhappily bound. In this context for a moment Hamlet's chair becomes again the empty chair of the murdered king, for which the tragic action took its rise.

The special function of the Laertes–Claudius subplot in the film, then, is to offer an alternative to the way Hamlet conceives of the father–son relationship. Instead of abuse, there is comfort; instead of distance and idealisation, there is human contact and admission of paternal weakness; instead of being consigned to empty spaces and imaginary relationships, the son is seated in his father's place by an authority that symbolically takes precedence over his father. For Laertes the conflict between generations is stabilised, the death of the father provides the key to the resolution of Oedipal conflict. For Hamlet, however, the deceased father has become a ghost, compromising his autonomy and contributing, finally, to the tragic Oedipal resolution of refusion with the mother. The value of this normative succession from father to son as an alternative to Hamlet's malaise is negated, however, by its origins in murder and its resort to treachery in the use of the poisoned foil. In a sense the film's exploration of the father–son bond between Claudius and Laertes remains limited by Hamlet's perspective. The film offers an instance of psychological health, but one so morally compromised as to invite us to prefer Hamlet's deeply brooding Oedipal perfectionism.

Hamlet's 'reconciliation' with Laertes before the fencing match is played so as to emphasise the unbridgeable distance between the two, Hamlet's exaggerated deference ('I'll be your foil, Laertes') masking contempt, as does his patronising apology for Polonius's death ('Did Hamlet wrong Laertes? Never Hamlet. Hamlet *denies* it.'). The mockery here is partly motivated by Hamlet's awareness that the positive relation to the father implied by the king's spon-sorship of Laertes is closed to him. His challenge of the pretentious term 'carriages' which Osric uses for the thongs attaching the sword to the belt likewise displays a rejection of manhood conceived as phallic competition. Hamlet understands the phallic symbolism of the rewards the king offers him for victory in the fencing match: 'The word would be more germane to the matter if we might carry a *cannon* by our side: I would it might be "hangers" till then – but on', the last two words spoken with a mocking lilt.

The contrast between Hamlet and Laertes is pressed home in Olivier's interpretation of the fatal touch. Laertes's weapon is, as we know, unbated and poisoned, and he is considered the better fencer; the king, in order to make the wager credible, has bet on Hamlet, but only with a substantial handicap as security. Nevertheless, Laertes cannot score a touch in fair combat, and it is only when trapped between the scornful disappointment in his manhood of Osric on one side and Claudius on the other that he strikes out in violation of the rules during a time out – 'Have at you *now*.' The shame Laertes feels when confronted with paternal disappointment is not unlike that which Hamlet has internalised, but it is momentary and calls forth instantaneous action.

There is note of victory in the death scene that follows: in Olivier's version (though not in Shakespeare) the queen drinks the poison knowingly and almost joyfully, defying the king and seizing on this opportunity for suicide as a kind of triumph whereby she extricates herself from the king and affirms her union with Hamlet. But Oedipal victories are defeats for the self.

The pattern of being cast down and reaching after the attacker with reproach and longing recurs here: Hamlet and Laertes, both dying, reach out for each other, and the motif of the extended hand now signals mutual forgiveness and recognition that 'the king's to blame'. The king himself, fatally wounded by Hamlet, repeats the gesture, but his reach is toward the crown he has lost and the lifeless queen. Olivier's fourteen-foot leap is the climax of the action and a summative use of the staircase as a symbol of violence visited from above – a violence with which Hamlet now identifies himself. The leap exemplifies a pattern in Olivier's life and art in which the fear of passivity and indecision is allayed by a masculine daring that offers only an equivocal solution because of its association with self-destruction. It seems appropriate that for the final act of this character, whose uniqueness is so much a part of both his pathology and his greatness, Olivier should have chosen an acrobatic move impossible to repeat.

The film ends with an extended reference to the opening sequence: Hamlet's body is carried up the narrow, winding steps to the top of the central tower. On the way the camera trails the procession behind the bearers as if it were a mourner, and as they ascend it breaks off from their upward course several times to revisit for the last time the symbolic locales: Hamlet's chair seen close-up in an upwardly spiralling camera movement, Ophelia's chamber, the chapel, the queen's bed. But there is no one left for whom these scenes will have the same importance and the endless play of possibility that they had for Hamlet. Elsinore has been presented from a point of view so close to that of Hamlet that his death drains meaning from the setting. In this context the final shot of the staircase to nowhere takes on its full value as an emblem of narcissistic self-enclosure: the tragedy of a man who could not make up his mind is the tragedy of a self that, for reasons we are meant to feel as valid and powerful, cannot give up the illusion of its own centrality and uniqueness, cannot invest itself in a symbolic order based on filial succession and the substitution of objects, and for whom, therefore, death is the destruction not only of the physical self but of the world of significances the self has sustained.

Olivier's film is thus firmly grounded in the Freud/Jones reading of *Hamlet* and incorporates the central insights of that reading: the erotic treatment of the mother–son relationship, the attribution of Hamlet's delay to an implicit equation between usurper and would-be revenger, and the understanding of Hamlet's final 'success' as a kind of self-destruction. But the tragic quality of the film and its value as an interpretation of Shakespeare derives at least as much from the director's exploration of aspects of the play's Oedipal theme that had special relevance to his own early life. The tragedy here is located in the failure of Hamlet's relation to his father, which leaves him with a sense of fundamental defect, uncertain boundaries, and a powerful impulse toward merger, evident in his identification with the invasive ghost early in the film and in his mystical bond with his mother later. Olivier's Hamlet displays both the greatness of spirit and the tragic waste of his gifts that Shakespeare's text calls for. He is vigorous, courageous, intellectually powerful, and ethically sensitive. But neither his mission nor his factitious Oedipal victory can supply a firm sense of worth or provide a stable connection between this brilliant but isolated character and the human world around him. Olivier's *Hamlet,* unlike Freud's, is a tragedy not of guilt but of the grandiose self and its unmet need for context and validation, of a son unable to find a non-abusive relation to his father.

From Peter S. Donaldson, *Shakespearean Films/Shakespearean Directors* (Boston, 1990), pp. 31–67.

NOTES

[In this extract from his full-length study *Shakespearean Films/Shakespearean Directors*, Peter Donaldson responds to Olivier's emphatically Freudian reading of *Hamlet* with a detailed psychoanalytic reading of the film. Although, in the preface to his book, Donaldson professes a degree of scepticism about the *auteurist* approach to film criticism, his analysis in places pursues a strongly biographical line. Drawing upon a distinction which is central to Freudian dream theory, Donaldson differentiates between the manifestly Freudian content of the film (phallic symbolism, the bed motif, incestuous hints in the interplay between Hamlet and Gertrude) and its latent meaning, a less immediately visible, densely coded subtext of anxiety and sexual abuse. Donaldson proposes a close identification between Olivier and Hamlet, and argues that the film plays out the director's sexual and gender confusions, and his troubled relationship with his own father. Quotations from *Hamlet* in the essay are from *The Riverside Shakespeare*, ed. G. Blakemore Evans (Boston, 1974). Ed.]

1. Noticed, for example, by John Ashworth in 'Olivier, Freud and Hamlet', *Atlantic Monthly*, 183 (May 1949), 30; Jay Halio, 'Three Filmed Hamlets', *Literature/Film Quarterly*, 1 (1973), 317; Bernice W. Kliman, 'The Spiral of Influence: "One Defect" in *Hamlet'*, *Literature/Film Quarterly*, 11 (1983), 159–66.

2. *The Standard Edition of the Complete Psychological Works of Sigmund Freud*, ed. and trans. James Strachey (London, 1953), 24 vols, vol. 4, pp. 264–6. Hereafter cited as *S.E.*

3. Ernest Jones, 'The Oedipus Complex as an Explanation of Hamlet's Mystery', *American Journal of Psychology*, 21 (January 1910); *Das Problem des Hamlet und der Oedipus-Komplex* (Leipzig and Vienna, 1911); *Essays in Applied Psychoanalysis* (London, 1923); *Hamlet by William Shakespeare with a Psycho-analytical Study by Ernest Jones, MD* (London, 1947); *Hamlet and Oedipus* (London, 1949, rpr. new York, 1976).

4. Laurence Olivier, *Confessions of an Actor* (London, 1982), p. 102.

5. *S.E.*, vol. 17, pp. 6, 27–8, 35–6, 45–6; vol. 19, 31–3.

6. Olivier, *Confessions*, pp. 31–2.

7. Brenda Cross (ed.), *The Film Hamlet: A Record of its Production* (London, 1948), p. 12.

8. Ibid., p. 15

9. Ibid.

10. Ibid., p. 11.

11. J. Dover Wilson, *What Happens in Hamlet* (Cambridge, 1953), p. 106. Compare Olivier, *Confessions*, p. 101.

12. Cross, *The Film Hamlet*, p. 12.

7

Branagh and the Prince, or a 'royal fellowship of death'

CURTIS BREIGHT

I

In a recent essay on Kenneth Branagh's 1989 film adaptation of Shakespeare's *Henry V*, Peter Donaldson claims that 'the political, even cynical aspects of the decision to go to war are emphasised: there is little celebration of "England" as a sacrosanct community; many of the trenchant ironies that the text directs *against* the king and his conduct are allowed to stand, and are even extended, as when the king himself gives the order for Bardolph's execution and unflinchingly watches his death throes; the battles are unglamorous and brutal. Branagh's *Henry V* speaks to us in the idiom and in the imagery of leftist critique and liberal pacifism.' The opening technique is said to be 'allying the film to the cinema of Godard and other practitioners and theorists of the avant-garde, for whom "revealing the apparatus" is closely linked to unmasking the presumptions and ideological function of Hollywood or bourgeois film aesthetics'. Near the conclusion, however, Donaldson asserts that Branagh's 'critical stance undergoes a gradual *aphanisis*, or fading, in the course of the narrative, as Branagh moves from Brechtian counter-cinema to an affirmation of cinema's traditional claim to present real people with authentic feelings; from cynicism about the war to something like acceptance of its tragic necessities'. Unlike the chapter on Olivier's *Henry V* in his recent book, in which he views the film not in its most self-evident terms as a blatant appropriation

of Shakespeare's history play for the exigencies of British militarism
in World War II but largely as an expression of Olivier's boyhood
biography and gender confusion, Donaldson confronts the political
surface of Branagh's film but does not plumb its schizophrenic
depths. Branagh clearly seeks to become the next Olivier, but why
challenge Olivier's *Henry V* rather than his *Hamlet* or *Richard III* or
Othello or *As You Like It?*[1]

Olivier's agenda in *Henry V* is apparent and excusable. England
embattled by a demonic regime, despite the historical casualties
generated by the British Empire, was sufficient cause for a patriotic
version of Shakespeare's play. But Olivier's choice of *Henry V*,
Shakespeare's most patriotic play in the view of traditional conservative critics, also signals his subservience to the reigning powers of
British society. Hence *Sir* Laurence Olivier. Branagh's *Henry V* is
more complex yet ultimately similar to Olivier's representation of
political power. Branagh may actually feel that he has made an
anti-war film,[2] but his personal ambition has led him to construct a
film ideologically conducive to Thatcherism. The explanation for
Branagh's schizophrenic *Henry V* lies in his autobiography entitled
Beginning, which reveals that he divorced himself from one royal
'patron' (the Royal Shakespeare Company) only to find that he
needed another – Prince Charles. Branagh's careerism and need for
patronage, curiously evocative of the conditions under which
Elizabethan playwrights operated, involve subordinating any supposed 'leftist critique and liberal pacifism' about war to dubious
overlapping ideologies conceivable as *responsibility of leadership*
and *militaristic brotherhood.*

The concluding chapter of Branagh's autobiography is 'a rough
diary account' of the filming of *Henry V*. Under 9 December (1988)
he records an anecdote: 'Enter Paul Scofield. If ever anyone was
born to play kings, then it was this Titan, with his regal frame and
haunted majestic face. I was more in awe of him than of any of the
other legends working on the film, and yet he was the shyest of
them all. He had no choice. Brian Blessed broke up any potential
for undue reverence with his midday yell across the floor after I had
given him some notes as Exeter. "You never give Paul Scofield any
fucking notes. You're just a bloody arse-licker. You've destroyed
my performance." Scofield helpless under his crown' (p. 237).
Blessed's comment is far more revealing about Branagh and his
film than a mere anecdote might suggest, even in the context of
Blessed's other irreverent comments (pp. 224, 226). Branagh *is* an

'arse-licker', but the 'arse' in question is not the regal Scofield's but Prince Charles's. Branagh's preoccupation with *Henry V* stretches back to the 1984 RSC season, in which he starred in the title role. Branagh's sense of himself, as indicated throughout the autobiography and in its final sentence ('The readiness is all'), involves identification with the 'recurring Hamlet in me' (p. 127). Henry V becomes a kind of Hamlet, at least in Branagh's 'sense of Hamletian doubt that runs through the part': Henry is 'haunted ... not just by his father and their troubled relationship, but also by the ghost of Richard II' (p. 137). Thus in a bizarre twist the least introspective of Shakespeare's royal figures is conflated with the most, but the difficulty of forcing this interpretation onto the character of Henry V led Branagh to seek a revealing encounter. He obtained an audience with Prince Charles for the purpose of answering the question, 'what was it *like* being a king?' (p. 141).

Branagh laid out a lengthy interpretation for the prince, in which Henry was characterised as isolated, betrayed, lonely: 'Through the course of the play a number of betrayals take place: his "bed-fellow", Lord Scroop, is discovered leading an assassination attempt; his former mentor, Falstaff, dies; and later still he is *required* to order the execution of another drinking companion, Bardolph. *His loneliness is intense* and *his hurt* at the various *betrayals and losses* is *very acute*. I asked Prince Charles whether the various newspaper betrayals of events, dramatic and mundane, had changed him. Yes, it had, profoundly. And it had, as I suspected was true of Henry, produced an extraordinary melancholy. It was a sadness that could produce bitterness or a more useful but painful *wisdom*, and Prince Charles had clearly developed the latter. He bore the *inevitable bruises* of his position with great courage, and although, sitting opposite him, I could detect the *haunted look of responsibility*, the very fact that he was speaking to me was an indication of his continuing desire to give people the benefit of the doubt' (p. 143; emphases mine). Although Branagh had prefaced his interpretation by affirming that his Henry V would not be an 'impersonation' of Prince Charles, he clearly felt the need to conflate the two. On meeting the prince he 'felt an instant rapport', having 'never encountered such an extraordinary and genuine humility' (p. 142). Henry too was a prince of 'genuine humility in relation to God', which 'would be a cornerstone' of Branagh's 'interpretation' (p. 138). In describing Henry's encounter with the three common soldiers, Branagh asserted that Henry 'wants to be one of them, but he can't be; he wants them to understand his position but they resist it. Had Prince Charles ever felt like doing the same? Yes, while he was at Cambridge he'd attempted to do the same thing, but the results were disastrous' (p. 143). Thus 'Henry's only real comfort could be his faith, and Prince Charles was in total agreement. Some kind of belief in God was the only practical way of living from day to day, it was the only way to deal with his position' (p. 143). Branagh converts Shakespeare's least meditative king into 'a complex psychological portrait ... which included guilt, doubt and self-questioning' (p. 143), and he 'had the impression' that Charles 'shared with Shakespeare's Henry a desire to strike a delicate balance between responsibility and compassion' (pp. 143–4).

Branagh, would-be prince of players, exists in awe of Scofield, not to mention of Henry, Hamlet, and Prince Charles, because he has a remarkably schizophrenic yet ultimately conservative view of royal power. He grasps that Henry is a 'ruthless killer' but feels compelled to perceive him also as a 'Christian king' (p. 144). In the Southampton scene, in which Henry so piously and hollowly thanks God for revealing what the Elizabethan security apparatuses discovered, imagined or manufactured, Cambridge asserts that 'Never was monarch better feared and loved/Than is your majesty' (II.ii.37–8), tipping us off to Shakespeare's awareness of Machiavelli's famous pronouncement: 'it is far better to be feared than loved if you cannot be both'. Another Machiavellian dictum is that the prince must always seem, if not necessarily be, religious: a prince 'should appear a man of compassion, a man of good faith, a man of integrity, a kind and a religious man. And there is nothing so important as to seem to have this last quality.'[3] The problem with Branagh is that his research on Shakespeare seems similar to his research for a role in an adaptation of Virginia Woolf, '"O" Level "Study Notes"' (p. 103). He cannot grasp Shakespearean irony and ignores Shakespeare's engagement with late Elizabethan culture, especially the murderous Elizabethan wars that had wasted tens of thousands of Englishmen, not to mention a huge number of the Irish. In doing research for the 1984 *Henry V*, Branagh read 'every biography of Henry V' he 'could get his hands on' (p. 140), and to understand war he read 'Clausewitz, Sassoon, historical documents about the combat detail at Agincourt' (p. 141). He listened to descriptions of the 'Second World War' (p. 141) and the 'First World War' (p. 229) – everything *except* any description of the brutal 'campaigns' in which so many Englishmen died during the more or less formal war period between 1585 and 1603. When Shakespeare's Henry tells Montjoy that 'My people are with sickness much enfeebled,/My numbers lessened' (III.vi.153–4), we should recall that according to one contemporary estimate, less than 10 per cent of the 11,000 Elizabethan Englishmen killed in France in a three-year period died in battle, the majority having been wasted by hunger, sickness, and injury.[4] Branagh ignores contemporary military debates in which Sir John Smythe accused Elizabethan captains of getting their men killed in order to pocket their pay. He does not seem to know that even the reactionary Matthew Sutcliffe, apologist for the Elizabethan politico-religious hierarchy, excused vagabond soldiers (like Bardolph) for theft. He ignores the fact that a phrase from one military treatise written in 1592 but not published until 1604 (when Elizabeth was safely dead) claimed that the conduct of contemporary war was 'murdering our men'.[5] When Shakespeare's Henry, in a line cut from Branagh's film, asserts that 'War is his [God's] beadle, war is his vengeance' (IV.i.173–4), Henry is not trying to make his men 'understand his position'; he is trying to mystify war and displace responsibility for gratuitous butchery. Shakespeare's Henry, in fact, spends much of the play not assuming royal responsibility but evading it. He displaces responsibility onto Canterbury (I.ii.96), onto the Dauphin (I.ii.259–97), onto the citizens of Harfleur (III.iii.1–43), onto the soldiers themselves and finally onto God (IV.i). Thus while Branagh attempts to manufacture both a religious and a responsible Henry, Shakespeare problematises the first and absolutely negates the second.

Branagh's appeal to Prince Charles, however, had its pay-off. The explicit reason for Branagh's initial encounter with the prince was advice, but the implicit reason was an appeal for patronage. Thus Charles attended a production of *Henry V*: 'I spoke to the Prince and his wife afterwards. He seemed much moved by the evening and said as much in a letter which he wrote some weeks later. Not only did he feel a very personal connection with the story, but both he and Princess Diana were both fascinated by the process of acting, by what you actually *feel* when you're being angry, sad, or whatever. It was a satisfying and all too brief conversation that confirmed our rapport and intensified my admiration for the man who was about to fight his way through the ten thousand-strong crowd that had gathered outside the theatre since news of the visit had swept round Stratford' (pp. 151–2). Prince Charles, 'our Royal Patron', also attended the 'Royal Gala Preview of *Twelfth Night*' for Branagh's new theatre company, Renaissance, on Branagh's invitation (p. 199). The prince later reciprocated by asking 'if Renaissance could provide a Shakespearian entertainment for a private party at Windsor' (p. 211), and of course Branagh obliged with a 'fifty-minute programme' (p. 212). Charles aided Branagh's plans for the film of *Henry V* through a personal 'recommendation' (p. 216), and attended Branagh's production of *Hamlet* in Denmark (p. 217). And most appropriately of all, Prince Charles arrived on the set when Branagh was doing a second shot of the 'Upon the King' speech from Act IV, scene i: 'He certainly was a Patron, and a great supporter' (p. 230). The British monarchy is given a human(e) face through Branagh's version of the Ceremony scene, but this face serves to mask the brutality of high political power.

II

At first glance Branagh's film seems radically divided between cynicism in the first half and idealisation in the second. The film's version of Shakespeare's first three acts seems to demystify high politics. Here unmasking the apparatus is akin to exposing the strategies underpinning political power, as when Canterbury manipulates Henry or Henry his three traitorous councillors. The open door at the end of Derek Jacobi's choral Prologue slides into Canterbury checking outside his door for spies hiding in the corridor. Canterbury and Ely whisper to each other to avoid informers, or the symbolic eyes and ears of the monarchy represented in Elizabeth's 'Rainbow Portrait'. Branagh stages treason at Southampton in ways remarkably similar to the stage-managed trials, executions, and post-mortem narratives of Elizabethan London, in which the traitor's willing confession (whether induced by torture or not) was a key element of the show. In imaginary flashbacks to the *Henry IV* plays, comic laughter in the Boar's Head tavern is displaced by Falstaff's and Bardolph's horrible recognition of Henry's ruthlessness. The Harfleur speech is not suppressed, and the battle at Agincourt seems grim. But by the end of the film *realpolitik* has disappeared. The Machiavellian machinations of vile politicians are purified by the honest blood-letting of hand-to-hand combat. Distinctions of social class conveniently disappear as the cult(ure) of military honour is established. On the battlefield it doesn't matter who you are as long as you kill the enemy effectively. Heroic (and victorious) survivors are thereby allowed to be 'on the team' or, in Henry V's words, a 'band of brothers' (p. 99). As an added bonus, hostile casualties are extremely high while the victors' are unbelievably low, attesting to the obvious fact that 'God fought for us' (p. 112). Finally, Henry ineptly yet charmingly woos Katharine, and thus the horrors of useless militarism are erased by a sanitised and boyish king.

At second glance the shift remains evident, but it is less radical and more subtly prepared by Branagh. The Prologue which supposedly unmasks the apparatus also discloses background props suggesting a connection between religion and militarism. When Henry says 'We charge you in the name of God take heed' (p. 21) and 'May I with right and conscience make this claim?' (p. 23), Branagh looks cold and grim but also sincere: ruthless killer and Christian king. Moreover, Henry at least seeks the counsel of supposedly spiritual advisers. When the film shifts to the French court, the first moments include Scofield's subtle dismissal of two prelates who look remarkably similar to Canterbury and Ely. The French court is thus purely secular in its handling of high politics. But the major shift toward mystification of politics and militarism occurs at the crucial juncture of the eve before Agincourt. Branagh begins to adopt rather than emulate Olivier. He starts seeking to humanise Henry, ironically enough, at precisely that moment when Shakespeare's Henry is least willing to implicate himself in common humanity. In a brilliant article Thomas Cartelli analyses what he calls the 'set speech' in Act IV, scene i, otherwise known as the 'Ceremony' speech, vis-à-vis Henry's encounter with three common soldiers: 'When Henry refers to Williams's vision of the dismembered body politic at all, he does so by bequeathing it the dreamless sleep of fools, wretches, slaves, lackeys, and peasants – a king's idea of an Elysium for commoners in exchange for their "profitable labour". In short, Henry responds to his soldiers' concern for their own welfare and salvation, first, by privileging the weight of his own royal burdens and, then, by reducing the soldiers to a state of bestial oblivion ... The feudal relationship between sovereign and subject ... is suddenly made equivalent to the relationship between master and slave, indeed, becomes identified with the same insofar as the ground of its being is made plain.' Cartelli concludes by arguing that 'Henry's reversion to a religious idiom and a provi-

dentialist approach to political affairs' ceremonially counter-
acts Williams's speech on dismembered bodies and Henry's own
exposure of the master–slave relationship. Sovereignty is thereby
reconsecrated, and its accountrements 'revalidated on the heels of
their own demystification'.[6] *Shakespeare (c)(ambri)(cs)Henry*

Cartelli makes this argument to expose precisely how the king is
remystified, not to further the process of remystification. Branagh,
however, uses Act IV, scene i to realign his film with Olivier's.
When Henry refers to the 'wretched slave' sleeping on a full
stomach, Branagh (like Olivier) gives Henry a referent for his description. In fact, he includes more than one slumbering lackey. The
sleeping soldier as a film prop is far more prominent in Olivier's
version but no less significant to Branagh's ideological project. By
realigning his film with Olivier's at this juncture Branagh begins to
endorse Henry as a human being by rendering the speech as honest
meditation rather than rhetorical evasion. Significantly, Branagh
cuts the final four lines of the original speech:

> The slave, a member of the country's peace,
> Enjoys it; but in gross brain little wots
> What watch the king keeps to maintain the peace,
> Whose hours the peasant best advantages.
>
> (IV.i.286–9)

Even Branagh must have understood the danger of high irony at
this moment in his film. Henry's encounter with three common soldiers – sleepless, worried, and probably hungry – negates the very
premises of the Ceremony speech.

The scene is performed as a levelling rather than a mystifying
moment: the king is just like his men, except for the outward orna-
ments of royal status. Shakespeare's Henry evades responsibility for
killing, while asserting (even in Branagh's version) that 'Every
subject's duty is the king's' (p. 90); but Branagh's Henry takes on
the emotional burden of his position, while simultaneously becoming a mere soldier. Thus Branagh cleverly seeks to collapse distinctions of social class. For instance, he picks up and deploys the
repetitive French references to the 'English' in the scene preceding
Act IV, and this aids the process of erasing class divisions while promoting nationalism. But Branagh is not ultimately concerned to level
all class distinctions. In the Introduction to his printed adaptation,
he repeatedly discusses his film in contrast to Olivier's, claiming that

the latter's 'seeming nationalistic and militaristic emphasis had created a great deal of suspicion and doubt about the value of *Henry V* for a late twentieth-century audience' (p. 9). Branagh apparently congratulates himself for 'including some significant scenes that Olivier's film, for obvious reasons, had left out: in particular, the conspirators' scene ... the savage threat to the Governor of Harfleur where the king talks of possible rape and infanticide, a speech which underlines the crueller aspects of an increasingly desperate English military campaign' (p. 12). But the central Thatcherite foundation of Branagh's film, and his failure to deviate from Olivier's vision, lies exactly in his treatment of the *deviant*. In seemingly innocuous fashion Branagh claims that the play's advantages for the screen include 'a rich mixture of *low-life sleaze*, foreign sophistication, romance, action, philosophy and humour' (p. 10; emphasis mine). 'Low-life sleaze' refers to the activities of Pistol, Nym, and Bardolph. It is not so much the case that Branagh, in a departure from Shakespeare's text, programmatically excludes them from the 'band of brothers' as that he uses the 'three low-lifers' (p. 56) to define a militaristic brotherhood that includes every other Englishman in the film.

Despite the fact that Branagh effectively frames the treachery of three noblemen to Henry with the loyalty of 'three low-lifers' to Falstaff, and that he generates audience sympathy during the ghastly execution of Bardolph, the 'stage directions' to his adaptation indicate that Branagh is consistently concerned to foreground what he terms, in describing Henry's impending self-mystification of ceremonial kingship, 'the ever-present ache of his responsibility' (p. 91). When Henry, even in the words of Branagh's Introduction, 'stage-manages a public cashiering of the bosom friends who have been revealed as traitors' (p. 12), he does so 'with terrible sadness and grim resolution' (p. 41). When Henry damns Bardolph to execution, 'a public trial of strength is provided for the King. Watched by his sodden soldiers, he must enforce his decree that any form of theft or pillage of the French countryside will be punished by death. Any favouritism or sentiment shown here will be disastrous for discipline amongst these poor soldiers' (p. 71). If the 'cost to the King is enormous' (p. 71) and 'tears stain his cheeks' (p. 73), these are effects of the king's first or personal body, not his second or public one. Branagh seeks to combine the king's two bodies in a harmonious package, yet always by privileging what we in the late twentieth century ought to regard with deep suspicion – the old 'responsibility of kingship' or 'burden of leadership' idea that characterises traditional conservative criticism of Shakespearean drama as well as the public philosophy (or rather ideology) generated by ruling classes and their apologists. Such an ideology is useful in derailing interrogation of murderous militarism. Rulers have sometimes found it essential to 'busy giddy minds with foreign quarrels'.

Quite simply, *royal responsibility* and *militaristic brotherhood* are predicated on exclusion of the economically dispossessed, the 'low-lifers'. For example, with no immediate textual authority Branagh introduces the encounter between Pistol and the disguised king thus: 'The figure of a man rummaging through some bags in the shadows ... Pistol looks out from under the awning to check he isn't being seen before getting back to his thieving' (p. 83). Although Shakespeare's Pistol claims that he will be 'sutler' to the army and 'profits will accrue' (II.i.114–15) the language here suggests that he is on guard duty. Branagh's strategy involves making the 'low-lifers' lower than they really are, while simultaneously homogenising other characters into fraternal warriors. Branagh seems unaware that the entire *Henriad* is deeply implicated in Elizabethan debates over contemporary military abuses, specifically those committed by corrupt captains. Falstaff, irresponsibly given a company by Hal in *1 Henry IV*, engages in corrupt recruiting practices and manages to murder nearly all his men in order to steal their pay. Falstaff again participates in corrupt recruitment in *2 Henry IV*, but in a significant advance over Hal's connivance at military murder in the first play, Prince John is the active source of militaristic terror, despatching unwilling rebels even after their leaders have surrendered. In *Henry V* the captains do not fight, and Fluellen in particular endorses 'military discipline', including the martial law that was so murderous to Shakespeare's contemporaries. So, while Shakespeare's *Henriad* can be viewed as an indictment of the Elizabethan military system, Branagh strives to render the captains not simply dignified but heroic. In his diary entry for the Harfleur scene, he mentions the 'four national captains' and 'a marvellous sense of impending danger in the British ranks' (p. 229). In 1599 there was no 'Britain'; in fact, there was little sense of 'England', at least to all those men who refused to be incorporated in a national military draft and instead emphasised that their sole military duty was to the shire. On Branagh's version of the field of Agincourt, British militarism in a temporarily classless society – with the exception of the kind of 'low-lifers' increasingly seen in the streets and alleys of Thatcher's London – is embraced.

If the Ceremony speech is a private ideological construction that Branagh distorts in order to humanise Henry, the king's great speech to his troops on the morn of battle is a public ideological construction that allows the now humanised Henry to view his soldiers as a 'band of brothers' (p. 99). The mutuality of militarism that levels class distinctions requires throat-cutting. (Shakespeare's play has more references to the cutting of throats than any other play in the canon, thereby rendering *Henry V*, in the words of Macbeth, 'the best o' th' cut-throats'.) In the extensive battlefield scenes, often shot in slow motion, the English warriors – Henry himself, his nobles, captains, and common soldiers – engage the enemy in similar fashion. Here is part of Branagh's lengthy description: 'On the ground the captains and foot soldiers are ... fighting for their lives ... *Pistol* and *Nym* are found crawling through the mud, their concern not to fight the French but to pillage the bodies of the dead soldiers for valuables, as the battle rages round them. *Bates* is drowning a French soldier in one of the huge muddy puddles which have built up on the battlefield. *Williams* has taken on a huge Frenchman, but with superior sword work, slits the man's stomach. *Henry* is fighting ferociously, surrounded by French horsemen ... *Nym*, finding another body under some trees, is about to secure another purse, when he is stabbed in the back and slumps over the branches ... *York* is now on his feet and cornered. His assailants rush towards him, plunging their knives in as if sticking a pig. We return once more to the dead face of *Nym* who has been found by *Pistol*. The old man's anguish at the loss of his companion is uncontrollable' (pp. 104–5). There is no textual authority for Branagh's representation of Nym and Pistol as cowardly cutpurses on the battlefield. In fact, Shakespeare's first battle scene involves Pistol capturing a Frenchman, and, despite the Boy's commentary on Pistol's cowardice, the scene is rendered at least ambiguous by the text's direct allusion to the chronicle: when the French soldier kneels to Pistol, Shakespeare invokes Holinshed's 'Englishmen ... so busied in fighting and taking of the prisoners at hand ... many [Frenchmen] on their knees desired to have their lives saved' (Signet edn, pp. 196–7). Holinshed's Henry 'hoped it would so happen that the Frenchmen should be glad to common rather with the Englishmen for their ransoms, than the English to take thought for their deliverance' (p. 194). Shakespeare's Pistol thus engages in activity deemed acceptable not only in the chronicle but also in Elizabethan military practice. (Even Sir Francis Drake, the hero of '88, abdicated his primary naval responsibility and engaged in prize-taking during night-time pursuit of the Armada.) Shakespeare's Nym, like Bardolph, is hanged for theft by martial law. Branagh's Nym is stabbed in the back, in military terms the badge of cowardice.

If Branagh seeks to degrade the 'low-lifers' far more extensively than Shakespeare does, he simultaneously ennobles a character who, in Shakespeare's text, does no fighting whatsoever. In screen moments omitted from Branagh's description, Fluellen and Henry are each represented killing a French soldier in similar fashion: both are standing (i.e., not mounted), and both shots represent the English warrior pulling his sword out of a Frenchman in slow motion. Branagh thus equates Henry with Fluellen, and moments later solidifies this view by having the two men 'hug each other' after the battle (p. 111). The crucial message is encapsulated in the subsequent juxtapositions.

> As **Henry** leads **Fluellen** back into the camp, signalling to **Exeter** to follow them, we discover a very broken and battered **Pistol** beside a tree, contemplating his inevitably empty future.
>
> **Pistol** Doth fortune play the housewife with me now?
> News have I that my Nell is dead.
> Old I do wax, and from my weary limbs
> Honour is cudgelled.
> Well, bawd I'll turn,
> And something lean to cut-purse of quick hand.
> To England will I steal and there I'll ... steal.
>
> From this crumpled figure we cut to **Henry** as he sits down with **Exeter, Montjoy** and **Fluellen** beside him as the rest of the army gather around to listen.
>
> (pp. 111–12)

In his Introduction Branagh explains that he cut the leek scene because it is 'resoundingly unfunny' (p. 11), but he fails to mention that he deploys the end of that scene to cement one aspect of his ideological project. Shakespeare's Fluellen cudgels Pistol in a manner stageable either as a simple beating (the Elizabethan 'basti-nado') or a kind of ambush (the modern 'sucker-punch'). But in any case Shakespeare's scene is a personal confrontation stretching back to a personal insult. Branagh omits this scene and substitutes tableaux. Pistol's brief speech (which ought anyway to have instructed Branagh that Pistol is not currently a thief) is sandwiched between two visual moments intended to suggest the *enactment*, not just the *verbalisation*, of the military brotherhood: Henry, Exeter, and Fluellen – king, nobleman, and captain – walk off together and leave Pistol alone, excluded from the brotherhood. Then these men join 'the rest of the army' to solidify the message. 'Honour is cudgelled' from Pistol not for private cowardice but for public abdication of the responsibility to kill Frenchmen. Branagh cements his brotherhood of military honour by rendering Pistol a figure of dishonour. As a lonely 'low-life' coward whose friends are all dead, Pistol is not even allowed to remain a comic figure.

In other words Henry, 'brave York', Fluellen, and Williams – signifying king, nobility, captaincy, and commons – all fight heroically as a 'band of brothers'. Branagh levels all these types into 'warriors for the working-day' (p. 100), with the notable exclusion of Hal's former drinking-buddies. This ideological project involves increasing distortion of both text and history. Despite Branagh's willingness to include at least a version of all the unpleasant episodes before Act IV, scene i – Machiavellian prelates, Southampton, Harfleur – he now completely erases all such episodes that follow Act IV, scene i. Henry is not shown ordering the summary execution of all French prisoners (III.vi.36–7), and the 'martial law' (or glove) scene involving Henry, Williams, and Fluellen is almost completely cut (IV.viii). Branagh's version of this scene is a mere visual moment: 'As Henry stands up, the rest of the army begin to move out into the field beyond, some taking the bodies of the dead boys with them. He walks over to where *Williams* is standing and hands back the glove with which he had challenged him the night before. *Williams* takes the glove gratefully, then suddenly realises that the hooded figure with whom he argued was none other than *Henry* himself. Shaking his head in disbelief, he moves out with the others' (p. 113). Shakespeare's willingness to subvert the moment of Agincourt by invoking the ever-present Elizabethan policy of summary execution by martial law for even minor offences (IV.viii.44) is erased by Branagh's mutuality of militarism.

The ideological high point of the film is not the final wooing scene but Henry's trudge across the battlefield, 'one of the longest tracking shots in cinema history, Tarkovskian in its post-apocalyptic sweep':[7] 'As the "Non Nobis" continues, building into a crescendo of voices and orchestra, we remain with *Henry* and the dead *Boy* as he walks slowly and painfully through the carnage and wreckage of the battle' (p. 113). Branagh's choral 'Non Nobis' evokes the final moments of Olivier's film, in which the Bishop of Ely directs a boys' chorus. One could argue that Henry, a *dead* boy, and a chorus ironically emulate Olivier, but such an argument would miss Branagh's consistent deployment of religious symbols in his film. From the opening shot, in which the Chorus strolls through a film studio featuring a church pew juxtaposed with weaponry, Branagh emphasises the connection between Church and State (or religion and militarism). Given the representation of the politic prelates, who in the council scene thrust their faces uncomfortably close to the enthroned Henry and thereby recall Shakespeare's (and Olivier's) Richard III, standing ''tween two clergymen', it is possible to argue that Branagh critiques the play's reliance on piety. But Branagh's treatment of the 'sacred' parallels that of the 'secular'. There is a general movement from critical exposure to mystification. In the Southampton scene, for instance, Branagh fully exposes the stage-management of a secular event that simultaneously relies upon a cynical invocation of divine intervention. When Henry says 'God', there is no trace of religious feeling. Providence is simply used – as in the staging of numerous Elizabethan 'conspiracies' by Parry, Hacket, Lopez, Squire, etc. – to explain a purely political moment. 'The king hath note of all that they intend,/By interception which they dream not of' (p. 37). By filming Westmoreland looking 'through a spy-hole in a partition' (p. 36), Branagh nicely represents the reality of intelligence apparatuses (as opposed to Providence) for both ourselves and the Elizabethans.

On the eve of Agincourt, however, Branagh adds a solemn representation of religion to the encounter between Henry and the three common soldiers: 'He moves off towards them, as we hear the sound of confession being taken. *Michael Williams* finishes making his confession and joins two of the other soldiers' (p. 87). Branagh even includes the Latin blessing: 'In nomine patris, et filii, et spiritus sancti.' Significantly, Williams kneels and thereby submits to the sacred authority of the priest, and it is not coincidental that Branagh chooses to render this particular soldier as piously subservient. Williams subsequently raises the most subversive series of images in dialogue with the disguised king, of 'legs and arms and heads chopped off in a battle', of 'wives left poor' and 'children rawly left' (p. 89). Most crucially, 'if these men do not die well, it will be a black matter for the king that led them to it' (p. 90). Henry's lame retort to Williams's stark reverie fails to answer at least the secular or familial aspect of the accusation, but Henry's assertion that 'every subject's soul's his own' results in Williams's partial intellectual submission: ''Tis certain, every man that dies ill,/the ill upon his own head; the king is/not to answer it' (p. 90). The hooded Henry, reminiscent of a medieval religious figure, thus gains the same kind of submission to authority that Williams had given to the priest. The implicit message is that commoners must not think for themselves but yield to authority, whether sacred or secular. As if to solidify this message, Branagh stages additional gratuitous piety immediately before the battle: 'Henry leads his men as they go down on their knees to cross themselves and kiss the ground upon which they will fight. A final prayer' (p. 101).

A common-sense response to these moments might be 'well, there are no atheists in foxholes', but such a response would over-look the sheer gratuitousness of Branagh's religious symbols. It is the modern Branagh, not the Renaissance Shakespeare, who chooses to stress that the suitably pious are rewarded with provi-dentially sanctioned military slaughter. This is not an anti-war film, but a glorification of male bonding through divinely endorsed blood-letting. An anti-war film would have stressed the cowardice of the captains, especially Fluellen, who compels the 'low-lifers' to attack the Harfleur breach while retreating to a position of relative safety and attempting to engage Macmorris in 'a few disputations' concerning the 'military discipline' (III.ii.96ff). An anti-war film would have discovered a way to represent how Henry's troops have been decimated by the conditions of medieval (and Elizabethan) campaigns – 'Sorry am I his numbers are so few,/His soldiers sick, and famished in their march' (III.v.56–7). An anti-war film would not have sentimentalised Henry in the final scene, which renders him, through flashbacks, a man of tender memory (vs the Henry who says, in an earlier flashback, 'I know thee not, old man') and a boyish wooer. As Branagh reveals, 'I wanted to make him as human as possible, but as vulnerable as possible.' The problem is that Shakespeare's Henry is precisely inhuman and invulnerable. Branagh tries to capture the 'unsettled inner man', but there is no inner man to capture.[8] This is not Hamlet but Fortinbras, a man willing to fight for nothing, as the choral Epilogue so ironically suggests. Shakespeare's Henry is a cold-blooded killer concerned to busy giddy minds with foreign quarrels by seizing upon the thinnest of pretexts as *casus belli*. Mass slaugh-ter is the result.

III

On one level Branagh's second Henry V *is* an 'impersonation' of
Prince Charles, constituting reciprocation for the prince's involvement in promoting Branagh's career. In Anthony Holden's biography
we learn that Prince Charles encountered opposition before his in-
vestiture as Prince of Wales at Caernarvon – '"Go home, Charlie";
"You're not too brilliant, are you?"; "You got into university on just
two A levels"' – and spent some six years in the British military, in
which 'there was the camaraderie of life in the services, which made
him more genuinely than at any other time in his life "one of the
boys"'.[9] In this context we can understand why Branagh made the
Welsh Fluellen and Henry V such pals, and why warfare is represented as a form of male bonding. But on a larger and darker level
Branagh's *Henry V* appeals viscerally to a significant percentage of its
audience. Branagh released his film through Samuel Goldwyn 'on the
eve of Veterans' Day in America', coinciding 'with the 75th and 50th
anniversaries of the outbreaks of the First and Second World Wars'.
He claims that his 'great desire was to make it look like a film of
today, to take the curse of medievalism off it, so that the *Batman* audiences could conceivably be persuaded to see it'.[10] The film is thus
directed at least as much to a popular American as a British audience,
and it arrives at the historical moment of what we might call,
borrowing from Susan Jeffords, the 'Remasculinisation of America'.[11]
A plethora of pro-military films, countless TV commercials featuring
military themes such as the troop-like discipline of fast-food workers,
even a morning aerobics show called 'Basic Training' – in which a
svelte woman leads men and women in work-outs framed by US military hardware such as ships or helicopters – all attest to the relentless
militarisation of American culture. Branagh's film speaks to contemporary culture precisely because it follows a crude 'Ramboesque' line
of development, almost as though all the *Rambo* films were collapsed
into *Henry V*: Johnny Rambo human and vulnerable, then insulted
and attacked, hence violent; Rambo on the offensive against all odds;
Rambo betrayed by his own side; Rambo killing huge numbers of
Russians and Vietnamese, with the help of sickly POWs, and sustaining few casualties. The only element missing is Rambo (successfully)
in love.

Writing this essay in the aftermath of what the Bush Administration
called 'Operation: Desert Storm', it is both haunting and uncanny
how the seemingly miraculous English casualty rate in *Henry V*

matches the casualty disjuncture occasioned by technological slaughter in the Middle East. On the eve of the slaughter Bush called for a national day of prayer, and in the aftermath, in Glasgow Cathedral, Queen Elizabeth and Prince Philip joined Margaret Thatcher in a supposedly solemn memorial service. During her subsequent American tour, Queen Elizabeth conferred an honorary knighthood on General Norman Schwarzkopf, commander of the Allied forces. Branagh's film is ultimately Thatcherite, spawned by a decade that featured the resurgence of Anglo-American hegemony founded upon massive military expenditures and a cold willingness to deploy overwhelming force combined with technological superiority against virtually defenceless Third World nations. English victory in the Falklands War, partially enabled by US intelligence, and events such as the Grenada invasion were mere warm-ups for strategic terrorisation, aka Bush's 'New World Order'. The 1989 Panama operation followed hard upon the 1989 FMLN offensive in the streets of San Salvador and the murder of six Jesuit professors by US-backed troops, and preceded the 'elections' in a Nicaragua decimated by a decade of US-sponsored civil war. Who can doubt that the blitzkrieg of Panama functioned to terrorise all of Central America and, indeed, an entire hemisphere still conceived as a 'sphere of interest'? After all, El Salvador, Nicaragua, and Guatemala alone have been the site of around 200,000 casualties – mostly civilian, many the result of butchery by right-wing military and death squads – since 1979–80, or the period featuring the revival of 'conservatism' in England and America under Thatcher and Reagan. The ongoing Cambodianisation of Iraq renders the Middle East not different from but grimly analogous to South-east Asia in the 1960s and '70s. Vietnam was a limited military loss but a huge political win for US foreign policy precisely because an entire region was terrorised and subdued: the Communist PKI was literally wiped out in Indonesia at an estimated cost of some 500,000 lives, and Cambodia was so destabilised that its successive regimes engaged in genocide. Vietnam itself has never recovered from its battle against neo-colonialism. Throughout the 1980s the 'special relationship' between Britain and the US has been characterised by the British government's absolute willingness to support the brutal policies of its imperial heir.

Divinely endorsed militarism is probably the most potent defence for a culture's unwillingness to acknowledge its complicity in holocaustal slaughter. Thus Branagh's *Henry V* seeks to excuse militarism by manufacturing a Christian context, and modern vile politicians put a Christian gloss on mass murder. Branagh claims that he wanted to create a 'truly popular film' (p. 220), but unless he is thoroughly dense about modern America, he must understand that the United States is a culture of violence, in the 1980s especially prone to the revival of military violence. Young American men who constitute a large percentage of cinema audiences (and British too, I suspect) do not flee in horror from representations of gratuitous butchery. They revel in it. By choosing to emulate the young Olivier through a male-dominated militaristic play – rather than the even younger Olivier of *As You Like It*, a comedy that gives women and romance a central role – Branagh makes a film that appeals to American and British citizens, the majority of whom subsequently supported techno-slaughter in the Middle East.

While the Irish Republican Army – heroically or unheroically, depending on one's judgement of centuries of ongoing atrocities occasioned by England's desire to dominate Ireland – lobs shells at 10 Downing Street from the vicinity of the spot where Charles I was decapitated, the Northern Irish Protestant Branagh signals his artistic subservience to Thatcherite ideology in a film far less justifiable, and hence far more suspicious, than Oliver's.

From *Critical Quarterly*, 33:4 (1991), 95–111.

NOTES

[Breight's essay is one of a number of responses to Branagh's 1989 *Henry V* which dispute its ostensibly liberal and progressive credentials as an 'anti-war' film. Like Peter Donaldson, whose essay on Branagh he cites, Breight adopts a psychobiographical approach to his subject. Branagh's account of his consultation with Prince Charles is seen to underpin his portrayal of Henry, as are conflicts generated by his efforts to move from a Protestant Irish working-class background into the English cultural establishment. The result is a film which is deeply divided and ambivalent, but nonetheless ultimately subservient to Thatcherite and militarist ideology. In a polemical conclusion, Brieght suggests a number of historical and cultural factors that may well account for the popularity of Branagh's film. Quotations from *Henry V* in this essay are from the Signet edition, ed. John Russell Brown (New York, 1965). Ed.]

1. Peter Donaldson, 'Taking on Shakespeare: Kenneth Branagh's *Henry V*', *Shakespeare Quarterly*, 42 (1991), 61, 62–3, 71. Donaldson's essay on Olivier constitutes the first chapter of his *Shakespearean Films/Shakespearean Directors* (Boston, 1990). For citations of Branagh's film see *William Shakespeare, Henry V: A*

Screen Adaptation by Kenneth Branagh (London, 1989). All citations will be by page number in the main body of the text.

2. See Kenneth Branagh, *Beginning* (London, 1989), p. 236. All further citations of Branagh's autobiography will be by page number in the main body of the text.

3. Machiavelli, *The Prince*, trans. George Bull (Harmondsworth, 1981), pp. 96, 101.

4. R. B. Wernham, *After the Armada: Elizabethan England and the Struggle for Western Europe, 1588–1595* (Oxford, 1984), p. 407.

5. Sir John Smythe, *Certain Discourses Military* (1590); Matthew Sutcliffe, *The Practice, Proceedings, and Lawes of Armes* (1593); Thomas and Dudley Digges, *Foure Paradoxes* (1604).

6. Thomas Cartelli, 'Ideology and Subversion in the Shakespearean Set Speech', *ELH*, 53 (1986), 9–10.

7. Graham Fuller, 'Two Kings', *Film Comment*, 25 (1989), p. 6.

8. Ibid., p. 7.

9. Anthony Holden, *Prince Charles* (New York, 1979), pp. 166, 202.

10. Fuller, 'Two Kings', pp. 2, 6.

11. See Susan Jeffords, *The Remasculinisation of America: Gender and the Vietnam War* (Bloomington, IN, 1989).

8

A Post-National European Cinema: A Consideration of Derek Jarman's *The Tempest* and *Edward II*

COLIN MacCABE

In some senses it is almost impossible to question the notion of European culture; the two terms seem to necessarily define each other. But this definition of culture is specifically European: it relates to the great national cultures of Europe and to their founding fathers, the Dantes, Shakespeare and Goethes. But you only have to sit, as I have sat, in conferences on Europe with Europeans whose forebears come from the Caribbean or from the South Asian continent to realise how pointless such a litany can sound, how far removed those national cultures are from the contemporary realities of multinational and multi-ethnic Europe. The real question is, how are we to understand the founding moments of those great national cultures in conjunction with a Europe whose other founding moment has come back to haunt it? If we think back to that period in the sixteenth century when Western Europe expanded to asset-strip the globe, what comes back in the twentieth century is the fundamental asset of labour which is now imported to service late capitalism.

The problem is that if we wish to grasp the reality of this moment it becomes difficult to know, or to understand, how we can define it as specifically European. In the movement from the sixteenth to the twentieth century we pass from a European to a global perspective, a perspective which demands that we analyse contemporary culture in terms of an imperialist imposition of authoritative norms which are then contested, negotiated, mimicked in the crucial emphases of our post-modernity. But that post-modernity would seem to have no more time for European than for national cultures as the crucial terms become the global and the local.

It might seem that we can short-circuit these theoretical difficulties by appealing to a practical political level at which European culture makes sense. Independently of the particular political rows about the single currency, or the powers of the European Commission, the European Community is becoming an ever-increasing political reality, and it is that political reality which is increasingly part of any European cultural agenda. It is such pragmatic realities which dominate much of our institutional concerns at the British Film Institute and have dominated the multitude of conferences on Europe which this theatre has hosted. And these concerns and conferences are not without their successes. The MEDIA 95 programme proliferates, growing new arms like a monster from a fifties sci-fi movie. But it is when one reflects on an initiative like MEDIA 95 that one realises that there is no real way to short-cut the theoretical problems by appeals to political reality. All the discussions around Media 95 make two massive cultural assumptions: the first is that American cinema is a cultural threat, and the second, as a necessary corollary, is that there is some evident meaning to the notion of European cinema and European culture. Within such forums any attempts to raise genuine questions about European culture are treated both as impertinent and irrelevant. Impertinent because we all know what European culture is, irrelevant because we must eschew such intellectual levity for the realistic rigours of 'policy'. In fact, almost all appeals to 'policy', like its repellent semantic cousin 'management', are appeals away from a reality which is too various and too demanding. But it is the cultural reality of Europe which must be faced, and faced urgently, if we are not to bungle the enormous possibilities offered by the growing movement towards political unification.

To understand our current cultural situation, it is my own deep belief that one must step into the 'dark backward abysm of time'. These are the words that Prospero uses at the beginning of *The Tempest* as he reveals to his daughter the world beyond their island. The world that we need to understand is not the Milanese court and its intrigues, which Prospero addresses, but the cultural space of the Elizabethan and Jacobean theatre which Prospero and Miranda inhabit. The film-maker who has been most preoccupied with this historical reality is Derek Jarman ever since, in *Jubilee*, the magus John Dee escorted Elizabeth I on a tour of her kingdom four hundred years on. For Jarman the investigation of what it is to be English is inseparable from a reworking of the controlling myths of the English Renaissance. Three years after *Jubilee*, Jarman made his own version of *The Tempest*.

Let us start with Shakespeare's version. The play starts eponymously with a tempest and a consequent shipwreck. The ship carrying the King of Naples back from the wedding of his daughter to an African (itself an interesting fact in the light of the play's concerns) is separated from its flotilla and wrecked on an island. The wreck itself divides the passengers and crew: Ferdinand, the heir, finds himself alone; the nobles form one group and the crew, with the exception of Trinculo, are confined to the ship and kept there for the duration of the play. It is at this point that we learn from Prospero, the magician who rules the island, the history of the island, or rather the history of his arrival and conquest of the island. He disposes of the former ruler of the island, the witch Sycorax, frees her captive Ariel, the airy spirit, who is then bound to him for twelve years (a period which will coincide with the end of the play), and enslaves her son Caliban, this 'thing of earth'. The play then pursues two sub-plots in which the nobles plot against the king and Caliban conspires with Trinculo to overthrow Prospero, while the main theme follows the courtship of Ferdinand and Miranda, all these events obsessively supervised by Prospero with the help of his spy Ariel.

While the play may seem entirely European, set in the Mediterranean, its source is not (as for almost all of Shakespeare's other work) a European story but a contemporary event in the Caribbean. In 1609, while sailing off Bermuda, an expedition led by Sir Thomas Gates was caught in a tempest, his ship was separated from the rest, and he was presumed lost. A year later Gates arrived in Virginia, having spent the intervening year on a magical island, which furnished the survivors with all they needed to eat and drink. It is from this contemporary story that Shakespeare actually weaves his tale. In this context it becomes clear that the problematic of *The Tempest* is the problematic of the relationship between Europe and the New World which had only been discovered a century before and was in the process of colonial appropriation. Caliban is not simply this 'thing of earth', the savage man who has a long history in European thought, but also an anagram of his own name: the cannibal, the inhabitant of this new world. Prospero's relationship with him is evidently, among other things, an allegory of Europe's relation with the New World.

It is fashionable at the moment, in the current jargon of post-coloniality, to read *The Tempest* entirely in relation to Caliban, to stress the extent to which one must understand the play as Shakespeare's meditation on the particular way in which the colonial is constituted as what is not civilised but then, in a complicated and reciprocal moment, is considered to be that which defines civilisation. In the contemporary critical climate this is defined as the political reading. From this point of view Jarman's *Tempest* is an embarass-ment, for his Caliban is white and the concerns of colonialism are largely absent from his film. But these contemporary readings ignore another, and as important, political reading which concentrates on the formation of the new nation-states which will dominate global history for the next four centuries. Explicitly, these concerns are present in *The Tempest* in terms of the politics of the court of Milan. Jarman rigorously excludes all such concerns from his film.

In *The Tempest*, however, he makes clear how Prospero's reign is one of terror. It was, not that long ago, fashionable to imagine the Elizabethan age as one of social harmony. More recently, and in the wake of the new historicism, political divisions have been un-derstood as contained by cultural power. What both ignore are the twin foundations of the Elizabethan terror state, torture and espi-onage. If one wants to think of London at that time then what I always think of first are the gates, the walls of the city, outside which are the theatres along with the brothels and the new facto-ries, but mounted on which are the bleeding quarters of those who have just been executed – noted by contemporary Protestant tourists to London as signs of England's civilisation. The crucial element in this machinery of terror was Walsingham's secret service, and we can read Ariel in *The Tempest* as an allegory of that secret service, forced under pitiless conditions to spy on every corner of the island and to bring to his master Prospero that infor-mation which underpins his power. It is for this reason that Jarman's *Tempest* concentrates on the relationship between Prospero and Ariel with its barely supressed sexual undertones. Jarman's homosexuality is what leads him to concentrate on the repression at the heart of the English state from which all the other repressions follow. The complete containment of sexuality within sanctified heterosexual marriage, the rigorous policing of desire and excess, the focusing of male sexuality and the denial of female sexuality. These are the fundamental themes of *The Tempest*, the sexual politics which underpin the birth of capitalism as it appropriates its colonial surplus.

But Jarman clearly understands, even more clearly in his art than in his discourse, how this sexuality is linked to certain traditions of representation. For if the security apparatus is the skeleton of the state, then the new national culture is the flesh. At the heart of this culture is a rigorous divorce between representation and audience. The traditional, and much mocked, reading of *The Tempest* is that it is autobiographical, that Prospero is Shakespeare and that when Prospero at the end says that 'every third thought shall be my grave', it is Shakespeare's own voice that we should hear as he bids adieu to his audience. In fact, if that traditional autobiographical account is placed within the wider context of theatrical history then it once again becomes very plausible. The theatre in which Shakespeare started to work at the beginning of the 1590s and in which Marlowe was already the transgressive star was a very different theatre from that to which he bid farewell in 1611. Not only was it more directly popular and addressed a much wider social audience but it was also one which posed direct political and cultural threats to the state. By the time he wrote *The Tempest*, Shakespeare was writing for a representational space which was much more contained both aesthetically and socially. That is the crucial point of the masque that Prospero puts on for the lovers in Act IV, the masque that will celebrate their wedding. In his instructions to Ferdinand and Miranda, his attempts to control them as they sit, his order that 'No tongue! all eyes! be silent', Prospero reproduces the new relationship to the audience, a relationship where without tongues, reduced to vision, the audience is excluded from the representational space. It is this space, directly filiated to an aristocratic culture, which disinherits the popular traditions on which Shakespeare had drawn so contradictorily. The biographical nature of the farewell comes in the recognition of what has been repressed and disinherited.

It is the fracturing of that representational space which makes *The Tempest* such a subversive film, for it sets itself not on an island but in a ruined aristocratic house, an imperial monument. If the viewer grasps that this is a house, there is no way in which he or she can organise the space that is presented. We cannot connect room to room or inside to outside. And, as if to make the point even more explicit, Caliban is played by Jack Birkett, the blind actor. It is this Caliban's blindness which places him categorically outside Prospero's cultural space. But if we can understand Jarman's undoing of the space of *The Tempest*, if we can see him using the cinema to undo the rigid distinctions of culture and sexuality which *The Tempest* so brilliantly performs, we must also admit that, in many ways, and whatever the borrowings from the popular culture of the twentieth century, it remains caught within that exclusive cultural space that it seeks to undermine. Brecht's 'fundamental reproach' to the cinema was that it could never escape that divorce between representation and audience which he termed 'Aristotelian' but which is more properly understood in terms of the Renaissance theatre.

In the aftermath of *The Tempest*, one could be left wondering where this filmic subversion of the relation between representation and audience could ever do more than endlessly interrogate itself. Jarman's disruption of cinematic space (in terms of costumes, sets, and articulation of shots and scenes) seems to invite (like so many leftist critiques) a nostalgic Utopia in which the ideal is a carnivalesque union of audience and representation, a return to a moment before any of the divisions of labour on which capitalism constructs itself. That carnival is, of course, realised for Jarman in the super-8 films of the 70s, but they remain irredeemably private, films which can only be truly enjoyed (as in their original screenings) by an audience entirely composed of their actors.

The counterpart of this personal privacy is the absence of any real public political sphere in *The Tempest*. Jarman excises the power politics of the kingdoms of Naples and Milan, but the film is then left in a curious vacuum in which the critique of representation and sexuality remains curiously unanchored. Jarman triumphantly solves this problem in *Edward II* when the political plot is made to turn (and turn even more emphatically in Jarman's version than Marlowe's) on direct sexual repression. *Edward II* would seem to mark a final settling of accounts with Jarman's chosen historical space: that interface between the Renaissance and the present which was first unveiled by John Dee in *Jubilee* and which has been investigated again and again, in *The Tempest*, in *The Angelic Conversation*, in *Caravaggio*. But all these films fade into 'prentice works beside the achievement of *Edward*. Christopher Hobbs's sets and Sandy Powell's costumes triumphantly realise what one now sees was only hinted at in *Caravaggio* (and Italy may always have been a diversion): a world which is always both now and then (both twentieth and sixteenth century) but is always England. At its heart is the constitutive relation which founds the modern English state on a repressive security apparatus and a repressed homosexuality. Jarman makes all these arguments with the deftness and lightness of a painter's hand. From the moment that Mortimer appears with the dress and bearing of an SAS officer in Northern Ireland, the equations between past and present, between state and sexuality, are clearly visible on the screen.

Jarman's *Edward* continues a debate about national and sexual identity which goes back four centuries to that moment at the beginning of the 1590s when the Elizabethan stage became the privileged symbolic space for a whole society. The exact date of Marlowe's play might seem of interest only to the most pedantic of scholars but, in fact, it is crucial to the play's significance that it comes right at the end of Marlowe's career, probably in 1592. Crucial, both personally and culturally, for by 1592 Marlowe was a man deeply engaged not only with the Elizabethan theatre but also with that other alternative employment for a man of letters who did not want to join the church or to occupy the position of learned scholar in a great lord's house: he was deeply implicated in the modern foundations of the Elizabethan state – Walsingham's secret service.

Culturally the play can be seen as a direct response to Marlowe's new rival Shakespeare whose trilogy *Henry VI* had attempted to produce a version of English history which would find ethical and political meaning in the bloody shambles which had produced the Tudor dynasty. Marlowe's response is that of the arrogant intellectual who has known the pleasures of both political and sexual transgression. There is no meaning to be deduced from these chronicles of blood and treachery, except Mortimer's wheel of fortune (a sixteenth-century version of Ford's dictum that 'History is bunk' but with none of that twentieth-century tycoon's optimism), and to emphasise the nihilism Marlowe places a perverse love at the centre of his story. But for Marlowe this perversity is very closely linked to the new learning from which he draws his own legitimacy. There is absolutely no warrant in the chronicles for turning Gaveston and Spenser into intellectual parvenus. Edward's minions they may have been, but they were as well born as Mortimer and the other barons. For Marlowe they represent the new class, of which he is a prominent member, who will sell their learning to the new state but will, in the end, be crushed by that very same state. It is Gaveston's and not Edward's death which uncannily foreshadows Marlowe's own end, that great reckoning in a small room when Ingram Frisar, almost certainly with the Privy Council's blessing, stabbed Marlowe days before he was to appear before that same Council to answer charges of blasphemy. Four hundred years on, Marlowe's death remains no less of a mystery but it is not unreasonable to speculate (as has become wearingly and repetitively obvious in our own century) that political and sexual secrets make the most likely of bedfellows and that in an age when sodomy was a capital offence there may have been more than one member of the Council who was concerned that Marlowe's testimony might end with a lethal outing.

Jarman's film is not, however, Marlowe's play. Marlowe's identification with new knowledge and learning of the Renaissance gets no response from the director ('such an intellectual queen', as Jarman remarks in a marginal note to the script), and Derek's Gaveston and Spenser are not overlearned smart young men working for M15 but very rough trade indeed. What Jarman has always insisted on is that he be recognised for what he is, and *Edward II* is, in that sense, unquestionably his most autobiographical work in what has been a consistently autobiographical *oeuvre*. But it is the bovine, middle-class ox Edward that Jarman identifies with, not the street-smart Gaveston whom he loves but who is here presented without redeeming feature except that 'he loves me more than all the world'. The film is also much more unambiguous in its misogyny than ever before. In that gay dialectic where identification with the position of the woman is set against rejection of the woman's body, *Edward II* is entirely, and without any textual foundation, on the side of rejection. For Marlowe, as for his age, the love of boys is merely the ultimate sexual transgression, not in any sense an alternative to heterosexual sex. It is here that Jarman does violence to his source, making Edward's passion for Gaveston a consequence of his inability to be roused by the queen's body, a truly chilling scene at the beginning of the film. This is itself horribly overtrumped at the end, however, by the murder of Kent when Tilda Swinton's magnificent Isabella literally tears the life out of him with her teeth; every fantasy of the castrating woman, the *vagina dentata*, rendered into all too palpable image.

But there is love in this film, and a love which redeems history. The film is punctuated by scenes from the end of the play as Edward and his murderer-to-be, Lightborn, discourse in the bowels of the castle where the king is imprisoned. We await throughout the film the fabled end, the vicious poker which will leave a king dead and humiliated and without a mark on him. It is this end that the film has prepared us for as we see the homophobia which courses as a vicious lifeblood through our history and our culture. No fault of Gaveston's can possibly excuse or justify the hatred which is spat out at him as he is forced through a gauntlet of hatred on his way to exile and a death unbearable in its explosion of destructive violence. As Mortimer comes to upbraid the king for his moral turpitude, the barons at his back suddenly reveal themselves as a moral majority stretching back and forth across the centuries, an endless, and endlessly unpleasant, Festival of Light.

But after the end that Marlowe and history has prepared us for, Jarman has contrived a happy end from the resources of his own fight against death. As Lightborn approaches the king for a second time with the dreaded poker in his hand, it falls from his hands and in a moment of real tenderness he bends and kisses the king. With this kiss a whole history of homophobia and violence is annulled, a whole new history becomes possible.

It is at this point that *Edward II* becomes possible, drawing the audience into the most private of worlds, not merely as spectator but as participant (and in this respect the published screenplay is an integral part of the film). The Outrage slogans which punctuate the text, like the film itself, demand reaction. It is in the multiplication of the forms of address around the text that Jarman provides a solution to Brecht's 'fundamental reproach'. For Brecht, the theatrical setting is still a unity, the alienation devices simply fragment that unity from within. Jarman, here working with the grain of advanced capitalism, breaks the unity of the cinema experience from without. The celebrity interview, that crucial tool of marketing, is here turned into a method of disrupting any separation of public and private, and thus depriving the moment of viewing of any simple aesthetic unity.

It is this multiplication of address, and its refusal of the divorce between public and private, which enables Jarman to solve the problems of *The Tempest* in *Edward II*. The private is made public and, as a result, the public sphere can be incorporated into the film. The state, which disappears from his *Tempest*, is now centre stage but that stage can also be the most public proponents of the abolition of privacy, the militants of Outrage. It is not, I think, unreasonable to suggest that it is the pressure of death, that unique meeting of the public and private, that has been the catalyst for the extraordinary experiments that have marked the last five years of Jarman's work. This is signalled within the film itself when, as the screen dims, the final lines, which are Jarman's rather than Edward's or Marlowe's, are:

> Come death, and with thy fingers close my eyes,
> Or if I live let me forget myself.

It is striking at this point, and in the context of the politics of any future European film, to compare Jarman's film with Branagh's *Henry V*. *Henry V* is a crucial play for Shakespeare – both the final answer to the problems that Marlowe had posed him seven years earlier in *Edward II* and the first play in the new Globe theatre. The power politics with which the bishops open the play is transcended by the national divinity which Henry represents. And the final farewell to an older cultural space is witnessed in the death of Falstaff, standing in for Will Kemp's (the great clown who had embodied Falstaff) refusal to join the new company. It can come as a surprise only to those who refuse to understand the links between sexuality and representation that it is in this play that the formal mastering of the female body is accomplished by the naming of Katherine's body in English and her marriage to the English king. It says a lot about the sheer bad taste of Branagh's film that his idea of taking licence with the text is to have Falstaff appear in flashback and to rehearse the famous Chimes at Midnight speech (which only makes sense as a conversation between two old men) as a dialogue between Hal and Falstaff. But this is all of a piece with the cultural nostalgia of Branagh's project (which is exactly captured in the name of his company). The Renaissance theatre will now use the cinema to reproduce the Elizabethan stage shorn of all its contradictions. What in Olivier's magnificent film is the cultural corollary of the last tragic moment of the English state (extinguishing its own empire in the fight against Fascist Germany) becomes in Branagh's tepid offering the farcical analogue of Thatcher's hideous mimicry of Churchill. Jarman's use of his Renaissance model has absolutely nothing to do with Branagh's. *Edward II* (as in Olivier's *Henry V*) is placed at the service of pressing contemporary concerns. Unlike

Olivier, however, Jarman's film responds to both public and private need and calls the very distinction into question.

I think that these reflections should enable us to understand something of the specificity of European film. What is specific to Europe, within a global context which emphasises the local and the international, is the question of the nation-state. It is no accident that Jarman never hesitates to stress his cultural conservatism, for what he returns to, again and again, are the founding myths of Englishness. Jarman, it could be argued, is trying to rescue, from underneath the monument of the nation, the last ethnic minority – the English. It is exactly the release of these buried ethnicities which constitutes the reality and risks of European culture and politics today. This is not to say that there is no question of cultural pre-scriptivism, that all European film-makers should now address the question of the nation. What it does say is that in so far that European film-makers make films that are specifically European, those films will focus on the reality of national identities and the possibilities that are contained in their transgression.

From *Screening Europe: Image and Identity in Contemporary European Cinema*, ed. Duncan Petrie (London, 1992), pp. 9–18.

NOTES

[In this essay, which was originally presented at a British Film Institute conference on the subject of cinema and national identity, Colin MacCabe offers readings of Jarman's versions of *The Tempest* and Marlowe's *Edward II* which draw upon postcolonial theory, new historicism, and gender studies to explore the films' complex negotiations between the historical provenance of the texts and their contemporary reproduction. Contrasting the plays' original conditions of production with the assertively contemporary style of the films, MacCabe traces a dialectical relationship between the early modern and the postmodern in Jarman's work, paying particular attention to the role of sexuality in the formation of English national and cultural identities. Invoking poststructuralist terms of reference (as does Catherine Belsey above in essay 3), MacCabe concludes his reading of *Edward II* with the suggestion that Jarman's non-realist and anachronistic mode of representation renders it an open, multiple text. Ed.]

9

Katherina Bound; or, Play(K)ating the Strictures of Everyday Life

BARBARA HODGDON

I

When Kate delineates a wife's duties to 'her loving lord' within a hierarchical configuration of marriage, Shakespeare's *Taming of the Shrew* ends in a 'frenzy of the social', putting on offer an image of 'woman' that the play's male characters use as a means of speaking to one another about themselves. As one among many texts, non-dramatic as well as dramatic, that participate in a conversation about the organisation of sexual difference in early modern England, *Shrew* demonstrates precisely the 'fine surge of historical intelligibility' that Roland Barthes attributes to Sade's writing.[1] Today, the anxiety over gender roles and attributes that characterised *Shrew*'s original historical moment is once again the focus of intense cultural negotiation. Given the increasing difficulty of standing outside the containments and contradictions of representation and history, *Shrew*'s obsessive attempt to circumscribe woman's 'place' has especially fatal attractions for late-twentieth-century feminist readers and spectators.

What are the conditions of readability for a play in which the 'problem' of woman is not her exclusion but her radical inclusion? Reading *Shrew* against the grain to resist its heavily gendered stereotyping has certain limitations. After all, if this particular play

can be reconfigured progressively, why should its seemingly co-
ercive no-choice politics matter? My interest lies in mapping the tra-
jectory of the grain, in rethinking how *Shrew* not only manipulates
its textual subjects but gets caught up and shaped, at particular historical moments, to secure or contest the sociocultural subjectivities
at work in women's lives. I explore a layered reading of *Shrew*'s
continuing cultural renewal as a popular pleasure, first, by unpack-
ing several texts that lurk in its margins and, then, by considering a
number of film and video performances. By multiplying the texts
that adhere to Shakespeare's play and paying special, though not
exclusive, attention to the ending, I want to extend the questions
Shrew raises. What figures of 'woman's' position in the order of
things does it make available? to whom are they addressed? and
what purposes do they serve? What I propose is akin to Michel de
Certeau's 'poaching', which Henry Jenkins characterises as 'an impertinent raid on [a canonical] preserve that takes away only those
things that seem useful or pleasurable to the reader'.[2] Insofar as
such plundering is a figure for rape, that metaphor suits the 'over-
reading' with which I wish to begin – the 'reading in excess' that
goes beyond 'acceptable' structures of representation.[3]

Noting traces of sadistic violence in *Shrew*'s taming plot, Shirley
Nelson Garner sees the play as a spectacle of dominance mapped
out on a (cross-dressed) female body and concluding with a
woman's abject submission to male mastery.[4] Moreover, the
Induction – with its 'wanton pictures', images of hunt-and-chase violence, and erotic Ovidian lures of near rape (Ind.i.43, ii.45–56) –
incorporates what Linda Williams terms the most distinguishable
feature of sadomasochistic fantasy: 'the education of one person in
the sexual fantasy of another through complex role-playing cued to
works of art and imagination'.[5] Elsewhere, too, *Shrew* evokes the
classic pornographic repertoire. The image of Bianca tied and
bound, at the mercy of Kate the torturer (II.i), hints at a mild 'sadie-
max' lesbian fantasy; and at the 'taming school', which editors
often locate in a 'country house' reminiscent of remote Sadean terri-
tories, Petruchio displaces his sadistic fantasies by humiliating his
servants and by verbally (in the theatre, literally) dismembering
Kate's dress (IV.ii.3). However playfully *Shrew* suspends sado-
masochism in fantasy, it shares affinities with pornographic films in
'relentlessly repropos[ing] sexuality as the field of knowledge and
power [and] woman as scene, rather than subject, of sexuality'.[6]

Ultimately, however, this exercise in 'aesthetic sadomasochism' concerns its characters' relation to and use of sadomasochistic images to negotiate their shifting sexual identities.[7] While the phallus articulates meaning and difference symbolically, *Shrew* collapses the sexual into the social to keep 'verité' sex just beyond representation. [...]

II

Just as 'woman', in her mixed functions of activity and passivity, most interests the genre of heterosexual pornography, so does this oscillation between dominance and submission interest the Elizabethan comedy of remarriage called *Shrew*. In its Elizabethan guise, played out on a stage that 'takes boys for women',[8] the play can be imagined as particularly multivalent: 'pleasing stuff', says Sly, that 'let[s] the world slip' (Ind.ii.134, 138). The Induction not only authorises such slippage within class as well as gender (at the Lord's will, as a joke on Sly) but teaches that there is no such thing as a discrete sexed or classed identity. Such identifications, *Shrew*'s frame insists, are themselves constructed in fluid relation to fictional 'others'. In the taming plot, gender codes move with equal ease across the boy actor's androgynous presence and the adult player's male body. On at least three occasions, the space of 'woman-shrew' is doubly occupied, doubly gendered: when Petruchio outdresses Kate at her wedding and turns ceremony to carnival (III.ii) and when he assumes a shrewish guise, first, on the journey to his house ('By this reckoning he is more shrew than she', remarks Curtis [IV.i.63]), and, later, with his servants and with the haberdasher and tailor (IV.i; IV.iii). Yet however bizarre his behaviour, Petruchio, like the boy actor who plays Kate's role, can move between masculine and feminine positions because his own subjectivity is never at risk. On the one hand, such cross-coding disperses 'shrewness' and the attendant social anxieties onto the male body; on the other, it hollows out the category 'woman' and suggests that no unified model of female subjectivity exists, while contradictorily affirming shrewness as *the* ground of feminine representation. For by the play's 'law', shrewness must be seen and spoken as feminine: only when Kate slips out from under the sign of the shrew and moves toward that of the phallus can 'she' be admired as a spectacle ('a wonder', according to Lucentio [v.ii.189]) and given a serious hearing.

I want to pause at this spectacle because, like the Induction, it calls particular attention to the boy actor. Here, claiming to *be* female is equivalent to claiming *from* the female. Part homily, part marriage rite, part confession, this curiously acrobatic speech, authored by a man for a boy to speak in order to sustain the illusion of femininity, recuperates male subjectivity by mapping the prerogatives of 'good husbandry' onto the body of a newly obedient wife. Since this is not soliloquy, the boy actor playing Kate is already set off, 'her' difference (and that of the other 'wives') clearly distinguished by the presence of adult male actors. Why, then, does the speech insistently rehearse women's attributes and include such special pleading – 'bodies soft, and weak, and smooth'; 'soft conditions and our hearts' (V.ii.165,167) – on behalf of the female body's 'truth'? Such excess betrays an intense anxiety to mark the speaker's body as feminine, and to do so, it pulls out all the culture's – and the theatre's – available capital. Toward the end of the speech, however, the illusion of femininity teeters on its head, threatening to tip 'woman' into the androgynous identity of the boy actor:

> But now I see our lances are but straws,
> Our strength as weak, our weakness past compare,
> That seeming to be most which we indeed least are.
> (V.ii.173–5)

Throughout, extraordinary syntactic clarity and balance characterise Kate's speech. Why, now, introduce a couplet requiring considerable sense-making effort? 'That seeming' elides the 'we' one assumes to be its subject; subject and object risk conflation; 'most' transforms to 'least'; comparisons fail altogether. Is it just accident that 'least are', together with other lines mentioning women's negative attributes, falls outside the iambic-pentameter beat and so would be called, in the Elizabethan age and (until fairly recently) in our own, 'feminine rhymes'? Spoken by the boy actor, these lines say that he is indeed the thing he is not, and they say it twice. He is the thing without a working phallus as well as the thing with nothing – that is, a woman.

The difficulty of taming these phrases analogises the difficulty central to both play and culture: the improbability of constructing a female subject (even a Queen?) except across a male identification and as a realisation of male desire. Framing the shrew-taming spectacle as a 'kind of history' staged, at the Lord's direction, for Christopher Sly's benefit (Ind.ii.136), the play seems specifically directed toward a male subject's 'visual pleasure'.[9] Although it also conceptualises, in Kate (and the wives she addresses), a female spectator, Kate is curiously silent and watchful, only occasionally protesting her assigned place in its victimising economy. But, whether for the figure of 'woman' that *Shrew* constructs or for the real women who attended the theatre, pleasure remains a somewhat muted term. Pleasure, *Shrew* teaches, is not owned by 'woman' but is arrived at secondhand: it depends on relative differentiations, not on absolute difference. Whether male or female, *Shrew*'s spectators remain conscious not just of power's unavoidable role in sex, gender, and representation but also of how oscillating gender identities may, on occasion, unfix that power and jostle it loose.

III

It is one thing to reconstruct past acts of comprehension with imaginary bodies and theorised spectators; it is quite another when *Shrew* is played out by and on the bodies of real women and observed by historically situated spectators of either gender. The difference lies in what Paul Smith calls 'discerning' the patriarchal symbol of 'woman' from the historical sociocultural experience of women. For twentieth-century representation, the ambivalent syntax that threatens to expose the gender-bent conventions of the Elizabethan stage marks a possible point of subversion. Like the shrew herself, the contention that we seem 'to be most [strong,] which we indeed least are' could turn to accommodate its opposite: we seem 'to be most [weak,] which we indeed least are'. However tempting, such momentary resistance seems only thinkable, not playable – an attempt to own property in a speech that, although it purports to negotiate an identity for 'woman', finally finds that identity non-negotiable, fixed rather than fluid. Indeed, Kate's speech resembles Stanley Fish's 'self-consuming artifact'. While in the Elizabethan theatre it appears to be an instance of speaking herself in his body, present-day representation reverses those terms. The address to froward wives reads like recipe discourse for a patriarchal dish to be swallowed whole, like a TV dinner; once Kate ventriloquises the voice of Shakespeare's culture and lets it colonise her body, she never speaks again. Looking for a Kate other than this apparently conformable one is like scanning the 'before' and 'after' images in ads for weight-loss programmes. Both are inescapably *there*: a viewer searches for the one in the other, wonders (like Lucentio) whether they do represent the same person, and attempts to merge the two images into a single, recognisably discrete entity.

Observing a similar phenomenon, Carol Neely cites the tendency of recent feminist readers to tame Kate's taming in order to fracture the play's patriarchal panopticism. Although, Neely writes, 'feminists cannot ... fail to rejoice at the spirit, wit and joy with which Kate accommodates herself to her wifely role', neither can they 'fail to note the radical asymmetry and inequality of the comic reconciliation and wish for Kate, as for [themselves], that choices were less limited, roles less rigid and unequal, accommodations more mutual and less coerced'.[10] Caught between a resistant desire for social equality and the conformist demands of comic form, Neely anticipates what Elizabeth Fox-Genovese, borrowing W. E. B. Du Bois's term, calls a 'lived twoness', the dialectic of sundered identity, the doubled consciousness of individuals who simultaneously identify with the dominant culture and with the marginal community or group to which they belong or to which that culture assigns them.[11] It is a curious place in which to live and from which to view *Shrew*'s finale – a spectacle (always) already endowed with enough accumulated cultural capital to enable women readers or spectators, stranded between incommensurable identities, to buy into its normative gender economy.

By crystallising images of dominance and submission in marriage, *Shrew*'s logic teaches that a shrew-wife has neither use- nor exchange-value and traces an especially canny broker's success in rolling over his initial investment. To find pleasure in this ending, a woman spectator must discover that *Shrew* inextricably weaves voyeurism, fantasy, and consumerism together to produce a dazzling constellation of viewing positions. If she takes the direct route that the play offers male spectators (through Sly), desiring herself as a fetish, she acknowledges not only the masculinity that conceptualises her access to activity and agency but the twists and turns in a woman's often circuitous route to pleasure. *Shrew* can also entice a woman spectator to regress imaginatively, responding as many do to *Gone with the Wind* or as a particular reading community does to Harlequin romances. By either gliding over the signs of the father in Kate's speech (accepting them as 'natural') or assuming that Kate is merely performing and does not believe what she says, readers can produce a scene similar to the happy rape, the fully authorised scene for female sexuality – authorised precisely because it is mastered and controlled. In such scenarios, Kate does not so much defeat the power of the phallus as take over its power in drag to play the 'good girl' and so get the 'bad girl's' pleasure; moreover, since she achieves pleasure as if against her will, she remains a good girl. Theoretically, *Shrew*'s aesthetic sado-masochism turns into a more acceptable social masochism through which one may negotiate pleasure from a position of relative powerlessness. In one way or another, each of these options is a self-consuming fantasy: as Lynne Joyrich observes of all present-day representation, perhaps the consumer's viewing role is the only one that remains stable.[12]

But the trouble is not that, by taking such pleasures in *Shrew*'s ending, one disavows critique and becomes the culture's dupe rather than its analyst. Instead, the danger is that such ethnographies of reading buy *Shrew* for a shared feminine mystique through which women may even further mystify their cultural positioning (or fate) as a trap, however tender. Thus women neutralise, in pleasant dreams or in nightmare fantasies that lie beyond the play's representational limits, whatever legitimate grievances they perceive, not only in *Shrew*'s Elizabethan patriarchy but in late-twentieth-century conditions of lived twoness. In 1594, when *Shrew* was first entered in the Stationers' Register, it was called 'a pleasant Conceyted historie', and its long performance history, through many alternative guises, suggests that it gives good conceits as well as good pleasure. It can also claim, like *Othello*, to have given the state some service. In the twentieth century as in the sixteenth, the public spectacle of a woman behaving properly stamps her with the culture's prerogatives, and being looked at, whether by male or female spectators, reconfirms her meaning.

How *Shrew*'s cultural capital has been reproduced, repackaged, and spent as a twentieth-century commodity is my concern in the rest of this essay. Because the models of 'looking' the play presupposes – voyeurism, fantasy, and consumerism – are all metaphors for film and television viewing, and because the viewing regimes of these media resonate with social and psychic codes of sexual difference, it is appropriate to consider how modern representations re-market and sanction *Shrew*'s social contract. After all, however carefully academic gender studies may construct or deconstruct images of women, in this more public territory *Shrew* continues to enfold 'woman', as well as 'women', within representation to make and remake new patriarchies and new cultural myths with which to negotiate her use.

IV

Famous as the first sound film of a Shakespearean play, Columbia Pictures' *Taming of the Shrew* (1929), starring the legendary Mary Pickford and Douglas Fairbanks, is perhaps even more infamous for its credit line, 'by William Shakespeare with additional dialogue by Samuel Taylor', the director. (A contemporary cartoon shows a bust of Shakespeare at the Library of Congress being replaced by one of Taylor.) Intriguingly, in the distribution of verbal property, Shakespeare's poetry goes to Fairbanks while Taylor's additions – except for a version of Kate's author-ised obedience speech – fall to Pickford, who complained that Fairbanks (once a Shakespearean actor) took advantage of her. According to Pickford's autobiography (and to her sympathetic biographers), Fairbanks tamed the 'shrew' in real life as well as dominated her before the cameras: he not only played jokes, delayed shooting schedules, and failed to learn his lines, wildly increasing production costs, but relegated his co-starring wife (also his co-producer and co-financer) to a lower place in the production hierarchy. Writes Pickford, 'The making of that film was my finish. My confidence was completely shattered, and I was never again at ease before the camera or microphone.'[13] Yet the film opens up contradictions in this confessional portrait of a woman at the mercy of both her husband and the camera apparatus. When the performer known for her golden curls and for a whole bag of coy 'Pickford tricks' first confronts Fairbanks's Robin Hood–Black Pirate Petruchio, a frieze depicting Herod's slaughter of the innocents frames her figure, perfectly troping her image as a grown woman pretending to be a little girl as well as her self-characterised victimisation. But her costume – a black skirted riding habit, boots, and a sweepingly feathered picture hat – draws on an equally familiar published identity, that of the androgynous tomboy (*Rebecca of Sunnybrook Farm* [1917]), according her the power associated with male masquerade; she, not Petruchio, cracks a mean whip.

However much the image of Fairbanks – clad in rags, a jackboot on his head, slouching against a column, and crunching an apple during the wedding – codes Petruchio's bravado, glossing his shrewish display with his already commodified identity, the film also mocks the alien, romantic manliness associated with his previous roles. After escorting Kate to her bridal chamber, Fairbanks's Petruchio returns to the dining table and attacks the food and drink he had previously rejected. Meanwhile, following a dissolve that transforms Pickford's dirtily dressed Kate into a bride wearing a virginal peignoir, she appears on a balcony overlooking the great hall, where she sees Petruchio sharing his taming strategy with a dog that has replaced her at the table; smiling mysteriously, she disappears before Petruchio asks, 'Dost thou know better how to tame a shrew?' and the dog barks in reply. Later, on finding Kate asleep, Petruchio slams the bedroom door, scatters the bedclothes, and bellows at Kate, who applauds his performance; then, after each opens a window, the couple argue over whether they're looking at the moon or the sun and quarrel over who gets the best bed pillow. If this Noel Coward-like bridal night offers audiences a voyeuristic glimpse of 'the most popular couple the world has ever known',[14] its finale also restages the gender codes of Shakespeare's *Shrew*: after bashing Petruchio's head with a stool, Kate coos, 'O Petruchio, beloved'; pats his face to revive him; and, cradling him in her arms, throws her whip into the fire and murmurs a soothing 'There, there' as he lays his head on her bosom. Gazing up at her with a puzzled look, Petruchio asks, 'The sun is shining bright?' and, reassuringly, Pickford's motherly Kate replies, 'Aye, the blessed sun'.

In the final wedding-banquet sequence, Petruchio, his head bound with a raffish bandage and looking immensely self-satisfied, sits with one leg hooked over his chair while Kate, standing beside him, swears to love, honour, and obey. As she finishes her vow, a cut to mid-close-up isolates her broad wink, which Bianca, in an ensuing mid-shot, acknowledges. Just as Petruchio is a son playacting the role of husband, Kate is a mother who plays a wife. By turning men into braggart boys with knowing mothers, Taylor's *Shrew* gives the Oedipal scenario a curious gender spin: while the son may get his mother, articulating that resolution from a woman's point of view turns the familiar plot into a variant of the Freudian joke, with women, not men, having the last laugh. Yet, although the wife's seizing the comic advantage and the mythic power of a heavily coded subject position skews the film's final deshrewing, it only momentarily dismantles the call of Shakespeare's patriarchal culture. In playing out what appear to be competing instructions for marital pleasure, Taylor's *Shrew* simply gives the emperor's text new (and newly contradictory) robes, cut from the cloth of a regressive fantasy about occupying – and performing – infantile roles. If Pickford's wink clears any space for real women spectators within *Shrew*'s ending, that space, like the entire film, is already traversed with questions of ownership, whether of Fairbanks's exotically masculine image or of Pickford's identity as 'America's Sweetheart'. Possessing either, however fleetingly, would effectively (and conventionally) mask whatever cultural tensions remained concerning those who, only a short ten years before, had been enfranchised. But any anxiety the film prompts about Kate's momentary 'triumph' is allayed when Petruchio pulls Kate across his lap for a final kiss, Baptista begins a song in which all join, and the camera pulls back, revealing the entire wedding party, to conclude on the sight – and sound – of full social harmony.

A rather different doubleness – or, more appropriately, a 'lived twoness' within what Richard Dyer calls 'star discourse' – informs Franco Zeffirelli's 1966 *Shrew*, a vehicle for the equally legendary couple Elizabeth Taylor and Richard Burton. Like other *Shrews*, Zeffirelli's circulates around the use- and exchange-value of a shrew-wife. But locating this image of 'woman' in Taylor's body – itself a site (or text) of sexual spectacle and spectatorly desire – lends particular resonance to this *Shrew*'s hyperactive narrative. As 'the most expensive, most beautiful, most married and divorced being in the world', Taylor both stands for the type 'star' and calls into question the ontological distinctions separating stars from 'ordinary people'. Her star category not only ignores how her off-screen experience models the late-twentieth-century crisis within heterosexual monogamy but fails to account for either her 'commonness' or her frequent successes in 'bitch' roles. Nevertheless, the star system, and Taylor within it, figures 'the decadence, sexual licence and extravagance' that characterise 1950s and 1960s American culture and anticipate Foucault's designation of sexuality as the area of human experience where we can learn the truth about ourselves.[15] As a fathomless icon of femininity, with stories in her eyes, her body carries meanings that may supersede, or fuse with, stardom's ability to embody social categories, especially to promote the idea (and ideal) of individual agency within culture by suggesting that a private self resides behind the role and that 'truth' lies just beyond the image.[16]

Shrew and the Taylor–Burton team are ideally suited to mapping this contradictory web of discourses and its equally contradictory pleasures. Most intriguingly, Zeffirelli's film grounds its particular negotiation between textual and social subjects, not just in Shakespeare's play but in reverberations of two other productions starring the couple: *Cleopatra* (1963; dir. Mankiewicz), whose filming embraced what Burton called *le scandale* that broke up both stars' previous marriages, and *Who's Afraid of Virginia Woolf?* (1966; dir. Nichols). Certainly the teaser for *Virginia Woolf* – 'You are cordially invited to George and Martha's for an evening of fun and games' – applies equally to *Shrew*. For the game in Zeffirelli's film is to exchange 'Hump the Hostess' for 'Get the Guests' and, by treading the edge of the madonna–whore dichotomy, to transform not just the unruly Kate but Taylor herself from a published 'scarlet woman' to a legitimate wife.

Appropriately, the film's first image of 'woman' is that of a blowsy whore, who replaces the figure of Lent in the opening spectacle of Paduan Carnival, which replaces Shakespeare's Sly Induction and thematises the licensed inversions of *Shrew*'s narrative. Aptly characterising Shakespeare's *Shrew* as 'a play not for a sober Monday morning but for a drunken Saturday night', Jack Jorgens calls Zeffirelli's film a version of Saturnalian Revel, with Burton and Taylor reigning as the Lord and Lady of Misrule.[17] Not only is Burton's smashed Welsh Petruchio (a parody of Charles Laughton's portrayal of Henry VIII in Alexander Korda's 1933 film) seldom without a wine goblet in his hand, but he throws away Shakespeare's lines with a panache that overpowers Taylor's more hesitant delivery. As with the Pickford–Fairbanks *Shrew*, the male star's ownership of Shakespeare's language reifies the text's linguistic logic; whereas Petruchio owns the words, silence codes his wife's presence until the play's end, when Kate talks and talks and talks. Here, however, Taylor's body language overmatches Burton's facility with Shakespeare: the film not only eroticises her spectacular body but capitalises on her attraction for Burton. Following the wooing scene, an extended romp that ends with the pair falling into a pile of feathers, a close-up sequence not only privileges Kate's point of view but, by including an extreme close-up of one of Taylor's famous violet eyes, turns her gaze into a spectacle in which viewers can meet their own voyeurism. Her look keys a high-angle full shot of Burton's Petruchio bragging to the other men that he has won her; then, drawing back from the window's 'eye', Kate sinks into a thoughtful pose; and a smile crosses her face as the sound track's soft, romantic music expresses her private pleasure, inviting spectators of either gender to share and, perhaps, extend her fantasy.

That fantasy culminates at Bianca's wedding banquet, where, following an exchange of sidelong glances between Kate and Petruchio, Kate's point of view keys a shot of several children playing; after a cut-in mid-shot of Kate, they reappear, this time with a large dog. She smiles fondly at them, then gazes tenderly at a bored, wine-drinking Petruchio and, with expressively downcast eyes, raises her own cup to her lips. Moments later, she disdainfully leads the women away from the men's locker-room talk about the Widow. In her eyes, marriage should breed increase, not bawdy puns: this Kate would 'keep/By children's eyes, her husband's shape in mind' (Shakespeare's sonnet 9). Indeed, this spectacle of fortunate issue seems to motivate her later obedience speech and so bends *Shrew*'s ending toward familial myth – and this particular *Shrew*'s intertextual connections.

For both Kate's mothering instinct and her refusal to listen to dirty jokes flood outward, encompassing *Virginia Woolf*'s loud-mouthed Martha and George and their imaginary child as well as Taylor's own history. After three cesarean sections, Taylor had decided, on the advice of her doctors, not to have another child, and during *Cleopatra*'s early filming, she arranged to adopt a severely crippled infant girl. Then, as her dangerous liaison with Burton became worldwide news, an open letter in the Vatican City weekly, *L'osservatore della dominica* (implicitly if not officially speaking with a papal voice), accused her of being 'an erotic vagrant and an unfit mother'.[18] Three years later, *Shrew*'s ending seemed specifically Taylor-ed to address those slurs and to prove her moral worth. When Taylor's Kate reappears at Petruchio's command, tugging Bianca, the Widow, and a train of (presumably) marginal wives, her spectacle of obedience becomes a serious pledge of wifely duty, complete with a cut-in mid-shot of a weeping peasant woman. As Kate kneels before Petruchio, joyful applause breaks out; after Petruchio raises her, the film cuts to a close-up kiss and then to a full shot of the entire assembly, smiling and applauding this conventional romantic-comedy ending. In close-up, Petruchio addresses his final lines to the less fortunate husbands and to the camera, but when he turns, expecting Kate to be at his side, she has disappeared, and he is trapped in a crowd of other wives. Kate–Taylor's desire for Petruchio–Burton, and for children, has apparently transferred to all women; and Burton's newly eroticised body must fight through this unruly mob to make his exit, much as Burton and Taylor were plagued by intrusive Roman paparazzi wherever they went. Finally, Grumio holds up his hands, as though to say 'that's all' and to stop the camera as well as the women from invading an imaginary offscreen bedroom. But it is not all, for out-takes from the hectically paced wooing scene provide a coda that not only restores farcical gaiety but shows what the filmed sequence does not: a pair of jolly, thriving wooers, a model star marriage that appropriates Shakespeare to authenticate a beautiful woman's transgressive body as that of a faithful wife and to confirm the jet-setting couple's Italian, if not international, respectability. 'All is [indeed] done in reverend care of her' (IV.i.175): within this *Shrew*'s doubled carnivalesque, that ideology prevails precisely because it awards pleasure to both textual and spectatorly subjects.

V

However much its box-office success capitalised on viewers' voyeuristic fascination with its stars, Zeffirelli's *Shrew* falls within a high-art tradition of filmed Shakespeare. But more popular representations of *Shrew* – by distancing, dispersing, or redirecting Shakespeare's cultural authority – can more easily accommodate the possibility of containment as well as of resistance: the 'double movement' of popular culture.[19] Although *Shrew* is (always) already popular culture, George Sidney's 1953 film of Cole Porter's *Kiss Me, Kate* (1948) moves 'Shakespeare' even more definitively toward its popular origins. Adapted to show how Lilli and Fred, a divorced star couple, come together (again), this *Shrew* quite literally swings to another tune. Like most musicals about making a musical, this one equates a couple's ability to perform together onstage with their successful offstage sexual performance, a convention well suited to address the decade's preoccupation with sexuality (1953 marked *Playboy*'s inaugural issue and Kinsey's report on American women's sexual behaviour) and to tinsel the pleasures and dangers of sex with a discourse of 'pure' entertainment.

Ultimately, *Kate* is less interested in shrewing around than in placating, through song and dance, the cultural tensions of screwing around: wiving it wealthily in Padua takes second place to floating desire, affecting unruly women ('I will take ... any Harry, Tom or Dick', sings Bianca–Lois) and ex-husbands alike (marriage is fine by day, 'But oh what a bore at night', mourns Petruchio–Fred). Although Kate–Lilli's 'I Hate Men' deconstructs macho stereotypes – Jack the Ripper; the athlete 'with his manner bold and brassy,/[Who] may have hair upon his chest but, sister, so has Lassie'; the travelling salesman 'who'll have the fun and thee the baby'; the executive whose 'bus'ness is with his pretty secretary'[20] – she finally accepts the contradictory 'twoness' of lived experience: 'from the mind, all womankind should rout 'em,/But ladies, ... what would we do without 'em?' Taking any Dick is not for Kate–Lilli, whose love-hate for Petruchio–Fred's philandering phallus makes her seem willingly complicit in repeated humiliations, including a public spanking ('So taunt me and hurt me,/Deceive me, desert me,/I'm yours 'til I die'). However playfully *Kate* extends *Shrew*'s brief to express women's and men's grievances against monogamy's material circumstances, it not only rigorously polices excessive desires but tolerates no ruptures within male dominance. A well-stuffed codpiece, a whip, and a banana code Petruchio–Fred's high visibility; and the film's original 3-D version heightens his subjectivity (never Kate–Lilli's), as well as his self-reflexive performance, through the emergence effect, which makes him seem about to break from the screen to become one with the viewers' reality. *Kate* reworks Shakespeare as sadistic bard through two Sly-surrogate hoodlums, whose advice – 'Brush up your Shakespeare, and they'll all kow-tow' – brushes in the tangled links between Shakespeare's titular erotics and mid-twentieth-century misogyny to recirculate *Shrew*'s discourse of phallic potency:

> If she says she won't buy it or tike it,
> Make her tike it, what's more, 'As You Like It',
> If she says your behaviour is heinous,
> Kick her right in the 'Coriolanus'
> ... ...
> Just recite an occasional sonnet,
> And your lap'll have 'Honey' upon it,
> When your baby is pleading for pleasure,
> Let her sample your 'Measure for Measure'.

Somewhat predictably, Lilli 'kow-tows', cancelling her proposed elopement with the travestied Texan cowboy whose limousine sports giant cattle horns and using Shakespeare's obedience speech (set to Porter's music) to tell Fred she loves him. When she waves Fred's little black book in his face, he laughs ('A pox on the life that late I led') and, as Lilli tosses away his record of past conquests, segues into the finale's 'Kiss Me, Kate', further confirming the myth of heterosexual monogamy and cheerfully accepting its strictures as structure. Superimposed over their playground–stage, the figures of Lilli and Fred, once again through the emergence effect, project into the 'eternal present' of both the film's phantom and its live spectators, joining two cultural spaces in a wedded bliss that has been mediated by, but finally suppresses, a dominant-submissive undertext. All are included guests at this celebratory marriage between the playwright Hollywood calls 'Billy Big Boy' and the big-hit, stage-to-screen musical. If *Kate* vents sado-masochistic fantasies in soft-shoe routines to teach that fighting phallic power can be fun, it also suggests that managing monogamy's double-toil-and-trouble standards is strictly women's business.

From *PMLA*, 107 (1992), 538–9, 540–7, 547–8.

NOTES

[In this edited version of an essay on the theatrical and cinematic history of *The Taming of the Shrew*, Barbara Hodgdon examines the sexual politics of three screen treatments of the play. Establishing a critical framework which draws upon feminist theories of the masculine gaze, pornography and sexual violence, Hodgdon argues that *The Shrew* is a culturally sanctioned sado-masochistic text; and that, moreover, its reinscription within the viewing regime of cinema has been particularly resonant in this regard. Thus the 1929 version plays with the elements of androgyny associated with Mary Pickford's screen identity, while the 1966 version foregrounds the star personas of Richard Burton and Elizabeth Taylor in an erotic, carnivalesque reading. In *Kiss Me, Kate*, Hodgdon suggests, the exchange between high and popular culture reflects the tensions within the institution of heterosexual monogamy during the 1950s. Quotations from *The Taming of the Shrew* are from the New Cambridge Shakespeare edition, ed. Ann Thompson (Cambridge, 1984). Ed.]

1. Roland Barthes, *Sade/Fourier/Loyola*, trans. Richard Miller (New York, 1976), p. 10.

2. Henry Jenkins, '*Star Trek* Rerun, Reread, Rewritten: Fan Writing as Textual Poaching', *Critical Studies in Mass Communication*, 5 (1988), 86.

3. See Nancy K. Miller, 'Arachnologies: The Woman, the Text, and the Critic', in *The Poetics of Gender*, ed. Miller (New York, 1986), p. 274; Carol Thomas Neely, 'Constructing the Subject: Feminist Practice and the New Renaissance Discourses', *ELR*, 18 (1988), 15.

4. Shirley Nelson Garner, '*The Taming of the Shrew*: Inside or Outside of the Joke?', in '*Bad*' *Shakespeare*, ed. Maurice Charney (London, 1988), pp. 107–8.

5. Linda Williams, *Hard Core: Power, Pleasure, and the 'Frenzy of the Visible'* (Berkeley, CA, 1989), p. 224.

6. Teresa de Lauretis, 'Through the Looking Glass', in *The Cinematic Apparatus*, ed. de Lauretis and Stephen Heath (New York, 1980), pp. 193–4.

7. See Williams, *Hard Core*, pp. 224–5.

8. Stephen Orgel, 'Nobody's Perfect; or, Why Did the English Stage Take Boys for Women?', *South Atlantic Quarterly*, 88 (1989), 7.

9. The now famous phrase is from Laura Mulvey, 'Visual Pleasure and Narrative Cinema', *Screen*, 16 (1975), 6–18, rpr. in *Feminism and Film Theory*, ed. Constance Penley (New York, 1988), pp. 57–68.

10. Carol Thomas Neely, *Broken Nuptials in Shakespeare's Plays* (New Haven, CT, 1985), pp. 218–19.

11. Elizabeth Fox-Genovese, *Feminism without Illusions* (Chapel Hill, NC, 1991), pp. 139–41.

12. Lynne Joyrich, quoted in *The Spectatrix*, special issue of *Camera Obscura*, 20–21 (1989), 193.

13. Mary Pickford, *Sunshine and Shadow* (Garden City, NY, 1955), p. 312.

14. Booton Herndon, *Mary Pickford and Douglas Fairbanks: The Most Popular Couple the World Has Ever Known* (New York, 1977).

15. Richard Dyer, *Stars* (London, 1979), pp. 49–50.

16. Richard Dyer, *Heavenly Bodies: Film Stars and Society* (London, 1987), pp. 11, 18.

17. Jack Jorgens, *Shakespeare on Film* (Bloomington, IN, 1977), pp. 67, 73, 78.

18. Dick Sheppard, *Elizabeth: The Life and Career of Elizabeth Taylor* (Garden City, NY, 1974), pp. 309–10.

19. Stuart Hall, 'Notes on Deconstructing "the Popular"', in *People's History and Socialist Theory*, ed. Raphael Samuel (London, 1981), p. 228.

20. The film bowdlerises some of Porter's lyrics in the staged version of *Kiss Me, Kate*, where the original line is 'His bus'ness is the bus'ness which he gives his secretary'.

10

Drowning the Book: *Prospero's Books* and the Textual Shakespeare

DOUGLAS LANIER

> In one of the rooms of the Fortuny Palace there are eight books from Prospero's Library. They are magical books. In many senses all books are magical. Fortuny had a library in which many of the books were manufactured by him, for he had the engrossing and engaging habit of booking every phenomena [*sic*] – photographs, texts, postcards, ephemera, which by their juxtaposition and organisation on consecutive pages of a book gave them the characteristics we expect of a book – display, sequence, order, chronology. A film has the same characteristics – display, sequence, order, chronology – but, in its linear, rolling, celluloid shape, the film may competently refer back to an earlier order of textual display that preceded the book – the scroll – a linear exhibition of facts and events. However the scroll, like the film, has a superb advantage. With a film the eye is only permitted to read one image at a time and the brain has to remember the sense of sequence. With a scroll the eye has no trouble at all in scanning the immediate past and the immediate future almost the same time as it views the present. Maybe we should re-invent the cinema as a scroll.[1]

For recent performance criticism, the phrase 'Shakespeare wrote for the stage, not for the page' has become something of a rallying cry. Questioning our conception of Shakespearean textual authority, at least as an ideal against which Shakespearean stagings might be judged, has become an enabling ritual of performance studies. The irony is that despite the ascendancy of performance the opposition of stage and page continues to shape Shakespearean criticism, although the polarity of that opposition has been largely reversed. Against the protocols of close reading, where from the comfort of the study a reader can tease out surpluses of textual meaning, we have learned to set the practical demands of theatrical performance, where an actor must render meaning in definite intonations and actions. Against the authority of the Shakespearean text – particularly that editorial chimera posited by earlier generations, the single definitive copy as it issued from the author's pen – we have learned to set the historical panoply of Shakespearean performances. For those critics willing to embrace the post-modern tiger, Shakespeare has become (indeed, always was) Shakespeares, a series of culturally specific, multiply-mediated historical events to which any given Shakespearean text is an incomplete and certainly not a regulatory guide. In fact, the question of how to conduct Shakespearean criticism in the absence of a determinant critical object has preoccupied many in our critical generation.

Nevertheless, for all its radical implications the adage 'Shakespeare wrote for the stage, not for the page' reveals, by the logic of negation, the very tenacity of the fact it seeks to efface: that Shakespeare has come to us principally as a book. Unlike Renaissance audiences, who experienced Shakespeare's work first and, for many, solely in performance, modern audiences almost invariably encounter Shakespeare first as a text or, at the very least, with an awareness that a 'literary' text subtends what they see on the stage. This simple phenomenological distinction has sweeping and stubborn implications. The extraordinary authority of the Shakespearean text, at least in the eyes of most outside the academy, has tended to render modern performances of Shakespeare supplemental, fleeting theatrical variations, of varying authenticity, on a prior, originary book. Thus it is not by chance that, as Michael Bristol observes, 'the historical success of textuality and of the powerful institutional apparatus that supports it coincides with the virtual collapse of theatre as a strong, independent centre of cultural authority'.[2] We can glimpse the intimidating shadow that the Shakespearean book casts upon the stage in a notice printed in Royal Shakespeare Company programmes: '*Please* would you bear in mind that following the text during the performance is very distracting to the performers especially when you are seated in rows close to the stage.' This plea acknowledges, in the very high temple of Shakespearean performance, the tension between the textual and the theatrical Shakespeare. Shakespeare can take the stage only insofar as the actors are not made to stand before the judgement of his book.

For this is not *a* book: it has become *the* quintessential text, the *Ur-book*, the model for English literary textuality, not a script but secular scripture. This book has functioned historically as a crucial touchstone for editorial and interpretive procedures which, being first successfully applied to the Shakespearean text, can then be extended to literary practice in general; that function has continued, ironically enough, with poststructuralism, cultural materialism, and even performance criticism itself. Its widespread status as a cultural icon is difficult to overestimate. An edition of Shakespeare is prominently displayed as a talisman in the ready room of *Star Trek's* Captain Jean-Luc Picard, our generation's most popular intellectual hero. The most important Shakespearean text, the First Folio, is, it is safe to say, the single most recognisable book in literary history, and its aura has come to underwrite everything from advertisements for beer and copying machines to the Folger Shakespeare Library. Even though the First Folio eschews many of the monumentalising strategies that characterise other Renaissance folio publications, it has nevertheless become, as Ben Jonson predicted, a 'moniment without a tombe'. In their letter to its first readers, Heminge and Condell purposely conflate the restored textual corpus and the resurrected authorial corpse when they promise a body of works 'now offer'd to your view cur'd, and perfect of their limbes ..., absolute in their numbers, as he conceived the[m]'. Even the rather plain Droeshout engraving of Shakespeare, a portrait without the typical accoutrements of laurel leaves, architectural frames, classical verses, or even a determinate background, has come to emblematise, with Shakespeare's eyes gazing out to meet ours, the book's promise to its readers: unmediated contact with its author. In short, for us Shakespeare has become his book, and in so doing has acquired the qualities of an artifact – physical presence, permanence, costliness, monumentality – qualities to be set against the ephemerality and twice-removedness of performance.

Little wonder, then, that performance criticism would cast the textual Shakespeare as its threatening *doppelganger*. One strategy for exorcising that threat has been to co-opt the text as a theatrical document; that is, to see it as a performance score, reading it, as John Barton and Cicely Berry do, as a meticulous blueprint for its stage performance, instructive to the actor in its every detail, down to fine points of metrics, line endings and punctuation. John Barton's *Playing Shakespeare* series, shrewdly discussed by William Worthen, provides an instructive example.[3] Barton sets his approach against that of literary critics, who tend to value sweeping pronouncements about meaning without much regard for practical matters of staging. Whereas the critic replaces the opaque text with his own commentary, standing in Shakespeare's stead, the actor, so Barton maintains, merely serves as a conduit for Shakespeare's voice encoded in the theatrical score. To demonstrate, Barton prompts David Suchet to read a high-flown critical passage about *Hamlet's* ambiguity, then directs Michael Pennington in mock earnest, 'come and follow that'. This critic-bashing gesture, one which, Worthen points out, also draws upon tensions between America and Britain for cultural authority over Shakespeare, reveals Barton's need to rob the textual Shakespeare of its power as a precondition for authorising the performative Shakespeare. As Worthen points out, Barton fails to acknowledge the extent to which his attention to 'commonsense' performability masks the ideological embeddedness of modern acting. One might add that Barton also fails to acknowledge that the 'score' his actors 'realise' comes to us, even in its earliest forms, mediated by interests arguably unconcerned with performability: copyeditors, typesetters, booksellers, readers. It is, in other words, as a condition of its preservation no longer merely a 'script'. More to the point, Barton's strategy of recasting the text as a theatrical 'score' paradoxically invests the text with even more authority, with the consequence that its every jot and tittle articulate a theatrical intent that any given enactment can only aspire to.

Another tactic for exorcising the textual Shakespeare has been to forge an affiliation between performance criticism and textual criticism. Like many performance critics, revisionist editors have sought to show that the various textual records we have inherited from the past do not point toward some single authentic Shakespeare but are, like performances, variants without a standard. Indeed, many have gone so far as to argue that textual differences have their beginnings, or at least their analogues, in different performances before different audiences. A superb summary of this approach can be found in Stephen Orgel's two articles on Shakespearean textual authority, 'What is a Text?' and 'The Authentic Shakespeare'. In the former Orgel stresses the lack of secure authorial imprimatur on any dramatic text we encounter from the Renaissance.[4] By 1988, however, the terms of his argument have subtly shifted. In 'The Authentic Shakespeare', Orgel argues that Shakespeare himself wrote anticipating the lack of final authorial control – wrote, in other words, assuming that his script would be cut or changed, in accordance with the conditions of Renaissance playhouse practice, 'a situation he understood, expected, and helped to perpetuate':

> And it implies as well that Shakespeare habitually began with more than he needed, that his scripts offered the company a range of possibilities, and that the process of production was a collaborative one of selection as well as of realisation and interpretation.[5]

Here Shakespeare's intent is extended over various performances of the script, in Orgel's words its 'range of possibilities', and by making the process 'collaborative' Orgel manages to retain Shakespeare the author as an integral part of the playhouse proceedings after the script left his hands. The effect of this argument is tacitly to suggest that Shakespeare anticipated and approved both textual and performative variations. Thus, in an article that outlines the problem of an authentic Shakespearean authorial imprimatur, Orgel offers a hypothesis suggesting that revisionist bibliographic and performance studies have the best claim to Shakespearean authenticity, or, more precisely, an authentically Shakespearean inauthenticity.

Thus for all their desire to do so, performance criticism and its allies have not quite left behind the problem of the author and the authoritative text. The battle cry 'Shakespeare wrote for the stage, not for the page' seeks to authenticate performance approaches by making them accord with Shakespeare's general (if not specific) *telos* for his work, by suggesting that since Shakespeare wrote anticipating variations we are warranted in studying them. Yet even this valorisation of Shakespearean *différance* has not had the effect of dispelling the immense authority of the Shakespearean text. Quite the contrary: by refetishising the textual archive in its every material particularity, the new New Bibliography has simply extended Shakespeare's cultural aura to ever more documents. In fact, the extraordinary attraction and authority of the 'document', increasingly a feature of the construction of editorial authority in revisionist circles, itself begs to be placed in a wider cultural perspective, that of the late capitalist nostalgia for the 'uniqueness' of hand-reproduced artifacts, a nostalgia particularly acute in an age of electronic reproduction. Arguably the rise of performance criticism is a recuperative response of literary institutions to the challenge of video and cinematic media as newly hegemonic bearers of cultural authority. So long as Shakespeare remains textual, his fate (and the fate of the institutional apparatus harnessed to him) is tied to a specific medium – the book – whose cultural supremacy is now under serious challenge. But once Shakespeare is (re)grafted on to performative media or textual documents (re)conceived as performative scores or unique artifacts, he and the cultural capital he represents can be uncoupled from the decline of the book in an increasingly post-literate society.

I rehearse this familiar competition between stage and page not to endorse the longstanding prejudice against the theatre chronicled by Jonas Barish[6] or to reinstate the Shakespearean text as an essentialist or transhistorical ideal. Rather, I want to observe that the Shakespearean book is part of the historical legacy under which modern Shakespearean performance has laboured. Because performance criticism has, as a gesture of self-authorisation, felt the need to push away from the monumentality of the Shakespearean book, it has been slow to recognise the ways in which the burden of the text manifests itself in Shakespearean production, at least in those productions that choose to confront it directly. In many ways the cinema has more readily taken up the challenge of textual authority than has the theatre, perhaps because filming Shakespeare entails more consciously translating the work from one medium (and cultural register) to another. As early as 1916, in one of the first feature-length Shakespearean films, Edwin Thanhouser confronts the textual Shakespeare by opening his *King Lear* with the shot of acclaimed Shakespearean actor Frederick B. Warde reading a book. In close-up that book is revealed to be *King Lear*, at which, via a camera trick, Warde dissolves into the character Lear and the narrative proper begins. Similarly, the burden of the book prompts a cinematic prologue for Kenneth Branagh's recent *Much Ado About Nothing*. The film opens with Emma Thompson as Beatrice reading the lines of the song 'Sigh no more, ladies', as the words flash, sing-a-long style, on the darkened screen. The first shot, of an idealised watercolour landscape, is transformed with a camera's turn into a lush panorama of the real Italian countryside. Both sequences serve the same end: to signal the subordination of a static artifact – the text, a painting – to its living enactment in the film. In both movies, the directors demonstrate, if only momentarily, the perennial struggle of Shakespearean cinema to free itself from the constraints of bookishness.

Of course, it has long been recognised that Shakespearean cinema has had to negotiate the problem of transferring stage performance into a fully cinematic vocabulary. Olivier's *Henry V*, to take a much-discussed example, addresses the issue from its very first shot of a wind-tossed playbill for the play's first performance at the Globe that emerges from a blue mist, as if blown from another time, to flatten itself against the movie screen. The image economically conflates theatre and film, Renaissance London and modern Britain, and prepares the viewer for the metamorphosis from Elizabethan stage performance to cinematic epic that Olivier effects in the first reel. Unlike Branagh's *Henry V*, where the central drama is whether the callow Henry can become an adult epic hero, the dramatic focus of Olivier's movie as it opens rests not on Henry V, who is represented as psychologically complete from the first, but on Olivier the actor and whether he can inhabit the larger-than-life dramatic role of Henry. The first shot of Olivier, about to enter the stage from the tiring room, shows us an unlikely heroic figure: rouge-cheeked and beardless, effeminate in manner, offering a weak cough. If there are credentials to be established in the opening scenes, in other words, they are Olivier's as a performer, not Henry's as a king, and in that regard the authority of the written text becomes a crucial foil. The bearer of that authority is the figure of the bespectacled prompter, a surrogate reader, the first of the acting company to cross the Globe's stage, bearing the script and acknowledging the viewer with a bow before seating himself stage-left. Throughout the Chorus's opening speech – indeed, throughout most of the first three scenes – we see the prompter at the edges of the frame, following the performance closely in his promptcopy. His function as a monitor of textual fidelity is confirmed when in the first scene someone misses the cue 'Is it four o'clock?', and he leaves his seat to check why four bells did not sound. His omnipresence is a reminder of the textual ideal that casts its shadow over the performance we are seeing.

Thus it is relevant that the second scene is conceived as a send-up of textual authority, punctuated by Ely's strewing of documents all over the stage. As if to underline the thematic link, we see the prompter pay assiduous attention to his script as Canterbury comically explicates the documents relating to Salic law – both act as bearers of textual authority. This farcical sequence ensures that we see Henry V's claim to power transcending anything conferred upon him by Canterbury and Ely's bundle of documents. Rather, his stature as royal authority rests upon his theatrical declamations of patriotism, displayed first in the grand rebuke he wrests from the Dauphin's insulting gift of tennis balls. In Olivier's film, this sequence also addresses Olivier's relation to the authority of the Shakespearean script, for as he replies to the French ambassador, launching into the first extended demonstration of his stature as a performer, our view of the prompter and his book is, for the first time in the movie, blocked by Henry and his onstage audience. This image marks, I think, the replacement of one source of authority – the Shakespearean text, the document – by another – the theatrical virtuosity of Laurence Olivier and/as Henry V. Indeed, after this moment the break between Olivier the actor and the epic character he portrays is no longer foregrounded: royal and thespian legends have been successfully conflated. Even more significant is Olivier's exit: as he exits stage left, the prompter, who, we see, has removed his glasses and attended to the actor's performance without reference to his script, nods in deference to the actor. Olivier hardly acknowledges the gesture. This small, telling nod sets the seal of *textual* approval upon Olivier's performance, marking his fidelity not only to the classical British theatrical tradition, but also to the text the prompter holds in his hand, even as the gesture implicitly approves the replacement of that text by the movie performance we are seeing. Later, for Henry's departure from Southampton, Olivier shifts the focus of the scene from Henry's denunciation of the traitors (which he cuts entirely) to a grand declamation of his French campaign. The climax occurs when Henry moves to the foreground to set his royal seal to a document, so that instead of documents conferring authority upon him, with a marvellously theatrical flourish Olivier/Henry confers *his* authority upon *them*. On this 'authentic' stage, where the authority of the original Shakespearean text over the stage is made especially visible, Olivier conspicuously establishes that the actor is king.

With the possible exception of Jean-Luc Godard's *King Lear*, the most thoroughgoing attempt to confront this onus of a textual Shakespeare, and certainly the most controversial, is Peter Greenaway's *Prospero's Books*. Perhaps because he was first trained as a painter and only later ventured into film and has consistently characterised himself as 'still, primarily, a painter who's working in cinema',[7] Greenaway has been especially sensitive to the gap between the immaterial, transitory nature of the cinema and the monumentality of other art forms, particularly painting and, in his last several films, books. In fact, his entire cinematic canon might be fruitfully seen as an extended interrogation of those representational codes by which we make order of reality. Those codes are, for him, exemplified by familiar masterworks of western art which constitute an ideal order of signification, masterworks Greenaway liberally recreates and deconstructs in his films. In *Prospero's Books* Greenaway recasts *The Tempest* within a filmic vocabulary that constantly acknowledges its competition with Shakespearean textuality while remaining faithful (or, perhaps more accurately, 'faithful') to the play's received text.

Greenaway's interest in this project might be profitably seen in light of his other 'high cultural' project, a video dramatisation of the first eight cantos of Dante's *Inferno*, entitled *TV Dante*. Like *Prospero's Books*, this work employs images manipulated by video paintbox technology to create a kaleidoscopic visual experience filled with Greenaway's characteristically jarring images. And, as in *Prospero's Books*, John Gielgud supplies the main voiceover as Virgil. Yet unlike *Prospero's Books*, *TV Dante* seems to concede that the textual condition of the *Commedia*, as well as its cultural distance from the modern age, cannot be overcome, for throughout the stunningly illustrated episodes, Greenaway intercuts explanatory lectures by more than twenty historical and literary scholars. Essentially video footnotes, the lectures are handled seriously and not ironically, with the final effect that the images and text, work and commentary, are at war with one another. Of course, this procedure may have been partly imposed upon Greenaway by the demands of the mass-market television audience for which this work was destined, but in any case in this context *Prospero's Books* would seem to address the very disjunction that characterises *TV Dante*, the gap between a historical text laden with cultural capital and scholarly commentary, and its modern performance or video realisation. Whether Greenaway has overcome that gap in *Prospero's Books* has remained the key issue in its reception, as the terms of the film's many negative reviews reveal.

The specific filmic vocabulary Greenaway adopts in *Prospero's Books* places the 'literary' linearities of narrative and character at the service of the image, the spoken word, and the body. In many ways, *The Tempest* is an apt choice for this recasting, for its bookishness is everywhere manifest. The play occupies pride of place in the First

Folio and, according to longstanding tradition, is Shakespeare's reflection upon and leave-taking of his writing career. Within the play itself, the power of books is ambivalently figured – Prospero's books give him access to powerful magic, but the seductive lure of retreat into those books also led to the loss of his dukedom, and Prospero's recognition of that temptation leads to his climactic vow to 'drown my book'. His ambivalence, we shall see, transfers to Greenaway's film in unexpected ways, at the most obvious level in Greenaway's insistence upon keeping books before our eyes while at the same time foregrounding the ways in which cinema as a visual and performative medium exceeds the formal capabilities of a written text. Greenaway's focus on the Shakespearean medium becomes clearer when one compares *Prospero's Books* with its avant-garde predecessor, Derek Jarman's 1979 film of *The Tempest*. Both productions share, as a reflex of their anti-realist cinematic aesthetics, an interest in the imagery of Renaissance hermeticism and a fascination with masque-like styles. Both are resolutely auteurist: Greenaway's central scenario, that Prospero imagines the events of the play, is an echo of Jarman's. One of the early scripts for Jarman's production featured Prospero as a mad Blakean magus, 'recreating the performances of each of the characters while they visited him' in an asylum;[8] as his film now stands, the last shot, of Prospero asleep in a chair, suggests that the entire film is his dream. In both of Jarman's scenarios, Collick argues, Prospero becomes a figure for the alienated bohemian intellectual, a reading which might easily be extended to Greenaway's treatment of Prospero. But whereas Jarman's approach critiques the politics of mainstream Shakespearean productions through camp, disrupting the play's status as an icon of straight high culture by irreverently mixing pop and high cultural references and stressing transgressive sexualities, Greenaway's attention is fixed on the question of the Shakespearean medium, experimenting with *how* the play's meaning is conveyed while essentially leaving the play's conventional heterosexual content and high cultural register intact. Jarman interrogates content, Greenaway form. Taking Prospero's books as his point of departure, Greenaway uses *The Tempest* to meditate upon the status of Shakespeare in an age of electronic performance. By problematising the oppositions among text, performance, and film, that meditation produces a self-consciously hybrid form for Shakespearean performance and draws our attention to many of the unarticulated premises and practices of contemporary performance criticism.

Greenaway adopts several strategies in the film for addressing the burden of the Shakespearean book. First, he puts before us Prospero's act of reciting and writing down what will eventually become the text of *The Tempest*, showing us not a finished Shakespearean book but the imaginative process by which that book is produced. Until the final act, Prospero speaks all of the character's lines as part of his process of visualising the work-in-progress. The play's action, much to the irritation of many reviewers, is radically de-narrativised, that is, handled as a series of static though visually sumptuous dumb shows that emblematise the text's imagery, rather than as the kind of drama of character familiar to twentieth-century audiences. The effect is to force a new relationship between spoken classical text and visual image: by eschewing the characterology of the realist stage and cinema, Greenaway is free to treat the text as a collection of intensely imagined verbal images that he can defamiliarise by (re)literalising them as arresting visual tableaux.

Central to Greenaway's technique is the image of the written text, kept obsessively before the viewer. In a *mise-en-scène* littered with antique tomes, again and again the camera returns to Prospero as he scribbles out the foul papers in his study. Periodically passages of the handwritten text flash across the screen or are written on parchment as we watch. The recurring dip of Prospero's quill in watery blue ink serves as an important leitmotif, reminding viewers of the writing process that lies behind all they see. At its simplest level, this picturing of writing allows Greenaway to convert the Shakespearean text into pure cinematic image, to focus on the image rather than the meaning of the handwritten words. The script we are shown is at times elaborately ornamented with calligraphic flourishes (in a relatively authentic Italic hand). The handwriting even features visual puns – the 'l' of the word 'sail' is, for example, drawn as a ship's mast – all of which tend to draw attention to the text's visual look, its status as a visual object, rather than to its meaning. More important, by reframing the text in this manner, Greenaway acknowledges his desire to be faithful to it while dismantling its received monumentality and authority. The text of *The Tempest* emerges from the film less an immutable, inevitable artifact than the record of a self-directed imaginative performance that unfolds within time, open to chance and revision. In the opening sequence, Greenaway highlights this gap between monumental text and performative process by having Prospero experiment with the word 'Boatswain', the first word of *The Tempest*, performing it as a kind of theatrical warm-up, savouring its sound to the delight of Ariel, and repeating it in different voices and different emotional registers. At the same time, we watch the word being written in Prospero's manuscript, and the juxtaposition draws our attention to the fact that its written form – 'b-o-a-t-s-w-a-i-n' – does not capture how it is pronounced – 'bo'sun'.

It might seem that the scenario of Prospero as author is designed to refashion *The Tempest* into something of an autotelic artifact, a work that leaves behind the problematic of Shakespearean author-ship by, in effect, writing itself. In reality, however, this scenario simply complicates the question of authorship. Greenaway is, of course, manipulating the traditional identification of Prospero with Shakespeare, but he adds to it a third variable, our awareness of John Gielgud's stature as the last of the great triumvirate of 'heroic' Shakespearean actors, one of the few capable of bringing off a per-formance of all the play's parts. The merging of author, character, and actor is deepened by our recognition that Gielgud, like Prospero and Shakespeare, is here giving a valedictory performance, playing a part with which his Shakespearean career has long been identified. Indeed, some of Greenaway's iconographic choices seem calculated to recall past glories of Gielgud's career. Robert Tanitch notes, for example, that the *Times* critic said of Gielgud's 1930 per-formance as Prospero that he 'looked like a Doge just stepped from the canvas of an Italian master'; that comparison is elaborated by Greenaway's allusion, through his costuming of Gielgud, to Giovanni Bellini's *Leonardo Loredan, Doge of Venice*. Similarly, Prospero's laughter in delight at his own creation early in the film recalls Gielgud's performance as the dying author Clive Langham in Alain Renais's *Providence* (1977).[9] By casting Gielgud as Shakespeare/Prospero and deepening the resonances of this triple identification, Greenaway manages to conflate virtuoso performing with the act of writing: at least within the fiction of *Prospero's Books*, Gielgud's performance becomes the source of *The Tempest*'s text, rather than that text the source of his performance. The overall scenario is designed, in sum, to deconstruct the text–per-formance nexus. It taps into the insight that performances tend to 'textualise' the script, that is, fix its interpretive possibilities into one definitive shape, so that to all intents and purposes the actor becomes, for those who encounter the play first through him, the work's 'author', the final arbiter of its meaning; equally, it recasts the text as a fossilised record of what amounts to a performance by the author, directed in his imagination to himself.[10]

Elaborating upon Prospero's passing references to the library allows Greenaway another means to refashion the textual Shakespeare. One by one he interjects into the narrative of *The Tempest* Prospero's library of twenty-four magical books, representing each as a source of the text we witness being written. In the film's opening sequence, for example, the Book of Water, a collection of Da Vinci's sketches of water, provides the source material for Prospero's magical tempest; Prospero's mention of his dead wife Susanna is prompted by his Alphabetical Inventory of the Dead; Gonzalo's famous set-speech outlining his ideal island commonweal, we observe, is culled from the Book of Utopias. Through such allusions Greenaway makes visible *The Tempest*'s intertextuality, its status as a collection of discourses culled from a variety of prior sources rather than a unified, freestanding artwork. This technique allows Greenaway to claim Shakespeare/Prospero as a precursor and warrant for his own postmodern bricolage aesthetic. Prospero's source texts are themselves not conventional books, but rather encyclopaedic gatherings of imagery and lore on various topics, compendia of Renaissance discourses. And because Prospero's books are collections primarily of images, not words, they allow Greenaway to reverse the priority of text to image he faces as a latter-day Shakespearean, confronted (as every Shakespearean director and actor are) with the task of making the text visible: in *Prospero's Books*, images, put into play in Prospero's magical imagination, are the source of the text, rather than the text the source of the image. As Prospero's books are revealed to us, they change from inert textual objects into magically animated pictures, melding the qualities of cinema and book to produce a third form. Their illustrations spring to life as we watch; the Book of Motion, literally a collection of moving pictures, will not sit still on the bookshelf, and the Book of Colours features a spectrum of shades that transmute before the eye. As if to underline this hybridity, several of the books feature moving images that allude to Muybridge's experiments with taking still photos and converting them into movies. In fact, at every opportunity Greenaway makes books move and thus transcend their status as fixed objects. The opening tempest, for instance, is imaged as a rain of pages in Prospero's library, an image that literally dismantles the book in order to make it into a cinematic metaphor for the storm. That Prospero's library numbers twenty-four volumes is itself significant, for, Greenaway helpfully glosses, twenty-four alludes to the number of frames per second that constitute moving pictures. Prospero's 'books', 'textual' collections of images that become cinematically animated, provide the model for the kind of hybrid Shakespearean 'text' Greenaway seeks to produce in this film. After all, the book of *The Tempest* we witness being written joins the other works in Prospero's library in the final reel, and the very process of production from Prospero's books allows filmic 'texts' to become the sources for *The Tempest*, rather than the other way around.

Perhaps most important, in a number of provocative ways Greenaway stresses the 'bodily' – i.e., non-textual – medium of the performance text Prospero creates. *Prospero's Books* relentlessly draws our attention to performers' bodies; it converts Shakespearean narrative into non-narrative, non-verbal bodily forms, into mime, acrobatics, static live tableaux, masque-like processionals, hyper-theatrical costuming, and abstract dance movement, in what amounts to a survey of bodily performance arts. The effect is magnified by virtue of the fact that the production recasts the ratio between spoken text and visual spectacle in favour of the latter. Caliban, for example, is portrayed by avant-garde dancer Michael Clarke entirely in terms of lithe and manic dance, his carnal nature indicated by his red and grotesquely swollen phallus; Greenaway's casting of Clarke appropriates the dancer's notoriously subversive relationship to the conservative world of the Royal Ballet, where he trained. Ariel's actions are performed by three different actors of differing ages, a gesture that draws our attention to the relationship of character to its bodily representation, an allusion and homage to a technique of avant-garde cinema.[11] Even the preposterous costumes of Alonso's royal party, with elaborate black doublets, ruffs the size of cartwheels, and corkheeled shoes with puffball tassels – costumes that severely inhibit the actors' ability to move – effectively convey their enervated overcivilisation. In fact Greenaway pushes the limits of his technique by using even bodily excretions for expressive purposes. Caliban shits, pisses, and vomits on books, and the opening tempest is conjured, memorably enough, by Ariel's urinating on a model ship.

What has drawn the most critical fire has been the production's nudity, a prominent feature in Greenaway's recent work – nearly all of Prospero's army of magical spirits are unclothed, a choice that the beleaguered Greenaway has defended in interviews as a homage to the idealised nude body of Renaissance art. Yet Greenaway's own remarks about nudity suggest that more than a mere homage is at work, particularly since many of the bodies Greenaway puts on display are pointedly *un*ideal. Nudity in Shakespearean productions, at least from a cursory survey of major productions of the last decade, has tended to be in the service of rather specific themes: sexuality (almost exclusively female sexuality), with Lady Macbeth, Cressida and Titania as prominent examples; and vulnerability, with Lady Macbeth (in her mad scene), Desdemona, Lear, the Fool, and Edgar as memorable instances. *Prospero's Books* stands as a notable exception. Its bodies are patently *not* in the service of thematics, a fact that explains why many have labelled the production's nudity gratuitous. Yet the controversy over this element of Greenaway's production reveals, I think, much about Shakespeare's status as a classic *text*. Nudity in Shakespeare, as a particularly insistent case of theatrical embodiedness, seems to many not merely a violation of decorum but an assertion of physical presence on the actor's part that can be justified only with a narrow and very special thematic warrant from the text. Greenaway has pointed out that cinema (and, we might add, theatre)

> usually uses people as personalities rather than bodies. You do see a lot of naked people but usually to reveal something about sexuality ... I want to see the physicality of an actor, the size, the bulk, the shadow they cast on the wall.[12]

Thus his interest in nudity in this production is not thematic or prurient, but formal, that is, in the physical body as a medium: in *Prospero's Books* the nude body becomes a formal element that, by its very insistence upon the bodiliness of the performer, forcefully counters Shakespeare's textual-ness even as it transmits the text's meaning. Branagh uses brief nudity in much the same way in the opening sequence of *Much Ado*, as yet another early signal of his film's movement away from bookishness toward embodiment; it is less troubling because Branagh gives it a thin veneer of thematic motivation. In the case of *Prospero's Books*, it is noteworthy that most of the nudity is confined to Prospero's spirits, the bodily media of his art, through whom he imagines his text and performs his magic. (The exception, the brief nudity of the royal party and Ferdinand after the tempest, is deployed far more conventionally to indicate their physical vulnerability to the storm.) Like books, nude bodies are never far out of the frame, and they serve the same purpose as the often shocking images to which Greenaway gravitates: to try to give the cinematic image the physical immediacy of live theatre, to overcome the text-like two-dimensionality of the screen.

Nevertheless, even in the case of nudity, Greenaway points as much to the link between body and book as to their differences. When Prospero imagines Antonio's *coup d'état*, he sees two conjoined waves of destruction, one of bloody bodies, the other of books. Throughout the film the pages of Prospero's books are filled with images of nude bodies, hovering between two- and three-dimensionality, moving pictures and static icons. In fact the title credit for the movie is projected over a giant book out of whose pages spring real people who slide down the book's spine. By merging the qualities of texts and physical bodies, words and things, Greenaway takes every opportunity to complicate the nature of Prospero's books. As we watch the Bestiary of Past, Present and Future Animals, for example, printed images of animals become real animals; the Book of Earth associated with Caliban is, we are told, 'impregnated with the minerals, acids, alkalis, gums, balms, and aphrodisiacs of the earth'; and Prospero's herbal, stuffed with actual plants, is a haven for real insects and fills the air with milkweed. This undecidability points to an ambivalence typical of Greenaway's *oeuvre*. He is, on the one hand, repulsed by the frailty of the human body and attracted to the ideal order of canonical art, its formal beauties, significance, and seeming permanence; yet, on the other hand, he is unconvinced that art offers anything more than a comforting illusion that does not correspond to an enigmatic, brutal reality. At the climax of Prospero's opening monologue, where he seems to retreat into the world of books out of grief for his wife's death, we learn of Vesalius's lost 'Anatomy of Birth' whose 'descriptive drawings of the human body ... move and throb and bleed' when its pages are turned: 'It is a banned book that queries the unnecessary processes of ageing, bemoans the wastages associated with progeneration, condemns the pains and anxieties of childbirth, and generally questions the efficiency of God.' This book, more than any other of Prospero's, seems to articulate the pathos of the evanescent human body, and Greenaway underlines that pathos with the image of Prospero's wife Susanna who, like some living version of a Renaissance anatomical drawing, peels away her skin to reveal her viscera, an image he follows with that of her face beneath a death shroud. The body's vulnerability and evanescence, Greenaway seems to suggest, demands an act of preservation that only an artistic work can provide. Yet the Shakespearean text, he suggests by his focus on the *act* of writing and imagining, is false to the very bodily processes that bring it into being. It is cinema, as an enduring record of the bodily process of creation, a hybrid of body and book, that serves as Greenaway's substitute for both.

The opening sequence of *Prospero's Books*, like that of Olivier's *Henry V*, functions as a sophisticated, if elliptical, prologue to the concerns of the work as a whole. The first image of the film, repeated several times, is a close-up of a water drop, an allusion to Harold Edgerton's famous strobe studies of water in motion. Throughout this opening sequence water – the basic material of the tempest – and film are metaphorically linked by virtue of the fact that both are fluid media, and in the case of water drops, ephemeral. By means of overlaid images, Greenaway builds up metonymic equivalences between the cinematic medium, water, and the process of writing (linked by Prospero's watery blue ink). These links converge in the first book in Prospero's library, the Book of Water, itself an exemplar of the kind of fluid, filmic text Greenaway is labouring to create. A volume of drawings that seek to capture the motion of water in still pen and ink images, the Book of Water transforms before our eyes into a genuine moving image of water. (Indeed, the repeated command 'bestir, bestir' in this opening sequence seems to address the images in the book as much as the doomed mariners.) A travelling shot reveals Prospero in a stylised bathhouse, his hand upraised to catch falling drops of water as an open book is superimposed. In a fleeting metaphor for Greenaway's own poise between text and performance, Prospero raises one hand to declaim his lines and to catch the water, while he rests his other hand on an open text. By doing so, Prospero himself becomes the medium in which text, performance, and water intersect. Prospero's experiments with 'Boatswain' usher in a textual fugue on the play's opening lines, as Ariel magically invokes the storm by urinating on a model ship. Besides being an elaborate visual pun on 'making water', and perhaps a comment on the almost puerile pleasure Prospero initially takes in his revenge, this pissing passage also offers wry commentary on the film's relation to Shakespearean textuality, for Ariel's water also falls on the antique text. The equation of Ariel's desecration of the book with Greenaway's as Shakespearean filmmaker becomes clearer when Greenaway flashes his directorial credit over an image of Ariel's pissing. As Ariel, so Greenaway: he embraces the violence his adaptation does to traditional textual authority as the necessary precondition for making his own cinematic 'book of water'.

In *The Tempest* Prospero famously vows to 'drown my book' (V.i.57), an act which, unlike the breaking of his staff, most productions do not stage. Given Greenaway's interest in the Shakespearean book, it is fitting that he should elect to make Prospero's fulfilment of that promise his climax. Prospero's fifth-act revelations to Alonso and company prepare for that moment. As Prospero reveals himself, newly dressed in ruff and doublet, we hear the characters speak in their own voices for the first time, as if Prospero is also ceding his control as author by entering history, becoming one character among many. This change is marked by Gonzalo's summary of the plot in V.i.208–13, the text scrolling across the screen in gold script as he utters the words. Certainly this image literalises Gonzalo's wish to set down the 'common joy', 'With gold on lasting pillars' (V.i.208), but the gold letters are recognisably in the typeface of the First Folio: we are watching the passage of Prospero's book from a bodily process of writing into a published, public artistic monument, and with it comes Prospero's authorial (self-)dispossession. As if to underline the point, Greenaway handles the breaking of Prospero's staff as the breaking of his quill, an act accompanied by images of the closing of his books.

This sequence paves the way for Prospero's spectacular drowning of his library, each book of which is tossed into the sea which consumes it in a tempest of images. The last two volumes, revealed only in this sequence, are the most precious to those who treasure the Shakespearean text. The first is Shakespeare's First Folio, identified by the initials W. S. and the Droeshout portrait but, tellingly, not by Shakespeare's name. In an instructive bit of business, Prospero's hand lingers over Jonson's prefatory poem that asks us to 'looke/Not on his Picture, but his Booke'. This particular folio has only thirty-five plays, with nineteen pages left blank at the front of the book, for the inclusion of the thirty-sixth. And the second book is that thirty-sixth text, the copy of *The Tempest* we watched being written during the course of the film. That text is also, we might note, that most authoritative, desired, and unavailable of artifacts, a Shakespearean holograph, the editor's dream of an ideal text fresh from the authenticating pen of the Bard himself, unsullied by the intervening hands of actors or copysetters. Both of these books Prospero tosses into the sea – a gesture directed as much against notions of textual purity or authenticity as against Prospero's relinquishment of magic. Yet the books are not wholly lost: they are retrieved by the barbaric man-fish Caliban, here a wry surrogate for the *enfant terrible* director himself. In Greenaway's hands, Prospero's act of destroying his text only authorises the film director's cinematic appropriation of it. 'Textual' transmission, thematised early in the film by a long travelling shot of an antique tome passed hand to hand between various creatures and ending with Greenaway's directorial credit, can now pass to the creature of the water, to a desecrater of books who nevertheless saves them from oblivion.

By stuffing every frame with allusive visual references, by overlaying and recombining images using high-definition television and video paintbox technology, Greenaway offers the visual equivalent of what Harry Berger Jr claims is our aural experience of the Shakespearean text:

> when Shakespeare is staged and you hear his language at performance tempo you are always haunted by the sense that you are receiving more information than you can process, and you wish you could slow the tempo down or have passages repeated or reach for a text.[13]

The frustration of trying to take in so overwhelming an experience has shaped the film's reception. For Greenaway demonstrates that in an age of videotape, one cannot speak of any simple triumph of the performative or cinematic over Shakespearean textuality. This adaptation demands to be pored over and explicated in detail as I have just done – to be given the kind of reading, as exasperated reviewers noted, possible only with the pause and rewind buttons of a VCR. In the end, Greenaway's film is itself destined to become a cinematic 'text', to be 'read' according to interpretive protocols of close reading and with many of the same assumptions about 'textual' monumentality. Greenaway anticipates this irony with his film's enigmatic ending. After Prospero/Gielgud begs us to set him free, the frame shrinking around him, we witness the applause of a recognisably Renaissance audience, an emblem of the historical moment of the work's 'original' production. Through this audience bursts Ariel, who runs toward the viewer as if to burst through the screen into the viewer's world. Throughout the film Ariel has been the symbol and agent of Prospero's artistic process, and his sprint toward us, getting progressively younger as he runs, memorably captures the work's impulse to break free from its 'original' moment of production. But Greenaway is sly in representing that impulse's ironies. As Ariel moves toward us, the screen-image flattens from three to two dimensions, and as the child Ariel seems to leap toward us, as if out of the screen and into our arms, he leaps literally upward and out of what has now become a screen-page, to leave the viewer with the final image of the film, a palimpsestic sheet of parchment, looking vaguely like a Renaissance map faded by contact with water, with just a hint of half-discernible animated graffiti. The price of surviving its historical moment is that the film must itself become a book, one from which the magical agency of Ariel, Prospero's prime image-maker and performer, has been 'set free'.

Greenaway's acknowledgement of his *Tempest's* passage from performance to text points, I believe, to what performance criticism, with the important exception of Harry Berger Jr,[14] has been slow to recognise about its own practice. For performance criticism has been enabled and sustained, in ways it has not fully acknowledged, not so much by a return to the theatre as by a revolution in the Shakespearean medium. As Samuel Crowl observes, serious critical attention to performative differences, particularly in our teaching, arose at the same time as 16 mm prints of Shakespearean films became available in the 1960s.[15] The availability of videotape technology a decade later has made performance studies widely possible, even dominant within the discipline, allowing us to pore over and compare performances as never before. Yet even as these media have democratised access to performances, they have also shaped our sense of them. Video and film have encouraged us to assimilate those performances to the condition of texts, stable artifacts rather than contingent, unstable, ephemeral experiences.[16] (For all its faults, the BBC Shakespeare series was forward-looking at least in its recognition of the 'canonising' power of the videocassette; the credits that roll at the first of these videos, in Renaissance typeface with head- and tailpieces on handmade paper, identify their 'textualising' intent, their status as substitutes for the canonical Shakespearean 'text', not a challenge to the power of its textual authority.) Even as we have hailed the death of the monolithic text in favour of performative variants, the technological apparatus that has encouraged this theoretical revolution – the VCR – has been subtly re-establishing, at another level, a new monolithic and stable 'text' – the ideal performance, recorded on tape, edited and re-shaped in post-production, available for re-viewing. If the central insight of performance criticism is that performance is radically contingent, open to historical and material pressures that may not outlast a performance (or even an act), the stability of the records from which we work may be false to the very historicity perform-ance criticism seeks to address. The run of a play is marked by night-to-night differences that spring from chance, design, and serendipity, differences that certainly shape reception and poten-tially reveal much about the performance process; yet the typical records of performance – promptbooks, set models, photographs, videotapes – tend to elide those differences, encouraging us instead to think of a given production as a self-consistent 'text'. Video does not capture the horizon of anxiety that live actor and audience share, the possibility that lines might be forgotten or mangled, props fall apart or become misplaced, cues missed, the anxiety that mundane material contingency may mar the performance. It thereby robs a live performance of some of its power, the sense that a potentially unpredictable situation has been made almost hero-ically to conform to an actor's bodily will. As the dominant medium through which we have come to study Shakespearean performance, the 'videotext' may encourage us to elide the very historicity and materiality we have sought to recover with the return to performance.

Prospero's Books thus is an instance of what we might call 'im-manent theory', an artifact meditating on the theoretical grounds of its own existence. Greenaway himself has characterised his own work in film, painting, and literature as 'an investigative procedure of approaching phenomenology on a very wide front'.[17] As such, *Prospero's Books* draws our attention to the medium within which our experience of Shakespeare takes place, and the interpretive practices that medium prompts. Greenaway has been taken to task for his adaptation's lack of an explicit politics, his failure, for example, to take into account recent postcolonial critiques of *The Tempest*. It is certainly true that Greenaway's essential interest is in the relationship between the artist and his representational appara-tus.[18] But that interest points, I think, to some of the ironies in our broadened sense of 'text' in the wake of Roland Barthes, for the poststructuralist concept of 'text' has enabled us to 'read' 'perform-ances' but only at the expense of their phenomenological specificity.

Prospero's Books confronts directly the issue of the Shakespearean medium, raising anew the crucial question of what forms the Shakespearean book and the cultural capital it represents can take in a post-literate age. By problematising (though certainly not escaping from) the hegemony that Shakespearean textualism continues to hold over our critical imaginations, even in an age of electronic reproduction, Greenaway points performance criticism toward a double challenge: a fuller account of the relation of performance criticism to recording technologies, and the shaping of a practice more attentive to the mundane specificities of the media that render performance capable of study: painting, sculpture, record, tape, CD-ROM, videotape, telecast, film, stage performance, still photos, promptbooks, production notes, *and text* – the complex phenomenological palimpsest that inescapably constitutes our Shakespearean book.

From *Shakespeare, Theory, and Performance*, ed. James C. Bulman (London, 1996), pp. 187–209.

NOTES

[This essay first appeared in a collection which aimed to address the relationship between Shakespearean performance, film and recent critical theory. Lanier contends that Shakespearean production (both cinematic and theatrical) has been historically overshadowed by the literary and cultural authority of the Shakespearean text, and that the negotiation of this burden of textuality has been central to (and visible within) Shakespearean cinema from the beginning. Lanier then offers a detailed close reading of Peter Greenaway's *Prospero's Books* as a sustained and adventurous attempt to displace the cultural authority of the textual Shakespeare, and one which presents a radical break with cinematic realism. In conclusion, Lanier proposes that Greenaway's film self-reflexively explores the new status of film as text in the context of VCR and multi-media technology, and that these technological developments themselves redefine the theoretical question of cinematic authorship. Ed.]

1. Peter Greenaway, *Watching Water*, Catalogue for the exhibition 'Watching Water', a special project for the Venice Biennale 48th International Exhibition of Art (Milan, 1993), pp. 22–3.

2. Michael Bristol, *Shakespeare's America/America's Shakespeare* (New York, 1990), p. 97.

3. See William Worthen, 'Deeper Meanings and Theatrical Technique: the Rhetoric of Performance Criticism', *Shakespeare Quarterly*, 40 (1989), 441–55.

4. Stephen Orgel, 'What is a Text?' *Research Opportunities in Renaissance Drama*, 24 (1981), 3–6.

5. Stephen Orgel, 'The Authentic Shakespeare', *Representations*, 21 (1988), 7.

6. See Jonas Barish, *The Anti-Theatrical Prejudice* (Berkeley, CA, 1981).

7. Gavin Smith, 'Food for Thought', *Film Comment*, 26 (1990), 60.

8. John Collick, *Shakespeare, Cinema and Society* (Manchester, 1989), p. 99.

9. Robert Tanitch, *Plays and Players*, 453 (November 1991), 22.

10. The verb 'textualise' is taken from Worthen, 'Deeper Meanings', p. 449. Set against the totality of performative possibilities offered by the written text, it is this tendency toward textualisation, particularly marked in film, that troubles Catherine Belsey [see pp. 61–70 above]. For a rebuttal, compare Holderness [pp. 71–82 above].

11. See Peggy Phelan, 'Numbering Prospero's Books', *Performing Arts Journal*, 41 (1992), 48.

12. Quoted in Marcia Pally, 'Cinema as a Total Art Form: An Interview with Peter Greenaway', *Cineaste*, 18 (1991), 47.

13. Harry Berger Jr, 'Bodies and Texts', *Representations*, 17 (1987), 146.

14. See Harry Berger Jr, *Imaginary Audition: Shakespeare on Stage and Page* (Berkeley, CA, 1989), pp. ix, 3–42.

15. Samuel Crowl, *Shakespeare Observed: Studies in Performance on Stage and Screen* (Athens, OH, 1992), pp. 3–4.

16. The ways in which the physical records of performances shape our notions of performances and performance criticism have been cogently addressed by, for example, Dennis Kennedy, *Looking at Shakespeare: A Visual History of Twentieth-Century Performance* (Cambridge, 1993), pp. 5–23; Marco de Marinis, '"A Faithful Betrayal of Performance": Notes on the Use of Video in Theatre', *New Theatre Quarterly*, 1 (1985), 383–9; and the essayists collected in the opening section of *Shakespeare on Television*, ed. James C. Bulman and H. R. Coursen (Hanover, New England, 1988).

17. Smith, 'Food for Thought', p. 55.

18. Phelan, 'Numbering Prospero's Books', pp. 48–9.

Further Reading

AUTHORED BOOKS AND EDITED COLLECTIONS

Robert Hamilton Ball, *Shakespeare on Silent Film: A Strange Eventful History* (London: Allen and Unwin, 1968).

Susan Bennett, *Performing Nostalgia: Shifting Shakespeare and the Contemporary Past* (London: Routledge, 1996).

Lynda E. Boose and Richard Burt (eds), *Shakespeare, The Movie: Popularizing the Plays on Film, TV and Video* (London: Routledge, 1997).

Lorne Buchman, *Still in Movement: Shakespeare on Screen* (Oxford: OUP, 1991).

Kate Chedgzoy, *Shakespeare's Queer Children: Sexual Politics and Contemporary Culture* (Manchester: MUP, 1995).

John Collick, *Shakespeare, Cinema and Society* (Manchester: MUP, 1989).

H. R. Coursen, *Shakespearean Performance as Interpretation* (Newark: University of Delaware Press, 1992).

Samuel Crowl, *Shakespeare Observed: Studies in Performance on Stage and Screen* (Athens: Ohio University Press, 1992).

Anthony Davies, *Filming Shakespeare's Plays: The Adaptations of Laurence Olivier, Orson Welles, Peter Brook and Akira Kurosawa* (Cambridge: CUP, 1988).

Peter S. Donaldson, *Shakespearean Films/Shakespearean Directors* (Boston: Unwin Hyman, 1990).

Charles Eckert (**ed.**), *Focus on Shakespearean Films* (Englewood Cliffs, NJ: Prentice-Hall, 1972).

Jack J. Jorgens, *Shakespeare on Film* (Bloomington: Indiana University Press, 1977).

Luke McKernan and Olwen Terris (**eds**), *Walking Shadows: Shakespeare in the National Film and Television Archive* (London: British Film Institute, 1994).

Roger Manvell, *Shakespeare and the Film* (London: Dent, 1971).

Ace G. Pilkington, *Screening Shakespeare from Richard II to Henry V* (Newark: University of Delaware Press, 1991).

Kenneth S. Rothwell and Annabelle Henkin Melzer, *Shakespeare on Screen: An International Filmography and Videography* (London: Mansell, 1990).

Stanley Wells and Anthony Davies (ed.), *Shakespeare and the Moving Image: the Plays on Film and Television* (Cambridge: CUP, 1994).

These volumes, which contain some material on Shakespearean film, are also worth consulting:

Morris Beja, *Film and Literature: An Introduction* (New York, Longman, 1979).
Deborah Cartmell, I. Q. Hunter, Heidi Kaye and Imelda Whelehan (eds), *Pulping Fictions: Consuming Culture across the Literature/Media Divide* (London: Pluto Press, 1996).
Robert Giddings, Keith Selby and Chris Wensley, *Screening the Novel: The Theory and Practice of Literary Dramatization* (Basingstoke: Macmillan, 1990).
Peter Reynolds (ed.), *Novel Images: Literature in Performance* (London: Routledge, 1993).
Neil Sinyard, *Filming Literature: The Art of Screen Adaptation* (London: Croom Helm, 1986).

SCREEN HISTORIES OF INDIVIDUAL PLAYS

The following feature discussions of one or more of the film versions of the plays in question:

Peter Davison, *Hamlet* (Basingstoke: Macmillan, 1983).
Harry M. Geduld, *Filmguide to Henry V* (Bloomington: Indiana University Press, 1973).
Julie Hankey, *Othello* (Bristol: Bristol Classical Press, 1987).
——, *Richard III*, 2nd edn (Bristol: Bristol Classical Press, 1988).
Barbara Hodgdon, *Henry IV, Part Two* (Manchester: MUP, 1993).
Graham Holderness, *The Taming of the Shrew* (Manchester: MUP, 1988).
Bernice W. Kliman, *Hamlet: Film, Television and Audio Performance* (London: Associated University Presses, 1988).
——, *Macbeth* (Manchester: MUP, 1992).
Grigori Kozintsev, *Shakespeare, Time and Conscience* (London: Denis Dobson, 1967).
——, *King Lear: The Space of Tragedy* (London: Heinemann, 1977).
Alexander Leggatt, *King Lear* (Manchester: MUP, 1991).
James N. Loehlin, *Henry V* (Manchester: MUP, 1996).
Jill Levenson, *Romeo and Juliet* (Manchester: MUP, 1987).
Scott McMillin, *Henry IV, Part One* (Manchester: MUP, 1991).
Hugh M. Richmond, *Richard III* (Manchester: MUP, 1989).
Marvin Rosenberg, *The Masks of King Lear* (Berkeley: University of California Press, 1971).
——, *The Masks of Macbeth* (Berkeley: University of California Press, 1978).
——, *The Masks of Hamlet* (London: Associated University Presses, 1993).
John Turner, *Macbeth* (Milton Keynes: Open University Press, 1992).
Virginia Mason Vaughan, *Othello: A Contextual History* (Cambridge: CUP, 1994).
Gordon Williams, *Macbeth* (Basingstoke: Macmillan, 1985).

ARTICLES AND ESSAYS

Traditional critical approaches to Shakespeare on film are well represented in the journals *Literature/Film Quarterly* (which has been running since 1974) and *Shakespeare Bulletin* (quarterly from 1982; in 1992 it incorporated the *Shakespeare on Film Newsletter*, which had been in existence since 1976). The following are examples of recent work which have drawn upon contemporary critical theory:

Curtis Breight, 'Elizabethan World Pictures', in *Shakespeare and National Culture*, ed. John Joughlin (Manchester: MUP, 1997).

Richard Burt, 'Baroque Down: the Trauma of Censorship in Psyschoanalysis and Queer Film Re-visions of Shakespeare', in *Shakespeare in the New Europe*, ed. Michael Hattaway, Boika Sokolova and Derek Roper (Sheffield: Sheffield Academic Press, 1994).

Peter S. Donaldson, 'Taking on Shakespeare: Kenneth Branagh's *Henry V*', *Shakespeare Quarterly*, 42 (1991), 60–71.

Chris Fitter, 'A Tale of Two Branaghs: *Henry V*, Ideology, and the Mekong Agincourt', in *Shakespeare Left and Right*, ed. Ivo Kamps (London: Routledge, 1991).

Graham Holderness, '"What ish my nation?": Shakespeare and National Identities', *Textual Practice*, 5 (1991), 74–93; rpr. in *Shakespeare Recycled: The Making of Historical Drama* (Hemel Hempstead: Harvester Wheatsheaf, 1992).

——, 'Shakespeare Rewound', *Shakespeare Survey*, 45 (1993), 63–74.

Robert Lane, '"When Blood is their Argument": Class, Character, and Historymaking in Shakespeare's and Branagh's *Henry V*', *ELH*, 61 (1994), 27–52.

FILM THEORY, CRITICISM AND HISTORY

J. Dudley Andrew, *Concepts in Film Theory* (Oxford: OUP, 1984).

David Bordwell and Kirstin Thompson, *Film Art: An Introduction*, 3rd edn (New York: McGraw-Hill, 1990).

Antony Easthope (ed.), *Contemporary Film Theory* (London: Longman, 1993).

Maggie Humm, *Feminism and Film* (Edinburgh: Edinburgh University Press, 1997).

Robert Lapsley and Michael Westlake, *Film Theory: An Introduction* (Manchester: MUP, 1988).

Gerald Mast, Marshall Cohen and Leo Braudy (eds), *Film Theory and Criticism: Introductory Readings*, 4th edn (Oxford: OUP, 1992).

James Monaco, *How to Read a Film*, rev. edn (Oxford: OUP, 1981).

Jill Nelmes (ed.), *An Introduction to Film Studies* (London: Routledge, 1996).

Notes on Contributors

Catherine Belsey is Professor of English Literature and Chair of the Centre for Critical and Cultural Theory at the University of Wales, Cardiff. She is the author of *Critical Practice* (London, 1980), *The Subject of Tragedy* (London, 1985), *John Milton: Language, Gender, Power* (Oxford, 1988), and *Desire: Love Stories in Western Culture* (Oxford, 1994). She is co-editor, with Jane Moore, of *The Feminist Reader* (Basingstoke, 1989; 2nd edn 1997).

Curtis Breight is Associate Professor of English at the University of Pittsburgh. He is the author of *Surveilliance and Militarism in the Elizabethan Era* (Basingstoke, 1996) and *Elizabethan World Pictures* (forthcoming).

John Collick teaches at the Waseda University, Tokyo. He has published essays and articles on Shakespeare, Keats, Emily Brontë and Angela Carter, and is the author of *Shakespeare, Cinema and Society* (Manchester, 1989).

Anthony Davies teaches at Victoria College, Jersey. He is the author of *Filming Shakespeare's Plays* (Cambridge, 1988), and co-editor, with Stanley Wells, of *Shakespeare and the Moving Image* (Cambridge, 1994), and has contributed to *Shakespeare: An Illustrated Stage History*, ed. Russell Jackson and Jonathan Bate (Oxford, 1996).

Peter S. Donaldson is Ann Fetter Friedlaender Professor of Humanities and Head of Literature at Massachussetts Institute of Technology, where he directs the Shakespeare Electronic Archive. He has published essays on Marlowe, Shakespeare, and Hypertext, critical editions of a number of Renaissance texts, and is the author of *Machiavelli and the Mystery of State* (Cambridge, 1988) and *Shakespearean Films/Shakespearean Directors* (Boston, 1990).

Barbara Hodgdon is Ellis and Nelle Levitt Distinguished Professor of English at Drake University. She is the author of *The End Crowns All: Closure and Contradiction in Shakespeare's History* (Princeton, NJ, 1991), *Henry IV, Part Two* in the Shakespeare in Performance series (Manchester, 1996), and *Restaging Shakespeare's Cultural Capital* (Pennsylvania, forthcoming). She is the editor of *The First Part of King Henry the Fourth: Texts and Contexts* (New York, 1997) and of the Arden 3 *Taming of the Shrew*.

Graham Holderness is Professor of Cultural Studies and Dean of Humanities at the University of Hertfordshire. His publications include *The Taming of the Shrew* in the Shakespeare in Performance series (Manchester, 1989), *Shakespeare Recycled* (Hemel Hempstead, 1992), and, with John Turner and Nick Potter, *Shakespeare: The Play of History* (Basingstoke, 1988) and *Shakespeare: Out of Court* (Basingstoke, 1990). He is the editor of *The Shakespeare Myth* (Manchester, 1988) and *The Politics of Theatre and Drama* (Basingstoke, 1992). He is one of the series editors of the Harvester Wheatsheaf Shakespeare Originals, and has edited *King Lear* (1995) and co-edited *Hamlet* (1992) and *Henry the fift* (1993).

Jack J. Jorgens is Professor of English at the American University, Washington. He has published numerous essays on Shakespeare and the cinema, and is the author of *Shakespeare on Film* (Bloomington, IN, 1977).

Douglas Lanier is Associate Professor of English at the University of New Hampshire. He has published articles on Shakespeare, Marston, Jonson and Milton, and is the author of *'Better Markes': Ben Jonson and the Institution of Authorship* (forthcoming).

Colin MacCabe is Head of Research at the British Film Institute. His numerous publications include *James Joyce and the Revolution of the Word* (London, 1979), and, as editor, *High Theory, Low Culture* (Manchester, 1986) and *Futures for English* (Manchester, 1988). He has been the editor of *Critical Quarterly* since 1987.

Index